FRANK HARRIS

Frank Harris.

FRANK HARRIS

By E. MERRILL ROOT

> *So we'll live,*
> *And pray, and sing, and tell old tales, and laugh*
> *At guilded butterflies, and hear poor rogues*
> *Talk of court news; and we'll talk with them too,*
> *Who loses and who wins; who's in, who's out;*
> *And take upon's the mystery of things*
> *As if we were God's spies. . . .*
>
> KING LEAR

THE ODYSSEY PRESS • 1947 • NEW YORK

To

EINAR LYNGKLIP
the Beloved Disciple

"Then in his misery and despair comes one man who accepts
his message as authentic-true; one man who shows in the very
words of his praise that he, too, has seen the Beatific Vision, has
listened to the Divine Voice. . . . Such a disciple is spoken of
ever afterward as the beloved and set apart and above all others."

FRANK HARRIS

CONTENTS

PREFACE

FRANK HARRIS, in the great words of Shakespeare which he so loved to quote, always considered himself to be "God's Spy."

He well knew the loneliness that is always the destiny of God's Spy in the world. And he knew that that loneliness is only supportable because, now and then and here and there, God's Spy finds one above all others who heeds and believes. That "one" Frank Harris called "the Beloved Disciple."

In Frank Harris's life that Beloved Disciple was Einar Lyngklip. And this psychographic study of Harris, based upon materials of incredible complexity and richness, is a testament to the hearty devotion of Einar Lyngklip—and to the equal devotion of his wife, Pauline Lyngklip. As a young man, Einar Lyngklip read *Pearson's Magazine;* he fell under the spell of Frank Harris; he gave up a highly paid position, just in order to be near Harris in New York; he followed Harris to Europe, and spent some time as his secretary. After his return to America, he gave the prime of his life to the gathering of every book, document, letter, clipping, source and statement that had any possible relation to the life and work of Frank Harris. He collected all the magazines that Harris had edited; every book and article about Harris; every scrap of information in the world's newspapers that touched upon Harris. He was indefatigable: for example, he persisted until he was able to secure the almost nonexistent pamphlet, *How to Beat the Boer*. He gathered into typescript copies of almost all the important letters Harris ever wrote. He met and talked with Kate Stephens, traveling out to Lawrence to investigate Harris's early life; he charmed her, although she was a hater and he a **lover of**

ix

Harris, and learned priceless facts concerning her knowledge and attitude. He centered his life about the lore of Harris, as disciples gather the sayings and relics of Gautama or Jesus. Then suddenly, in 1942, while still a relatively young man, he died, leaving the greatest collection of material about Frank Harris in existence anywhere in the world.

Einar Lyngklip brought great gifts to his deep concern with Frank Harris. He had intelligence, imagination, and love; he was unique in his vital interest.

His wife, Pauline Lyngklip, wished beyond all else that such devotion should find fulfillment, and that someone should write the first appreciative biography of Harris. Therefore, she gave as a free gift the bulk of his immense and rich collection to the New York City Public Library; and she wished also to make the material especially available to one whom she would choose out of all applicants—one who might write the life of Harris with the help of the great Lyngklip collection.

I was fortunate enough to be given first access to this material, and I have devoted four years to assimilating it and supplementing it by varied and wide research of my own. Ever since I reached intellectual maturity, I have reverenced the genius of Harris the artist and the man: thus all that I have written is predicated on a long apprenticeship of love. The result of all this is the first life that is sympathetic ever to be written of Frank Harris.

I am deeply grateful, also, to Mrs. Harris. She gave me graciously of her time and intimate knowledge, and supplied information and atmosphere that I could get nowhere else. Her statements in several instances have corrected current misinformation by former biographers, and have made real events definitive. Her never-failing faith in Frank Harris, the man and artist, has been a deep incentive to me to show him as he was—a star-finder and God's Spy. Her gracious permission to quote from his works and letters has made it possible at last to present him in his full stature.

I wish to thank Arthur Leonard Ross for his generous and untiring interest, for the rich material of letters and documents and information that he contributed, and for his permission, as Mrs. Harris's attorney, to quote from Harris's works. As he served Frank Harris alive, he serves his memory now.

And, after acknowledging my primary appreciation of Einar and Pauline Lyngklip, I wish also to thank several others who have greatly helped me. I owe much to the beautifully vital reminiscences of Allan Dowling, one of Harris's truest friends in his last years and himself a poet, and to the letters of Frank Harris which Allan Dowling gave me to read. I thank also the late Raymond Thomson, who gave me invaluable personal memories of Frank Harris. I am grateful to Elsa Gidlow for her memories of Frank Harris. I wish to acknowledge the gracious help of Howard C. Lewis, President of Dodd, Mead and Co., and the rare kindness and cooperation of Benjamin H. Stern. I am deeply grateful to Bernard Shaw for his permission to quote from his works and his letters.

E. M. R.

Putnam, Connecticut

Chapter I

INTO THE DANGEROUS WORLD

(1855-1869)

JAMES THOMAS HARRIS—later to be self-named Frank Harris—was born February 14, 1855. This date, like many of the events of his life, is debatable; but out of a flurry of three possible dates, each of which he himself gives in different places and at different times, it seems the most plausible.

In 1855 Tennyson published *Maud;* and Browning, still feeding on locusts and wild honey in the desert, the greater but only half-noticed *Men and Women.* Arnold brought out *Balder Dead;* William Morris was writing his first poems of nostalgic poignance about things Medieval. Carlyle, risen at last to an eminence that made his intrinsic greatness an extrinsic force, had gone to Germany to enter the valley of the shadow of Frederick. Dickens, passing from the genial adventures of Pickwick on the white roads or in the roaring inns of England, had traversed the grim Coketown of *Hard Times* and was now beginning the first installment of *Little Dorrit.* And in poignant symbol that half the century was over, Charlotte Brontë (last of the three gifted sisters) died on March 31. The old wild Decembers of Haworth were ended; a new age, which she and her greater sister Emily had presaged in their stormy eagle flights, was beginning.

Vincent van Gogh was two years old in Holland; Nietzsche

1

eleven in Germany. And across the ocean, 1855 was the birth year
of *Leaves of Grass,* in which America became a poem.

It was a great though a grim time to be born. War was stormy
in the Crimea: Balaclava, Inkerman, the Light Brigade were
then, or a little later, on all lips. The year was the watershed of
the century. The old Merry England lay on one side; the double,
double, toil and trouble of the Industrial Revolution on the other.
Wordsworth's worry and Ruskin's petulance about railroads had
not stayed the charge of the iron horses; Josiah Bounderby was
lord of Coketown, Tom Gradgrind schoolmaster of England;
coal and steam seemed Frankensteins in a world of dark satanic
mills. Industrial exploitation and the revolt of the workers were
already twins close to the birth hour. Science was shouting its
first raucous half-truths that overemphasis made malignantly
false: "struggle for existence," "survival of the fittest" (or fierc-
est?) into ears half indignant and half eager. Mechanism and
materialism, twin dogmas of agnosticism, seemed self-evident
truths to a blatant machine-made generation. Man (it seemed)
was an accident that happened to an amoeba; Capitalism (it
seemed) was the symbol of a social Mesozoic Age. Such was the
world climate of turmoil that affected the weather of the human
spirit; already the seismographs of prophets like Carlyle and
Ruskin had registered new earthquakes.

Men needed one who might bring Magic Glasses to smoke-
blinded eyes; who might raise the Veils of Isis, and show anew
the ever-living, ever-young Goddess; who might sail unpath'd
waters to undreamed of shores. Men needed some "rarer spirit"
who might evaluate the contemporary great, and be one of God's
Spies. Little did they guess, little could they foreknow, that such
an artist was even then being born. They would have said: "Can
any good thing come out of Galway?"

But for the present James Thomas Harris was safe from all
this, for he was on the rim of events. He was born in the western
seacoast city—provincial, historic, sleepy—of Galway, Ireland.

And Galway seems far from the hungry generations, treading each other down.

Galway, whose population in 1851 was only 24,967, stands on the almost exact middle shore of the deep indentation known as Galway Bay. The Islands of Arran bulk at the mouth like a sprawling breakwater. It is an ancient city, full of quaint angles of history. To commemorate the Roman justice of the Warden of Galway, who in 1524 executed his own son for piracy, this inscription was erected in Lombard Street:

1524

REMEMBER DEATH

ALL IS VANITY OF VANITIES

The stone was removed, but in 1854 was re-erected on the wall of Saint Nicholas's Churchyard. Little James Thomas spelled out the letters often: the melancholy touched him like a wind from beyond the world.

The port of Galway is the nearest roadstead in Ireland to America. It is 1636 miles from St. John's, 2700 miles from New York. Symbolically, Frank Harris was born in that part of Ireland nearest to the America which all his life he claimed and acclaimed with the poignant severity of love.

The part of Galway adjoining the harbor is the Claddagh. Its fishermen are the original Celts; they never intermarried with the "transplanters." They were formerly a distinct community, governed by their own "king." He was not hereditary but elected; at his election on the Eve of St. John there was tumult and shouting in the streets. "Bonfires were lighted round which young people danced in joyous hilarity, armed with long-handled brooms with which they gently touched each passerby who refused to obey the mandate: 'Honor the bonfire!' " [1]

James Thomas drank up many a salty word in the Claddagh, and marvelled at the dance of fire. His description of shipwreck

[1] Black's *Guide to Ireland*, 20th edition, p. 222.

in *Great Days*—the lights flaring on the midnight beach, the wind-beaten sailors black against the tossing flames—owes its color to this. And in a letter to Arnold Bennett the mature Harris wrote: "I should like to trace gigantic ebony figures out of the night itself with a flaming torch." It was an eruption of memory out of those nights in Galway when a wide-eyed little boy aglow with wonderlust stared at wild figures tracing their own gigantic ebony shapes with flaming brooms.

The boy grew up with the processional and recessional of tides always near, and in his nostrils the tang of the sea; the earth seemed only a larger anchored ship, precariously stable beside elemental tides.

Galway mingled modern squalor with grave old Spanish relics of sculptured façades and antique coats of arms. Lynch's Castle, in Shop Street, was one of the most interesting buildings: the ground floor was occupied by a grocery; but the windows and doors were ornamented with sculptures, and the roof had gargoyles to throw off the rain. Such beautiful old things nourished in him the grave beauty of his style, the brave integrity of his taste.

Ireland filled his soul—the pathos, the romance of heart and speech, the dreaming mysticism, the sharp lucid realism. "Like Shaw, most of the great men of this [Irish] renaissance . . . had to leave Ireland to prove their greatness, but at least they were born there. They breathed from infancy its strange air of realism and mysticism, its dignity with poverty, its love of scholarship, its wit as distinguished from gaiety, and never quite got any of it out of their systems."[2] It was so with him: he bore Ireland in his soul to the plains of Texas, the parlors of London, the azure coasts of the Riviera, and beyond the world's horizon.

Yet the land of one's birth is not the country of one's ancestry, and we must go farther than Ireland to find his red ancestral river.

In the *Western Mail* of Cardiff, Wales, for the 5th of Septem-

[2] Frank Harris, *Bernard Shaw*, p. 12. Simon and Schuster, 1931.

ber, 1931, the Rev. T. Lodwig Evans, formerly Baptist minister at Tenby, Wales, wrote:

"I am . . . able to solve the problem of his origin, and there is nothing in his ancestry that he should be ashamed of.

"Captain Harris, his father, was once a member of my church in Tenby. Then a retired commander of a Revenue Cutter of the British Navy, he was a most devout worshiper in my congregation, and very kind to his young minister—especially in providing him with books that came through his clever children.

"Frank's mother was the daughter of a very eminent Baptist minister, the Rev. T. H. Thomas, of the historic church at Molleston, near Narbeth, known as Thomas of Waterholms (his residence). Thomas of Waterholms was the pastor of the Baptist Church at Milford Haven when Captain Harris married his daughter.

"Captain Harris himself was born in a little farm called Gilfach, near Fishguard. He lived in Tenby with his daughter, who kept a kindergarten school, one of the first of the kind in Wales. When his daughter removed to London the Captain went with her, and he used to send me a copy of the *Fortnightly Review* every month during the time that his son Frank was its editor."

Harris's family, thus, was pure Welsh; he could say, racially, "How green was my valley!"

Captain Harris came from "Gilfach near Fishguard," his wife from a pleasant valley, green with the trees so dear to the Druids, where her father's house bore the cool delightful name of "Waterholms." Its sound suggests the psalm of peace, and the trees planted by the rivers of water.

The double Celt in Harris—Welsh blood, Irish breeding—is basic. He himself accented it often: "I am not one of the lions of Washington Square, but a sort of mongrel Welsh terrier breed, Celtic all through."[3] "I can only love any country in so far as it

---

[3] Letter to Michael Monahan, September 6, 1916. Published in "Recollections and Impressions of One Who Knew Him." The *Catholic World*, December, 1932, pp. 327-33.

stands for truth and beauty and humanity, and I come perilously near hating these savage Germanic peoples with their big bellies and combative instincts. I prefer the Celts, who cherish a humane ideal and can be moved by abstract ideal causes." [4]

Yet for all his love of his Welsh blood and Irish birth, he was not rooted in locality. He never knew Burns' fierce love of the Highlands, or Whitman's gusto for million-footed Manhattan. Harris was of the race of the Columbuses whose country is Passage to India; of the adventurers of the spirit who are farthest from the vegetable and nearest to the bird. He was like El Greco —a god in exile, an Olympian of wanderlust. He wrote to Hesketh Pearson: "The chief thing about great men is that they belong to no country and hardly to any time; they may be shadows, but, like all shadows, point to the sun." [5]

Though dynamic, Harris's parentage was not determinant. He was of the race of the super-born whose parentage is the genius that comes directly from God; he said of himself, like Napoleon, that other sons had found their line of ancestry waiting, but that he had *founded* his! The immaculate conception of genius. . . .

His father, Thomas Vernon Harris, was captain of a revenue cutter in the British Navy. Short, sturdy, weathered by wind and sun, half pickled by the brine of constant seas, he was an inarticulate stern sea-terrier. He had a brusque staccato bark that made fools fear his bite, but the staunch faithful valor of the terrier's heart.

His was a deep goodness, just but grimly kind. Outwardly he was hard as a shagbark hickory; inwardly, like the nut, he was full of sweet if scanty meat.

He mingled the skill of a master seaman with a canny goodness. He was a later descendant of Bunyan—the bonfire of fervor burned down to the steady coals of morality. The oath might leap

[4] Letter to Hesketh Pearson, November 4, 1915. Published in Hesketh Pearson, *Modern Men and Mummers*. Harcourt, Brace & Co., 1922.
[5] Letter to Hesketh Pearson, April 30, 1918. *Ibid.*

to his lips, but the quotation from the Gospels, or from the austere magnificence of the Old Testament, would flow as easily and more sincerely. He might once or twice get drunk on champagne, till the lewd comments of the sailors made his son ashamed; he was, however, a man of puritanic integrity in wedlock, whose life was as straight as it was narrow.

And with his arduous duties, and three boys and two girls growing into life while a beloved wife sank out of it, the captain had burdens to turn a saint into a cobra.

Captain Harris was forty-two when James Thomas was born. He was a hard man; he expected his son to be hard. A Lord of the Admiralty visited his ship. Little James Thomas, about eleven, came on deck in his boyish cocky way, an urchin not to be ignored; swimming was mentioned, and the captain, proud of the boy's grit and skill, bade him swim round the ship. The visitor marvelled that so small a boy could make so large a circuit; the captain's pride grew; when the boy was about to climb a rope after one round, he shouted: "Again!" The boy circled the ship once more, through troughs of waves grown higher and colder. Chilled and blue, he hoped to climb aboard, but his father bade him go again. The boy, for all his hot pride and strength, might have drowned, had not the visitor ordered him aboard.

Yet the captain asked nothing that he did not deeply feel was for the boy's good: James Thomas must know that life is not a snug harbor with unlimited shore leave, but a frigate with guns loaded, sailing in battle line.

Harris's mother remained his most gracious memory, yet she can have meant little in his life. From her comfortable home at Waterholms, she had come to be the lonely wife of a sailor, and to make his none too large pay cover the needs of a somewhat too large family. Behind her lay generations of lives in the mountains and valleys of Wales, touched with poetry of the heart and mysticism of the mind, nourished by noble aspects of nature and the superb art of the Bible.

She was frail—a chalice of alabaster where a flame precariously burned. She was often feeble with the tuberculosis from which she and three of her children were to die. Sometimes she walked into the sunlight of warm days, resting her too airy weight on James Thomas's shoulder as on a living crutch. He seems to have loved her deeply in a vague way. But he cannot have remembered much beyond a gracious woman already conscious of death, moving through a life she was too weak to direct.

The end came with cold terror. She had lain down to rest; as day darkened, James Thomas, not quite four, ran to the bed, whispered in her ear, and touched her forehead with his lips. She did not waken; her cold rigidity frightened him, and he started screaming.

This was more than death's chuckle in too young an ear. It shadowed the routine of his days: his father was at sea, and the lonely house had no mother to guide him; life became expediency —mere boarding here and there, without center of love. He drifted from school to school, sometimes living with his elder brother, Vernon, who worked in a bank. He went to Kingston, to Armagh (where he attended the Royal School), then back to Galway. Of his early schooling he himself said later: "Tetchy and wayward was my infancy, my schooldays frightful, desperate, wild, and furious."

He had two brothers, Willie and Vernon, and two sisters, Annie and Chrissie. They were good to him; but youth can never be really kind, for it has not learned how it hurts to live; it is callous with equal motivation of vitality and ignorance.

His brothers were, at best, only comrades. Willie was six years his senior, Vernon nine. Vernon was his favorite—an athletic boy, slender, dark, vivid: there was a white fire in his heart. It rose sometimes to his eyes; it was always in his heart. He was always seeking something he would never find. He had to work in a bank, which he hated; he longed for horizons. The fire would drive him, one day, to America; to attempted suicide; to lonely death in Louisiana. William was of more ordinary clay, though he was better to look at—even handsome. He would hitch his star to the world's wagons; he would grow conventionally pious—a church-goer on one day, a go-getter on seven.

The girls were touched with talent. Annie, who lived the longest of all save James Thomas, started the first kindergarten in Wales. Gracious, dignified, she flowered into her mother's poise and charm, but with a robust strength, a grave serenity. Chrissie, the youngest in life, was to be the youngest in death—killed by the blunder of a drunken doctor. She was precocious with a hectic brilliance; she had dark curls, flashing tender eyes, a lovely audacity.

The mature Harris recreates his family in his great autobiographical story, "The Ugly Duckling."

"My earliest memories" (it begins) "are neither very clear nor very interesting; but when still very young, I became conscious that I was unlike my brothers and sisters: I grew faster than they did and as soon as I out-topped them the tolerance they had hitherto shown me ceased; instead of kindness I got nothing but blame: whatever I did they found fault with: I was always getting in their way it seemed and always being snapped at. . . . At first I didn't mind this much: with the unconsciousness of youth I took it all as part of the unexpectedness of life and paid no particular attention to it, giving as good as I got. But day by day the differences between my brothers and sisters and myself grew more marked. . . . In my wretchedness I would wander away from the others. . . ."

The Ugly Duckling was meanwhile restless for some unknown goal—the destiny of the swan.

The glad animal movements of the normal boy began. The flesh wakened; out of this, the mind wakened; out of that, the soul awoke. Desire and curiosity stirred within him: the desire of the blood, the curiosity of the mind. Much of this—as usual in a boy—had to do with sex, which he accepted as normal, but which many have considered abnormal.

He believed that this awakening to sex was his initiation into beauty.

"I had never yet noticed the beauties of nature; indeed, whenever I came across descriptions of scenery in my reading, I always skipped them as wearisome. Now of a sudden, in a moment, my eyes were unsealed to natural beauties. I remember the scene and my rapt wonder as if it were yesterday. It was a bridge across the Dee River near Overton in full sunshine; on my right the river made a long curve, swirling deep under a wooded height, leaving a little tawny sandbank half bare just opposite me; on my left, both banks, thickly wooded, drew together and passed round a curve out of sight. I was entranced and speechless—enchanted by the sheer color-beauty of the scene—sunlit water there and shadowed here, reflecting the gorgeous vesture of the wooded height. And when I left the place and came out again and looked at the adjoining cornfields, golden against the green of the hedge-rows and scattered trees, the colors took on a charm that I had never noticed before: I could not understand what had happened to me.

"It was the awakening of the sex-life in me, I believe, that first revealed to me the beauty of inanimate nature." [6]

From that time on he sought beauty everywhere, and caught glimpses of it that turned his being into "a hymn of praise and joy."

Yet, being a man's man, he turned from beauty to action. If he reached Athens and Jerusalem, he set out from Sparta. Oscar Wilde might seem suited by the green carnation or languorous lily, but Harris sought the edelweiss dangerous upon Alpine heights. He wanted to be an athlete, to make his body an instrument of supple power and skill; he ran, he jumped, he boxed. He hardened his flesh into vigor that was to last, in spite of large

[6] *My Life and Loves*, Vol. I, pp. 62-63.

demands of adventure, passion, and work, for seventy-six years. Vernon was a good boxer; James Thomas learned so well from his tutoring that, though years younger and short and short-sighted, he could hold his own. At school his supple legs carried him swiftly over a hundred yards or lifted him like a swallow over the bar.

He used brains to supplement brawn. Reading descriptions of how to swim, he decided that it was a matter of faith: anyone could swim who believed he could. So when they went to the sea, he threw himself into deep water—and swam. Vernon asked him when he had learned; he replied: there and then! No wonder that, in "The Holy Man," he was to write that anyone could walk on the water who had faith and love.

The first disappointment of his life was the discovery that physical handicaps would keep him from becoming a great athlete. He was of the terrier breed—wiry, quick, small; his greatest height was to be five feet six. (Later he was to wear heels two inches high in an attempt to remedy nature.) He told Einar Lyngklip: "As a boy I added two years to my age and two inches to my height, and then tried to live up to both. But I was soon dissatisfied with that, and tried to grow beyond both."

Another defect that led to defeat was his short sight. His boxing suffered, and his prowess in games; later, on the plains, he was to discover that he could never be a marksman.

At the age of twelve he discovered that he was ugly. "As soon as I learned as a boy of twelve wherein beauty really consisted, I saw that I could have no claim to it; my features were irregular, my eyes only ordinary in size and gray-blue in color, and even my father's sailors always called me 'lug-sails' because of my over-large ears. The chief thing about my mug, as Rodin said, was that it had a certain life and energy." [7]

He believed, however, that "every handicap in natural deficiency turns out to be an advantage in life to the brave soul,

[7] *My Life and Loves,* Vol. III, p. 26.

whereas every natural gift is surely a handicap." So his physical limitations drove him down to the depths and up to the heights. "Every kite," he said, "goes up against the wind."

In those youthful years he heard whispers of strange things. Ireland, the land of broken hearts, was also the land of broken heads, the land of Mangin's *Dark Rosaleen* and of the romantic revolts that seemed a sort of political art-for-art's-sake.

An Irish boy pointed to the placards on the Court House offering a reward of 5000 pounds to anyone who would tell the whereabouts of James Stephens, the Fenian Head-Center. James Thomas—even if he had known him!—would not have betrayed him for all the treasures in Ali Baba's cave. This romantic symbol lay in his subconscious, later to grow into the red Bougainvillaea vine of Sonia and Louis Lingg.

Perhaps because of the boy's innocent babble about Fenians (which his father overheard)—perhaps because he realized that the boy was a thoroughbred colt in a country paddock, Captain Harris determined that the Irish life must end. He knew that there was no future in Ireland for one who desired wide horizons, and it was a wise decision. So Wilde and Shaw were to carry Ireland in their blood to the wider opportunities of England.

Captain Harris sent James Thomas to an English grammar school at Ruabon in Wales.

The boy suffered from and profited by his brief formal schooling there: he was never one who suffered schools gladly; yet he was eager for wisdom. He found a lack of love and light: English boys and masters were not kindly, spontaneous, intuitive, like the Irish. Learning was by rote of head, not by glow of heart; discipline was enforced not with sympathy and humor, but by mechanics of irony, superimposed tasks, and flogging.

He did his worst in languages, his best in mathematics. Greek and Latin were chores till hurt pride stirred him to passionate learning; but from the first, with Euclid, he looked on logic bare.

A chief irritation was fagging. To him, this was never the bluff, hearty abuse, amenable to bluff, hearty remedy, that it seems in *Tom Brown*. He instituted a revolution that failed. The young arch-rebel, however, had his spectacular individual gesture: at a big cricket match, as the teams were completing the preliminaries, he cried, "I won't play on your side, you big bully!" and flung the ball at the face of his captain, Jones, who was the chief of the Gestapo. Jones' face bled as the ball grazed it; but he was so startled by this blasphemy against tradition that he could only stand and stare. Thus Harris wrote in blood the prototype of *The Bomb,* and was himself the Louis Lingg of the schoolyard.

Another evil was homosexuality. At Ruabon it was mildly endemic, and at times violently epidemic. Harris reacted in indignant disgust. All his life he hated perversity; even in Oscar Wilde he hated the vice though he loved the victim; he took joy in proving that Shakespeare was free from perversion. Love to him was polarity between opposite sexes: a magical regeneration of individuals by the passionate tension of opposites that finds release in union; a glory of consummation that has none of the sick cowardly inbreeding between two of the same sex.

Meanwhile his real education proceeded, as it will in spite of schools. He began to read widely—"madly" he said—novels of adventure and romance, and finally poetry, his life's dearest love. Scott was a healthy champion of the chivalry of youth; Captain Marryat was a favorite, too: a bluff artist of pluck, tenacity, hardihood. He came to know his lord of language and life—Shakespeare. *The Merchant of Venice* was given, and the boy who was to have been Shylock was dubious about playing the Jew. To Harris that seemed the very part to play, so play it he did—even, by his own account, inventing a stage trick that Irving himself was later to employ. (Characteristically, he criticized Irving for using it!) He lost himself in those dying falls of cadence, those spells of beauty's white magic, that made his Celtic heart a swallow in the wind.

He clashed with his fellows and his teachers not upon the low plane of worldly interest, but upon high matters of justice and intellect. No boyish pranks (though such there were, to be sure) made him outcast or alien. An acceptance of school standards, plus the customary prankish intransigence, would have won him favor. He was not Beelzebub—but Lucifer.

Disgusted by a school where the life of the mind was scorned, he longed for "real" life. He asked his father to give him the nomination as midshipman in the British Navy: his father would not do so, nor would he explain why he would not. So James Thomas resolved to run away; for weeks he weighed South Africa (where diamonds had just been discovered) against western America and the hair-raising Sioux.

The final camel that bit the straw in two was an honest injustice which he thought characteristically English. He had taken the examination for one of the school's annual scholarships to Cambridge, and had won first place. But the professor from Cambridge who was to award the prize was unwillingly dissuaded by the head of the school. James Thomas was too young: he had two years of work to do before the price-tag could be sewed on the finished fabric. The professor, with some embarrassment, gave the scholarship to an older English boy who had won second place; to Harris he gave the second prize of ten pounds.

Harris was always furious at injustice. Though he loved to quote Housman—

> *Be still, my soul, be still, it is but for a season:*
> *Let us endure an hour and see injustice done. . . .*

he never endured, even for an instant: his soul was "still" only as the lightning is—because it precedes the thunder.

Now he was resolute for action. Pleading a desire to see his father, he excused himself from spending the ten pounds for the books it was supposed to buy; adding the five pounds that was his fare home, he set out ostensibly for Tenby in Wales—which he was to reach years later, by way of Chicago, Kansas, Paris, Berlin, and Athens.

His mood is suggested in "The Ugly Duckling." The Ugly Duckling has gone to visit the Anglo-Dorkings, who are distinguished by physical pugnacity and emotional prudery; finding no true companionship among them, he says: "I took to living more and more by myself, and resolved not to depend in any degree upon others. After all, I used to say, consoling myself, the sky does not belong to the Anglo-Dorkings, and the fields of air and the sunshine by day, and the winds and stars at night, were as much mine as theirs. If they made me an outcast and pariah, what, after all, did it matter: My life was mine to live as I chose, and the days were mine to spend nobly if I pleased. And so I took to the life of a solitary, and grew strong in loneliness, though always a little sad." At last he discovers that he is a swan. "Swans," he is told, are "the Children of the Light . . . and follow the sun around the world." Therefore "I went right up . . . on strong wing-stroke exulting, for . . . I felt that it was better a thousand times to be killed falling from heaven than to live in a duck pond."

He celebrated the nonchalance of chosen orphanhood by attending a loud, colorful play—*The Two Roses*—in Liverpool, as an aesthetic declaration of independence. Then, proving his right by the amazing bass of his voice sonorous in a child's throat, he purchased a steamship ticket with no more hindrance than a vaguely inquisitive stare from the clerk.

He divided his life, later, as follows: "I have always wanted to build Romance in the heart of Reality, making the incidents of my life an Earthly Pilgrimage; of my youth a great adventure; of my manhood a lyric of love; of my maturity the successful quest for El Dorado; and finally, of my old age, a prophetic vision." Such was his own conscious understanding of his life; now, unconsciously, he began the "great adventure."

He boarded the ship. He shook England from his feet. He breathed the air of the prairies afar, and saluted the Sierras in imagination. He was only a boy; he did not know the greatest poet of the new continent to which he was sailing; only later was he to write his salute to Walt Whitman. But he was already seeking what Whitman sought—Passage to India and the Open Road.

Chapter II

AMERICAN ADVENTURE

(1869-1876)

FRANK HARRIS tells in his autobiography many quaint and some salacious details of his voyage. Thus he forgot or ignored the purchase of bedding before the boat sailed; he made up for it by repeating verbatim, after one reading, an essay of Macaulay's; he made love in a lifeboat to the chief engineer's daughter; he so impressed an old gentleman that he was in danger of adoption. Spiced fact or truth-based fancy—who can tell?

Beyond such details lies the certain, because psychological, truth: he left England a boy; he landed in America a man.

It was 1869 or 1870. In the world toward which he sailed, modern America was in process of birth. The Civil War was over, the industrial North had won; slavery was abolished, Capitalism was master. The country was full of frustrations and desires, of forces let loose without direction, of violence turned suddenly from man and against nature. Even old men were going West. The lure of gold or the call of land roused diverse temperaments that were one in wanderlust. The Industrial Revolution was remaking America: trains were plowing their way through herds of bison, or fighting their way through the superb light cavalry of Comanche and Sioux; mills and mines and factories were blackening the East with smoke. Roaring camps—with or without luck—were raucous in the Far West; cattle were beginning to crowd the bison from the central plains. Literature was coming to rude birth in the Sierras with Bret Harte or on the Mississippi with Mark Twain. In the East it was the time of High Finance, in the West, of Expansive Action. Vanderbilt, Gould, and Fisk were arranging in New York a private Gold Rush of their own that was to send the price of the metal skyrocketing, to shake Wall Street, and to be ended only by government intervention. The West was hailing the completion of the Union Pacific, May 10, 1869, when the Union and the Central Pacific Railways were joined at Ogden. The United States was the Forge of Vulcan: it ceased to speak the word, and it rang with the deed. The Union Pacific was its *Song of Roland,* Brooklyn Bridge its *Iliad.*

Yet even then an artist was approaching who was first to share its deeds and then to speak its words. The name of the ship on which he sailed is lost; but we may call it the *Mayflower:* for he too was a Pilgrim, seeking a new world of freedom to worship life in his own way.

As the ship entered the harbor of New York, his eager eyes saw no modern sky line, no bold figure in bronze looming with Olympian torch; the canyoned streets, the skyscrapers, the bulk and loom of modern New York were latent.

In *The Bomb* Rudolph Schnaubelt, also an immigrant, thus describes his first day in New York: "The May morning had all the beauty and freshness of youth; the air was warm, and yet light and quick. I fell in love with the broad, sunny streets. The people, too, walked rapidly, the street cars spun past; everything was brisk and cheerful; I felt curiously exhilarated and light-hearted." [1] It was Harris's own mood. Later he affirmed that the American sky, higher and wider than the sky of Europe, lifts the heart in idealism. It is an intimation of his mood: he was a pilgrim for a vaster heaven.

[1] *The Bomb,* p. 20.

Here in New York (which another visitor of the time described as "a slice of honeycomb on the map") [2] young Harris was seeking the power and the glory; but his first problem was the daily bread. What was he to do?

He found a friendly Irish family who boarded him for almost nothing. He became a bootblack and made eighty cents an hour. Willingness to work, skill, deftness, and brains seemed sufficient to open a way in the world.

Though his motivation was not Rudolph Schnaubelt's last desperate need, James Thomas also got a job in the caissons driven into the underwater muck of the East River, as one of the sandhogs who were excavating for the foundations of Brooklyn Bridge. He was *pontifex,* or bridge builder, in the literal sense before he became bridge builder for the mind of man.

The first caisson had been sunk in 1866, under the direction of John A. Roebling, a Prussian, who had just completed the suspension bridge across the Ohio at Cincinnati. Two years later, injured in an accident, he died; his son, Washington A. Roebling, continued construction with vigor during the seventies. The bridge was opened in 1880; in 1869 it was still in its earlier stages, with excavations being dug for the deep foundations.

Work under the pressure of compressed air was exhausting, often crippling, sometimes fatal. The bends—that awful twisting of the flesh by the expansion of highly intensified air still bubbling in the blood after the body had reentered normal pressures—was a ghastly peril. Dizziness and deafness were cumulative, even if one did not succumb. The bends made a man fall down, writhe, knock his face on the floor till blood spurted from nose and mouth. A man's legs might be twisted like plaited hair. It might leave him a spidery invalid. It might even kill him. Harris tells of a young workman who, in a hurry to meet his girl, went into normal air without the slow necessary hour in the de-

[2] Max O'Rell.

compression chamber. When the men finally emerged, haste had made death: their impetuous fellow workman lay in a stertorous heap, puffing his life out through bubble-like lips.

It was terrible work for men; more terrible for a boy. Safeguards of labor were not then what they are now; but even then boys were not allowed to work in such lethal depths. The caisson was a hole hammered into Hell, a bubbling inferno of sand and muck, in atmospheres stepped up to fearful pressure. Yet the evidence of intimate knowledge, both in the autobiography and in *The Bomb,* proves that he experienced what he expresses. Somehow he made the foreman believe that he was sixteen and a man. He earned his five to ten dollars a day, and worked so well that his boss called him the best man in the shift, a "stout little pony," a Jack of all work.

The Bomb turns all this into an epic of labor.

Warned by the experience of senior workmen, and by pains in his head and difficulty in hearing, Harris ended his work in hammered Hell after the first month. Since the Mulligans, the kind Irish family with whom he stayed, were hesitant about taking even the three dollars a week which he insisted on paying for his room and board, he was able to lay aside considerable money. He had one hundred and fifty dollars in his pocket when he left his job.

New York did not satisfy him: America lay elsewhere—the bison in their shaggy myriads, the expanses of the prairies where the Sioux were still the truculent lords of the land. It was once supposed that to open a page of Virgil was to find an omen. Harris, bootblacking again on the sidewalks of New York, quoted a line of Virgil as he polished the boots of a Mr. Kendrick who, amazed, investigated his classical bootblack—and offered him a job in his Chicago hotel. Harris never hesitated as Hamlet did: in three days he left for Chicago.

Chicago, which became his favorite American city, was already more than a raw sprawl by a windy lake. It was a city of some

350,000, gathered in white-painted wooden houses (antecedent to Mrs. O'Leary's cow). There were huge box-like warehouses that did not yet rise in sky-scaling ladders of glass; there were houses and hotels, offices and banks, of brick or limestone. The outlying streets were full of blowing dust or flowing mud according to season. Yet concrete sidewalks had appeared; avenues like Michigan and Wabash had been widened into drives; cedar-block pavements had been laid, and a network of horsecar lines extended over the city. The streets were lighted by 2500 gas lamps—an illumination brighter than that of most eastern cities. In this metropolis of the prairie the older life of the East and the raw life of the West met and mingled. A stormy city!—lusty, savage, grandiose—fitting forerunner of today's dinosaur with epilepsy.

In the Fremont House, a "good but second-rate hotel," young Harris worked as night clerk, till he "practically managed it at $150 and board a month." [3] Yet nothing of spiritual importance happened to him: if his story had been that of another immigrant who made good, nothing would have failed like his success; but his destiny was not to make good, but to make best.

In his explorations of the city he encountered the avid ferocity of a man out of work and hungry, who showed him the savage primal violence close under the skin of American life; and he befriended a prostitute who tried to solicit him in order to keep her baby alive.

His departure was motivated by a romantic meeting. A Spanish family stopped in Chicago on their way to Chihuahua: Senor Vidal, his wife, a cousin, and Senorita Vidal. The girl was reserved, lovely, with fine dark eyes and black hair; at first one did not notice her enough, as one may fail to notice the first and loveliest star in a gently darkening sky. But there was about her "a proud grace of carriage," a "magical glance."

The Vidals were birds of passage, soon to fly. Harris saw the *senorita* only in transit; yet she so took his heart that, restless after

[3] *My Life and Loves,* Vol. I, Chap. VI.

she was gone, he found Chicago flat, stale, and impossible. At the back of his mind was the fixed resolve to reach Chihuahua "somehow or other in the near future"; and the resolve "shaped his life anew."

Such was his motivation; and he found the means. Three cattle-men—Reece, a tall dark Welshman; Dell, an ordinary English-man of middle height; and Ford, "the boss," six feet tall with a "hatchet-thin bronzed face and eagle profile," registered at the hotel. They became his intimates; they taught him tricks of rid-ing and told tall tales of cattle bought in southern Texas at a dol-lar a head and driven over the hazards of the trail to be sold in Chicago at fifteen or twenty dollars each. They recounted buffalo hunts and Indian fights. They seemed to speak of what he de-sired—the open road.

> *I give you my hand!*
> *I give you my love, more precious than money,*
> *I give you myself, before preaching or law;*
> *Will you give me yourself? Will you come travel with me?*

So his new friends seemed to speak. Was not this what he had come to America to find?

The three cattlemen were glad to have him accompany them: he was a personable youth, with command in his eyes and swag-gering quiet confidence in his manner; and he had saved $1800.

It was the best choice he could have made. His mother had died of tuberculosis, his own lungs were sensitive; life in the dry sunny air of the plains was bodily salvation. Suns tanned him and winds fanned him into bronze, enduring strength: the foun-dation for three quarters of a century. And in relation to litera-ture it was an advantage; he was to be no poet-scholar like Swinburne, no sedentary genius like Carlyle. Bernard Shaw was relatively an amateur of life: he had never killed a man at a thou-sand yards, knowing that—if he missed—the avalanche of the

Sioux, scorning his marksmanship, would ride him down. *Arms and the Man,* or Fabianism, would have been less albino if Shaw had known war. Chocolate instead of a revolver?—a bookman's idea! Finally, by his life on the trail Harris learned to find his own answers to his own questions: "I think first and read afterwards." His solid, authentic thought, like carving in oak that follows the grain of the wood, came from those days on the trail. He knew man in his elemental needs and deeds. He had killed men to keep his own life. He had known that thought is not a game, but a way of life or of death. On the trail, a man had to keep his head—or lose his hair.

It was a life of grave adventure that sparkled like the sunlight over the plains—a life shadowed here by clouds looming in thunderheads of heat, shimmering there with illusion of mirage, and again cool with wide sluggish rivers and green cottonwoods. Through that thesaurus of adventure Harris's life moved full and flowing like the Missouri.

What characters he met! Notable was Wild Bill Hickok—the most marvelous gunman of the frontier, as legendary as Cyrano among swordsmen. Harris watched his superb prowess with a revolver from the back of a galloping horse. The deadly shooting of the Westerners was the true art of war: quantity of man-power cannot stand against quality of fire-power.

He saw life in the raw, in the rough. He watched his lust-crazed, drink-incited young comrades tangle with Mexicans; he praised their shooting, but was awed by the lethal Mexican knife. He hunted buffalo alone; he was hunted by Indians. He suffered siege with his fellow cattlemen, and helped stand off the swarming hundreds of the superb light horsemen of the plains. He made a fierce ride for rescue on his mare with the speed of wind and heart of iron, Blue Dick.

Amid these adventures his mind and spirit were growing. He read only a few books, but he read them thoroughly and he thought them through: Carlyle became his hero, and John Stuart

Mill challenged him to criticism. He learned, also, to evaluate men: he saw his companions throw their lives away with raw whisky and diseased women; he watched a half-breed die like stoic bronze under the bite of a rattler; he learned the venom in the heart of a quiet man. It was apprenticeship to life.

Years later he was talking to Guido Bruno. Bruno asked him: "Experience, then, counts most for the writer? . . . To know life, to know people, means more than artistry in words?"

"Of course," Harris answered. "Living and knowing life is uppermost, and then to tell others about it."

Those were great days when the lungs drank the western air like wine, and the muscles ached and thrilled to the miles of trail, and youth flirted with death as with a girl! (Always he remembered little details—the buffalo meat that, he said, was the best meat in all the world; the buffalo grass with the long tenuous roots that bound the arid prairie soil together.)

In October, 1871, he returned to Chicago with a large herd of cattle. He awoke next morning to the fury of the Chicago fire. The city with its flimsy wooden houses, and fanned by a stiff lake breeze, burned like a pocket edition of Hell. Harris was the prose Dante of that Inferno. Remembering it years later, he wrote: "Another thing I noticed almost immediately: the heat was so terrific that the water decomposed into its elements and the oxygen gas in the water burned vehemently on its own account. The water, in fact, added fuel to the flames." [4]

Harris noticed the anguish, the humor, the human gargoyles. Out of the chaos and courage: the stringing of a looter from a lamp-post—the humor of the Yankee who sold water under the sign: *"What do you think of our Hell? No drinks less than a dollar!"*—the concourse around the bread trains where women and children always went first—out of all this he came to the admiring conclusion that Americans were a great people. "This is the greatest people in the world, I said to myself, and was proud

[4] *My Life and Loves*, Vol. I, pp. 143-44.

to feel at one with them." He went into the fire "an Irish boy"—
he came out of it "a proud American." [5]

By quick thinking and quick doing, he drove his cattle to
safety; despite a slightly diminished herd, he made (he said)
about $12,000.

He returned to the trail once more, taking Carlyle and Mill
with him. But he was dissatisfied, restless; he caught an infection
that made him miserable with chills and fever; the rough men
and rougher life began to weary him.

He summed up—and dismissed—his life on the trail in the
single motto: *"He who wills, can."*

Meanwhile his brother William had come to America and established himself at Lawrence, Kansas. The probability is that
despite his bravado young Harris was homesick for English faces
and speech, and even for his family. In "The Sheriff and His
Partner" the young Englishman, evidently Harris, says: "In those
early days . . . I was often homesick, and gave myself up readily
to dreaming of English scenes and faces." So it was good to visit
William at Lawrence.

Lawrence, founded in 1854, had had a stormy history of raids
and lynchings by pro- and anti-slavery bands from Missouri. It
had finally become an Abolition stronghold and its soul went
marching on with the noble idealism and drastic action of a John
Brown. As the Civil War diluted the fervor of Abolition by the
liquidation of slavery, the old spirit became intellectual. As a symbol, the University of Kansas, founded in 1866, stood on a hill
above the city like a chaste crown flashing on a high ascetic head.

Harris, recovering from the chills and fever of the trail, rode
into Lawrence as one of Captain Kidd's men might have sailed
into Massachusetts Bay.

He came to find himself. For here he met the man who was to
waken him—Professor Byron C. Smith, who taught Greek Language and Literature at the University.

[5] *Ibid.,* pp. 147-48.

Byron Smith was a child not of Whitman but of Emerson. Stronger in mind than body, he had nothing of Whitman's fleshly turbulence: he was the American Scholar of Emerson's dream. He had studied in Germany. Influenced by Spinoza and Hegel, he saw history as the shadow cast by the progress of the spirit's self-unfoldment, and the world as the extension of the spirit's intention. He accepted the data of science as a rediscovery of the logic of the eternal spirit, the rereading of the moving finger. He would not cancel a single line; nor, by tears, blot out a single word. It was enough to "carry in our bosoms the imperishable sense of our identity at heart with that transcendent life which is not subject to, but which involves, necessity." *Self* was "iniquity"; he lived in and for the Oversoul, seeing the phenomena of the world and the limits of individual lives in the oblique light of eternity. He rose to a lyric immolation of Self before the All whose spirit filled substance and made the universe a poem—or a Euclidean theorem.

He accepted the continual challenge of "new difficulties, new sorrows, new limitations"; an athlete of the soul, he would rise by wrestling with them. The doubt and uncertainty of the age were to him agencies of regeneration. He sought no easy assurances of "snug-minded priests"—rather, the arctic heroism of the mind, surrendering its immortality to prevent the mortality of God. "The soul," he wrote, "is its own place"; it must not agitate itself as to any dogmatic solution of the world's process, whether mechanical or spiritual, but devote itself to endeavor and aspiration. From the battlements of this philosophy he blew trumpets of stoic bronze. He believed that the mere preaching of morality was obsolescent; that men no longer needed to hear the moral law, but at last to practice it. Culture, he thought, was no rose-scented cowardice claiming high prerogatives. Culture was not a Maginot Line but a perpetual *attack*—like the affirmation of a Socrates who died that man might awaken and who lived that the world might not fall asleep.

Smith's photograph reveals him. Character in every age has its temporal mask of manner that veils it from ages with different fashions. Whiskers and beards in those days made features quaint. Smith's face is hedged by a wealth of dark hair, full yet delicate. Dark hair is full over the forehead, also, and parted in the center; the brow is broad yet fine. The chiseled nose is too small to suggest boldness; the lips, hidden by the full dark mustache, seem easy in repose and not drawn tight by hurt of heart or doubt of mind. The chin, cleft by a deep dimple, completes the foundation of the face with quiet strength. The eyes are large and dark; they look from the picture with candor and the nobility of a mind made wise and not bitter by experience and thought. It is the face of a pure spirit, brave for all great things; yet about the eyes there is a hint and prescience of pain.

According to the records of the University of Kansas, Byron Smith was Professor of Greek Language and Literature from 1873 to 1876, but was on leave for the years 1874-1875 and 1875-1876.

Professor Smith was not an excavator of verbal fossils, but a poet of language like Gilbert Murray or Swinburne. He did not teach a "dead language"—for Greek was to him a language forever living. Greek was poetry, philosophy, life; he taught it splendidly, as a power and a glory, yet humbly too, as the daily bread of the spirit.

Harris came to Lawrence like Saul, who, going out to find his father's donkeys, stumbled on a kingdom.

He himself leaves no doubt of his debt. He says: "Smith led me as Virgil led Dante into the ideal world that surrounds our earth as with illimitable spaces of purple sky, wind-swept and star-blown." [6]

Harris believed the love mutual and equal, for his own love dazzled his eyes. It could scarcely have been so, however: he was an enigma to Lawrence, an ambiguous figure. He engaged in

[6] *My Life and Loves,* Vol. I, p. 216.

affairs with women that could not be hidden in the goldfish bowl
of a small university town. Byron Smith must have known of
them: he was not the man to like them. In a letter to his fiancée,
Kate Stephens, he specifically wrote: "You know I have no confidence in or respect for the moral character of the man and could
not therefore dream of making him a confidential friend. He
had, however, been persistently kind to me, and seemed to build
so much upon my good opinion, and besides wrote me so ardent
and eloquent a letter, that I could not find it in my heart to
answer in terms not somehow touched with warmth. But I was
careful to express only that enthusiasm for humanity which is
natural to me and goes out to everyone who appeals to it—without meaning to establish relations of personal confidence. Doubtless he understood me in a personal sense. I wished also to benefit
him by pointing out that the only foundation of friendship which
I recognize is that of personal honor and devotion to great and
worthy aims. I overdid the matter and felt that I had before your
letter brought it home to me with such force." The letter is curious: Smith leans too far backward in denying a glow of friendship (he even "overdid" his own eloquence!); he is denying that
friendship largely because the girl he loves does not like the man
he loves. In such circumstances a man is seduced from the truth.
Yet, after all discount, the letter proves that Smith's love for Harris was less than Harris's for him. In every love, the French say,
there is one who loves and one who is loved.

It would have been hard to find *any* American intellectual of
that day who would not have been dismayed by the bold thought
and equally bold practice of Harris in relation to sex. In the time
of Stedman and Howells, and of a Mark Twain afraid of Mrs.
Grundy, who would have been able to understand such freedom?
Only Herman Melville, whom Harris was never to meet, or
Whitman, who was old! Melville never met the man who also
sailed against "the proud gods and commodores of this earth,
[and] ever stands forth his own inexorable self." In many ways

Harris was close to Melville—Melville who found freedom of
love in the South Seas; who hunted the White Whale of Nature's
strange demoniac power; who founded his faith only on the Titan courage of the spirit; who never dipped his flag to the proud
commodores but was "patriot only to Heaven." It is sad that they
never met, that Harris was never fully aware of Melville's genius;
yet perhaps they were too much alike ever to have liked each
other.

Frank Harris—he had now begun to sign himself "Frank" in
symbol that he was born again—did not then suspect the reserva-
tions in Byron Smith's heart, but only years later when he read
Smith's letters to Kate Stephens.

That Harris changed his name is significant. The undistin-
guished "James Thomas" was inadequate to a great artist and
man. Frank, however, was excellent: it suggested candor, integrity; its rhythm—the monosyllable before the dissyllable—was
good. The change was a date in his inner life, an outward and
visible sign of inward and invisible growth. He himself says:
"Now for the first time, when about 19 years of age, I came to
self-consciousness as Frank Harris and began to deal with life in
my own way and under this name, Frank." [7]

Meanwhile the newly born Frank sought the adventures of
the mind with the same ardor as he had sought the adventures of
the trail. Byron Smith was, like all great teachers, a catalyzing
agent: he caused a chemical precipitation between a sensitive
student and a great culture. By his necromancy Socrates became
a contemporary in a timeless world of truth and martyrdom, and
Antigone a magnificent rebel whose passion play was enacted in
Lawrence. Under the contagion of Smith's fervor, Harris learned
by heart many great choruses from the Greek dramatists, and
much of the *Apology* of Plato. His memory was prodigious—but
he said that this was a defect, since it made learning seem too
easy. He followed Smith beyond the lecture hall, and became that

[7] *My Life and Loves,* Vol. I, p. 241.

dream of every great teacher—a student about whom you need
not worry because he will not let you alone. He described himself
as a sponge, soaking up knowledge in ecstasy.

He absorbed the glory that was Greece. Himself Hebraic in
spirit (his style founded more on the King James Bible than on
Plato, his vision closer to Isaiah's than to Socrates'), he now
widened his learning and his life. He learned the lucid mathematics that differentiates a Greek temple from the charge of the
stone against the stars in a Gothic cathedral.

Yet even in the presence of his great teacher he remained original. Smith led him to the waters of Latin; but though Harris
drank, he declared them tepid and brackish. He never reverenced
the derivative, the second-best. He thought Horace a gossipy
worldling, and Virgil a moon beautiful with borrowed light.
Only Catullus, the lesser Villon of Rome, could hold him; or he
cared only for the bitter quintessential words of Tacitus, wrung
out of scanty, enduring granite.

Meanwhile he studied Kansas with care and with love. His
first volume, *Elder Conklin,* is retrospective evidence: it is vivid
with great landscapes that prove his loving intimacy with the
slow amplitude of Kansas. "On the horizon to their right, away
beyond the spears of yellow maize, the sun was sinking, a ball of
orange fire against the rose mist of the sky." And again: "Not a
cloud in the purple depths, no breath of air, no sound or stir of
life—peace absolute. . . . How the ivory light bathes the prairie
and shimmers on the sea of corn, and makes the little creek a rib-
band of silver. . . ." He knew many types of character in Kansas,
some (like Elder Conklin) the antithesis of his own, and he was
tolerant and just to all. Often, too, he refers to the dreadful heat
of the Middle West, which a European would know only if he
had endured it. He was fascinated by that fury of flame which
descends with summer over the scorching plains, to lay the country under intolerable burdens of temperature. "The sun," he

writes, "was pouring down rays of liquid flame; the road, covered inches deep in fine white dust, and the wooden sidewalks, glowed with heat." [8] Such salamander experiences are the shuddering memories of those who have endured them: not even Dante could have imagined Kansas heat out of his own heart. And Frank Harris noticed winter equally: "The snow-garment of winter protects the tender spring wheat." [9] Thus he set down lovingly his footnotes to Nature's Epic of Kansas.

Harris profoundly appreciated, too, the spirit of American democracy. There was a wastrel in Lawrence—a sort of ambulant sponge whose only distinction was that he had known Ulysses S. Grant when they were boys together: on that bright fragment from a black life, he based his pride. Suddenly it was announced that Grant, now President, was to visit Lawrence and dine at the Eldridge House. The youths of the University (who had often wondered if the wastrel was telling the truth) primed him with a round of free drinks and jockeyed him into position five minutes before the President was to arrive. When Grant appeared, accompanied by various dignitaries, the youngsters pushed the bleared, shambling wreck of a man forward, till he stood there in the light—blinking, holding out his hand with a deprecating smile, and saying, "Ulysses, Ulysses!"

"Grant's grim face did not relax. He looked at the human wreck with sharp little blue-gray eyes, taking him all in, his dirty threadbare clothes, frayed trousers, shabby boots and hat—everything—but not a gleam of recognition.

"The wastrel was ludicrous—pathetic. 'You hain't forgot Hap,' he said, grinning.

"Suddenly Grant's face changed. 'Are you so and so?' he said.

"'Sure,' quavered the wastrel, 'sure. I knew you'd remember me.'

---

[8] "The Sheriff and His Partner." In *Elder Conklin,* John Lane, 1930. P. 90.
[9] "A Modern Idyll." In *Elder Conklin.*

" 'Of course I do,' said the President, holding out his hand, 'of course I do. Yet it is twenty years or more since I saw you. You must come in and dine.'

"The wastrel's face quivered like jelly and he looked down at his clothes and hands.

" 'What's the matter?' Grant went on heartily. 'Come right in; these gentlemen will forgive your dress.' And in they went, to our amazement, the President and the drunken wastrel in the lead." [10]

Thus did Grant prove himself a great man. A lesson in democracy; a vindication of the American dream! Frank Harris cherished it and told it later to Balfour: something, he felt, "almost unthinkable to a European"—something poignant and great.

According to the records of the University of Kansas, "Mr. James (Frank) Harris entered the University September 9, 1874. He gave his age as nineteen, his home as Tenby, Wales, and a statement on the record indicates that he was born in Ireland. No date is given. He apparently only attended the University a few months in what is called a 'select' course. This apparently corresponds with what we now call a 'special student' who may take work but not toward any degree. We have no record of the courses in which he enrolled and in view of the fact that no grades appear on the record, it would indicate that he did not complete any work here at the University."

Thus Frank Harris got what he wanted at the University: incentive and direction. Formal training, a degree, a passport to social prestige or business connections, he did not get—for these he did not want. The University lit his torch and turned his face toward the horizon.

Meanwhile by shrewd skills impossible now to trace, he kept alive. By the money from his cattle-driving (though he unwisely loaned much of it to his brother), by working as "bouncer" in a gambling house, by possible but uncertain activity as entrepreneur

[10] *My Life and Loves,* Vol. III, pp. 364-65.

of billboards (this has been denied, but is utterly in character), by joining with his brother in running a butcher-shop he stayed alive. And he lived well.

He also loved well. At this time, by his own account, he possessed five women: the mature passionate wife of his employer in the gambling house, Lorna Mayhew; the ingenuous and charming Kate; the lovely Lily; the exquisite virginal Rose; the sense-ravishing mulatto, Sophie.

One must understand what he sought. Love to him was a sacrament, the very bread and wine of the body. It was renewal: a passionate release of poignant tension, a vital meeting of opposites that became more deeply individual because for an hour they had been more deeply one. He experienced these adventures of the flesh, which most men caricature on a level of dull release, with the ardor of a demigod and the artistry of a poet. And he never sought only his own easement, but to impart to the woman an equal joy. One should recall that even the Puritan, Carlyle, praised Mirabeau thus: "All manner of men he had gained . . . more especially all manner of women . . . for indeed hardly since the Arabian Prophet lay dead to Ali's admiration, was there such a love-hero with the strength of thirty men."

Frank Harris's body was vibrant with the ecstasy of love. He ached with the ardor of that ecstasy; the loveliness of Eve or Lilith drove him to sweet madness. He was insatiable, avid, love-drunken; he feasted eyes and hands upon love's body; he drank and drowned in the great rivers flowing to the sea. Each love, while it lasted, seemed central; in each he found a different door leading toward the same center. His joy purifies even the dross of his occasional words; the poetry of his love kindles even the prose of his lust. His lovesickness kept him healthy; his love-madness kept him sane. As saints and martyrs die in the white fire, the lover *lives* in the flame.

Meanwhile Byron Smith took leave of absence from the University. He had always been frail; now renal neuralgia left him wasted by restless nerves and residue of pain. He refused to marry Kate Stephens till he won the health he was never to regain. Harris ascribes his illness to a sexual wasting brought about by excess in Greece, years before. It is incredible that Smith would have confessed this, even if it had been true, to one of his students; the story has been traced to a man who, taking Smith's place, wished to keep it even by scandal. Harris, in his generous love, came to believe that Smith had told him the secret; his desire to be Smith's dearest friend was the paternity of his belief. It is curious that he was to make such incredible claims of confidence again, about Carlyle. Neither Smith nor Carlyle—proud, puritanic, taciturn about sex—would have revealed such things (even if they had existed) to anyone. Such confession would have violated their characters as surely as it would have violated Gauguin's to rise in prayer meeting and confess his "sins" like a Buchmanite. Why did Harris tell such things? Why did he believe them? The psychological genesis was that he loved and reverenced these men; yet they seemed to him one-sided, lacking in the sensuality necessary to genius: their lives, contradicting his own, convicted him of excess. As compensation for his own over-sexing, he found in them the flaw of under-sexing; their impossible confessions are the tacit confessions of Frank Harris.

Byron Smith went to Philadelphia to consult a doctor. Harris, restless without him, followed him there—and met a greater man. He heard Walt Whitman lecture to a small audience of workmen in a huge hall: thirty, where there was room for a thousand. The poet with his stiff slow walk, his short jacket cocked up behind, the tuft of gray hair showing under his parted collar, the margin of dirty white shirt visible under his vest, seemed comic, like "an old Cochin-China rooster I had seen when a boy; it stalked across the farmyard with the same slow, stiff gait and carried a stubby tail cocked up behind." But Whitman spoke slowly, with simple dignity. More and more with the years this meeting grew in meaning, till Whitman came to seem "the large unruffled soul of that great people manifestly called and chosen to exert an increasingly important influence on the destinies of mankind."

Whitman's great work was done. The harvest of his poetry was stored: he was like a farmer after autumn, contemplating his full barns. What if the world had no market?—he knew that it was a harvest to nourish a continent for ten thousand years. It is sad that he was too old and Harris too young for full comradeship: for here he met face to face the "dauntless rebel," the treader of open roads, the "turbulent and fleshly" apostle of life "immense in passion, pulse, and power," of whom he sang; and a man who was one day to be what he prophesied, one of a race of "splendid and savage old men." Whitman would have saluted, could he have foreseen them, *Montes* and *The Bomb* and *The Man Shakespeare*. It is sad, also, that Harris did not then fully know the greatness of Whitman.

Frank Harris returned to a half-life, fevered and brief, at the University. Smith grew weaker; caught pneumonia, which ended in tuberculosis; gave up his position on the Philadelphia *Press,* and went to Denver to seek health in that dry air. Passing through Lawrence, he met Harris. He spoke of himself as "finished"; he urged the younger man to take up the torch falling from his own hands; to become a scholar; to go to Germany and study with the masters of the mind.

Saddened by prescience of his friend's death, Harris was in no mood to conform. Almost immediately he quarreled with the University—he himself says it had to do with enforced chapel—and withdrew from classes. Whatever the casual excuse may have been, the causal reality was the absence of his one great teacher.

How was he to live? What was he to do? Law in the West of that time was both the most honored and the most lucrative profession. Why not discover some leading lawyer who was in need of an assistant—or even a partner, and educate himself into the profession? It is significant that again and again in the stories of the *Elder Conklin* volume, Harris speaks of law and lawyers. In several stories a young Englishman is a student in some lawyer's office, or a lawyer starting on his career. There is no reason for this unless it is a conscious or unconscious projection of Harris's own experience. He speaks of the law as if he had indeed cogitated it and worked with it: "The more I read the more clearly I see that law is only a sermon on various texts supplied by commonsense." [11]

Now Harris himself began to study law in the office of a friendly attorney, and finally presented himself for examination. In the period of 1874-1875, admissions to the bar in Kansas were made by the District Courts. The Journal of the Court in which they were recorded was the day by day record, kept in the handwriting of the clerk or judge, of whatever actions had been taken by the Court. Checking these records from 1872 through 1877, the secretary of the Douglas County Bar found no entry in the name of *Frank* Harris; but an entry dated June 22, 1875, says that *James T.* Harris was on that day admitted to the bar.[12] In official matters he still signed himself by the name given him at birth.

Harris gives his own account of his admission in *My Life and Loves*. He writes, "I was notified by Judge Bassett that I had passed the examination and told to present myself for admission on the 15th of June, I think, 1875." The fact that the date is not literally exact is the best possible evidence of the truth of his statement. He is evidently writing from memory—for he gets the year right, yet misses the day (narrowly); if he had been literally exact it would be surprising, or might suggest that he had merely looked up the record and copied the figures. His slight (natural) inaccuracy is one of those exceptions that prove the truth.

A picturesque footnote to his life as lawyer was his deliberate creation of a Kansas accent. His English speech, he was told, would prejudice a western jury; so he set himself to copy the

[11] "The Sheriff and His Partner," *op. cit.*
[12] Maxine Virtue, secretary of the Douglas County Bar, 1942.

speech of Hoysradt, a lawyer with the most pronounced western accent he had ever heard. He made it a rule always to use the slower western enunciation, the drawl of the prairies; till in a week or two everyone would have taken him for a man raised under Kansas sunflowers.

Harris says that his partner, Sommerfeld, a prominent lawyer of Lawrence, relieved him of much of the routine of the office and let him "get up the speeches." This was certainly a natural division of labor, if Sommerfeld was wise; Harris, with his knowledge of men and his vigor of speech, would have been at his best in such work. Before a jury his trenchant assurance, his fiery lion-eyes staring with the intensity of high spirit and short sight, would have made him a paragon. Pity the witness whom he cross-examined! In summing up or making a plea, his rich bass voice—now musical as a violin, now ringing with the resonance of an alarm bell—was an instrument unequaled in Kansas. He might have been an antecedent Clarence Darrow, rising to the height of his profession, and using his power in the service of those who labor and are heavy-laden.

One biographer, finding no record of the courts as to his appearance as counsel, decides that the whole story of his career as lawyer is "entirely fictitious." [13] But major declarations by Harris —for example, his visit to Carlyle, or his work for the Chesapeake and Ohio Railway—have been proved literal in substance. And his abilities, as well as the flexible nature of the law and its romantic attraction in the old West, would make it both possible and probable that he might turn to it and that he would do well in it. The evidence of his stories suggests that he had been a participant in the law. Even if he did not remain a lawyer long enough to appear himself as a counsel, he might well have been a brilliant young assistant who (as he says) "got up speeches" for Sommerfeld, and worked to perfect himself for future greatness.

[13] A. I. Tobin and Elmer Gertz, *Frank Harris: A Study in Black and White.* Madelaine Mendelsohn, 1931. P. 61.

It is ridiculous to suppose that such a man, after having been admitted to the bar, would not do well. Even his mediocre brother Will became a lawyer in Lawrence: could the brilliant Frank fail? It has too long been a tendency of Harris's biographers to make a molehill out of every mountain.

Harris did not become famous as a lawyer because his destiny lay elsewhere. He had not forgotten the urging of Byron Smith. Out of the tedium of the days and the hardening carapace of professional life, destiny called—now with a new voice. He often went to the Lawrence library. The librarian, a well-read and idealistic woman, was much interested in the brilliant young man. One day she showed him the last page of Emerson's advice to the scholars of Dartmouth College: "You will hear every day the maxims of a low prudence. You will hear that the first duty is to get land and money, place and name. 'What is this truth you seek? what is this beauty?' men will ask with derision. If nevertheless God have called any of you to explore truth and beauty, be bold, be firm, be true. When you shall say, 'As others do, so will I: I renounce, I am sorry for it, my early visions; I must eat the good of the land and let learning and romantic expectations go, until a more convenient season'; then dies the man in you; then once more perish the buds of art, and poetry and science, as they have died already in a thousand thousand men. The hour of that choice is the crisis of your history. . . . Why should you renounce your rights to traverse the starlit deserts of truth, for the premature comforts of an acre, house, and barn? Truth also has its roof, and bed, and board. Make yourself necessary to the world, and mankind will give you bread, and if not store of it, yet such as shall not take away your property in all men's affections, in art, in nature, and in hope."

Frank Harris saw the inertia of his present life hardening into tedium, into mere delight in nerve and sense, into momentum of "getting on," into lag of earth tangent to the soul's far trajectory. Lawrence had given him all it could. He was weary of too excessive passion, numbing the soul with final torpor; of scholarly decorum, now that the master of learning was gone; of professional ties that, with the years, would have turned his magic casements into windows opening on the dust of Main Streets.

Such is the motivation—but what of the means? One cannot be certain. Harris himself says that Byron Smith loaned him money to go to Europe; but Smith was sick and dying, he had given up his University salary and saw years of illness, perhaps, between him and death: could he have loaned the money even if he had had it? Certain biographers, leaping to the sceptical extreme, assume that Harris went East on the brake-rods of freight trains, and smuggled himself to Europe as a stowaway; but that violates his proud, aggressive character and his habit of success. He made his exits and his entrances not like some poor player, but magnificently—like a Macready. The explanation that best fits his character and circumstances is that the money he made driving cattle (through whatever transmigrations it may have gone) gave him sinews of war. His work as a lawyer may have aided him.

Where did he go, and how? He himself says that he traveled West, visiting the dying Smith in Denver, and sailed from San Francisco for the Orient. (Smith died May 4, 1877, in Denver.) The best evidence that he did not is Harris's own writing in *Confessional*. There, in an essay on "Great Cities of the World," he writes about cities that he visited about this time—Paris, Athens, Constantinople, Budapest, Vienna, London. But there is no account of any photography of the sun upon his soul in India, South Africa, or China—*at this time*. In his autobiography, too, there are vivid pages from his earlier years about all these cities; but a mere mention of visiting an undescribed East. If, as he says, he was too young to appreciate the Orient, why was he so vividly able to appreciate Europe?

Factual evidence is scanty. The State Department writes: "A search of the passport records covering the period [1874-1876] has failed to disclose the issue of an American passport to Mr. Harris to enable him to travel from the United States. However, it may be stated that passports were not required of American citizens traveling abroad during the period mentioned." Frank Harris says in his autobiography that his admission to the bar in Kansas, by the statement of a prominent judge, made him an American citizen; he would not, therefore, have required a passport. The probability which best fits his circumstances and his character (corroborated by his writings) is that he had saved a sum sufficient for his return to Europe, and that he sailed modestly but comfortably from New York to France.

However he went, Frank Harris returned to Europe richer because of America. He could never be wholly a European again: the amplitude of the prairies, the rush of great rivers, the majesty of the American sky, the energy of Chicago and New York, the voice of Whitman sounding over the roofs of the world, the idealism of a Smith and an Emerson, were part of him forever. The freedom and energy of the New World were his: could Columbus, after his voyages, ever be just a European? Frank Harris, too, had crossed unpath'd waters and had explored undreamed of shores—a second Columbus.

Chapter III

THE WANDER YEARS

(1876-1882)

IN *Confessional* Frank Harris selects Paris, among others of the few great cities of the world, for special realization: "Paris, too, is not likely to die, nor can it ever be forgotten. Here we grew sceptical of duty and laughed, and the light laughter—echoing hollow in the eternal silence—is called Voltaire. There is something of Rousseau and Voltaire, of Panurge and Figaro, in every man, and here is the city in which they lived their lives and faced their deaths. And what deaths they all met! A sort of convulsion of universal nature, during which the foundations of the earth were shaken, and the waters under the earth rose up to fill the vault of heaven. And all the while the blood-rain fell in sheets, till the earth shivered under its clammy mantle. But since the Revolution, Paris has become the ideal city. Profiting by its revolutionary experiences, France leads the world in social justice. It has no unemployed, few multimillionaires, and a love of the best in art, literature, and thought. . . . No! Paris is not likely to be forgotten while men live upon the earth." To this Paris he now came—to the city of Molière and Pascal, of Robespierre and the Knitting Women and the *Carmagnole,* of Napoleon, of Zola and Hugo and Baudelaire, of Corot and Renoir and Millet, of serene light and the soft music of Debussy. He felt the high lure of this

Gallic city that sparkled like the flame of a candle in which salt has been sprinkled.

He came in 1876.

In that decade the land of Napoleonic *élan* had crumbled like a country of hollow men before a new force in Europe: the Germans of the North, marching now not as a wild horde of valor, but with the disciplined might of the Legions. A new strong man had risen in Europe—Prussia; his prophet of blood and iron was Bismarck.

France was rekindling her eternal light from scattered hearths, amid the shadows of defeat. Outwardly broken, materially devastated, she was training herself to look into the eyes of Fate. In literature she was saying, "Be hard!" Realists, hiding the softness of their too tender hearts under the resolute hardness of their minds—de Maupassant, Zola—were seeing man as a political and social animal, and seeking to study him with the objective candor of science. Their champion in aesthetics was Taine, with his formula whereby the man, the race, the surroundings, the epoch, explain the work.

And in that land where eyes can see landscape, great painters were working: it seemed that France was seeking the consolation of loveliness in landscapes. Impressionists were seeing all that light shows upon a plane surface when reflected in the mirror of a mood. Among them yet beyond them, Cézanne, loneliest and last, was passing from surface to solid mass. As yet van Gogh, that Madman of the Sun, was working out his apprenticeship among the miners of the Borinage, or in the denser darkness of his father's home in Holland. Harris never met him. Rodin, master of clay and bronze and marble, was chiseling his rude tremendous elemental dreams, where stone surges out of the imprisoning earth to become idea. And him Harris did meet. In Paris, indeed, Frank Harris discovered his eyes: he looked at canvases where exquisite colors and firm lines freeze time into space. He saw also the frozen music of architecture: Notre Dame,

where the surge of the stones toward the stars took his eyes—
and his breath.

With equal eagerness he turned to the artists of the word. He
read the *Hernani* of Victor Hugo, and saw and heard it one
night with Sarah Bernhardt's "grave *traînante* voice" making it
music. He picked up a discarded copy of *Madame Bovary* (the
first eighty pages gone) and "swallowed it" in a couple of breathless hours. He read French literature from Rabelais and Montaigne (always a favorite) to Flaubert, Zola, and Balzac (that
genius of solid substance), with excursions into Pascal, Vauvenar-
gues, and Renan. This exhausted him, as Jacob was exhausted
after wrestling all night with God.

There was Taine, too, whose lectures at the University of Paris
on "The Philosophy of Art" and "The Ideal in Art" he attended.
Taine was famous throughout Europe—a critic, philosopher, and
historian, who in each capacity had done much for the new literature. (He was one of the first to acclaim Nietzsche.) Taine was
like Harris in his desire to discover genius; and Harris had intuition both for stars and for the telescopes of God who search them
out. Harris with his short supple body, his peering eyes that
seemed more aggressive because they had to stare in order to see,
his straight flesh-thick "rudder" of a nose, his fighter's chin that
he was already learning to mitigate by a mustache, his resonant
voice that could dominate a crowded room, listened with an appreciation mordant but sensitive to Taine's vivid words clothing
a vigorous intelligence. Among the more effervescent sons of
France, Harris sat with grave intensity kept salty by a sardonic
high disdain.

What words Taine spoke! The idea that lay at the heart of
anything, let an artist capture *that*. A lion, for example—what
was his *idea?*—lean, tawny, savage power: the lightning become
flesh; incarnate hunger, burning fierce. To realize him, the artist
might make his jaw a little longer or more terrible than nature;
might change him, by heightened emphasis, in the direction of

the lion's own meaning; but let a man distort the lion's intention or idea, even with grace, even with power, and it would be false art, for it would be the lie of the lion. Such words, salty with good sense, appealed to Harris; like all great teaching, they simply awakened what he had already known.

And Taine was no cloudy idealist drifting in a balloon of theory till he forgot the earth. When a student asked him if the universe revolved around some central axis to a divine fulfillment, he tartly answered: "My boy, there is only one thing around which the world revolves: a woman's body."

Taine noticed the mordant, deep-voiced youth—who smiled with grave eyes at his jests, and asked questions that startled even the teacher. Here was the disciple who might himself become a master! Interest warmed into intimacy, and led to letters of introduction, pregnant with insight, that proved not only the quality of Harris but equally of Taine.

Meanwhile Paris was beautiful. Girls of Paris were chic and dainty; the Seine, that artery of tradition, flowed with the blue blood of the aristocracy of rivers; there were good food and wine in the cafés. He found the wit and wisdom of a civilized people who, on the one hand, could say *"Bon homme, bon animal,"* and on the other perceive the distinctions of truth with Pascal or rise to devotion like that of the Maid of Orleans. The Celt in Harris and the type of his talent disposed him to love France. He loved the extremes of French genius, from the salty scepticism of Montaigne, measuring all with his *"Que sais-je?,"* to Jeanne la Romée, murmuring "Blessed Jesus!" among the flames. If America had given him space, energy, and material, France gave him grace, logic, and form.

In those marginal months he lit his world with the white candle of Paris that sparkled as Frenchmen dropped into the flame the salt of their wit. He lived delightfully on the Rue de Rivoli, that channel of human tides, that cascade of history.

He did not yet know his destiny; but already he was apprenticed to genius. He developed (for all his precocious audacity) slowly and late. He wished to keep his life forever fluid; later he wrote to Kate Stephens: "When a muscle becomes hard, it's a sign that it has ceased growing: which is another way of saying, 'Those whom the Gods love grow young.'" His fundamental desire was to follow the direction indicated by Byron Smith: to become a scholar. As yet it concealed his greater destiny: to become a creator. Meanwhile, in a more vital way than Matthew Arnold knew, he was seeking to *meet* the best that was being said or done in the world, incarnate in living men. Already he desired what he was later to formulate as his design: "The love of women and the reverence of great men." He wished to become the Boswell of man and superman.

The strenuous Jacob-wrestling of those days wearied him, and he fell ill. Only then did he remember his father and sister, and returned to the home he had so stridently left, a home now situated in Tenby, Wales.

There was little, however, to hold him there. His brothers were making a living and losing a life in America; Chrissie, his favorite, was dead; Annie was mistress of the first kindergarten in Wales. Captain Harris, quieter in speech, was more communicative: at last father and son could meet on a basis of experience that leveled the years. The Captain could tell Frank why he had not recommended him for the navy; could understand why the youngster had run away to be born again and named anew. He had known the devious ways by which one rose to be a Captain in the Queen's Navy; he had known that so spirited a lad would flare into disastrous revolt. A man of granite integrity! Yet his father was concerned with deeds done, with memories, with dreams in a night that was settling over the years. To Frank the past was the springboard of adventure: the ocean sparkled at his feet, inviting the strong swimmer.

Harris wandered in Ireland, and even attended Trinity College; but after the high clear skies of Kansas, Ireland seemed a drizzle of rain. And it was on the rim of events: he sought the center.

Fortified by a letter from Taine and helped by a new friend, Grant Allen, Harris became a teacher at Brighton College, in Brighton, that London-by-the-sea which was sometimes described as made of "wind, glare, and fashion."

He was one of the world's great teachers and one of the world's great scholars; but he had no formal degrees, and he was as alien to colleges as van Gogh or a timber wolf. His colleagues were the usual professors—a vacuum surrounded by an education. He was contemptuous of their ideal of the passionless pursuit of passionless intelligence; he disdained mediocrity, and reverenced only genius. He must have seemed to his colleagues some fantastic nemesis for their unknown sins.

His teaching was characteristic. In each class of thirty, "five or six were of real ability, and in the school three or four of astonishing minds, well graced, too, in manners and spirit. But six out of ten were stupid or obstinate." [1] An aristocrat of education, he ignored the dunces and taught the intelligent.

He was a strange "professor." His gray-green lion eyes, peering with the persistence of short sight, moved slowly over a class, seeking interest, intelligence. His magnetic virility and arrogance compelled discipline as an atmosphere, though he never asked it as a system. Not for nothing had he bested shipping clerks, sand-hogs, Indians, men who lived by their guns; he had the deadly assurance of Wild Bill Hickok: psychologically it seemed as if he had a six-shooter ready and was death on the draw. He held them by his voice—a voice to make Jericho fall. He held them by his originality: here was no prating from notes, no patter of dates and labels; here was literature come to life, as a character comes to life when a great actor lives it on the stage. Literature was not sawdust but star dust. And from star dust worlds and suns are made. To hear Harris read literature was to know music from the violin of a master. His students were entranced; they

[1] *My Life and Loves,* Vol. I, p. 328.

forgot grades, examinations, even the hungers and lusts of the flesh. And Harris did not seek from them the usual answers out of the dustbins of scholarship; he wanted them to think and live. Who was this man with the fierce glance and the fighter's jaw, who sometimes had tears in his eyes and who was unashamed of poetry? Pouring his voice abroad in such an ecstasy!

His students were held and compelled. The bookish and academic, though they could not patronize him (no one could ever patronize Harris!), discussed him before their other professors, who were happy to listen. Could this be "learning" if it came from such energy and joy? Did he have a system, complete a schedule, give them "facts"? To a few—the shy or lonely, or the bold and vital—he brought magic glasses, and lifted the Veil of Isis. They forgot him—but they never escaped him. All their lives, though inland far, they remembered that mighty voice, rolling forevermore.

At the suggestion of a wise woman, Harris gave extra classes for girls; these grew in size and favor, and made him more money in a week than the college paid him in a month. Thus, as usual, he fared well; and, knowing America, he invested his savings in Chilean bonds.

During one of his vacations, Frank Harris came to London on a quest begun in Texas. He had encountered Carlyle in his books —stormy prophet of doom, and heavyweight champion among critics. The dour Scotchman—a Titan hurling mountains amid twisted lightnings of pain, a Cromwell of the pen calling for new Ironsides to ride down the dilettanti of sham and set up integrity in word and deed—won his heart wholly and his mind partly. Here was a genuine man; a Prometheus with the vulture of dyspepsia gnawing at his vitals, hanging on the smoky Caucasus of London. With sure intuition of greatness, Harris knew that Carlyle spoke the height of contemporary England. So he went to meet Carlyle, in January, 1877.

Carlyle was eighty-two, Harris twenty-two. Carlyle had won

to the heights at last and stood alone upon a mountain top; through rifts of cloud he could see the future—the deserts humanity must cross, the battlefields, the green valleys far on the horizon. At times he saw a blood-red sun and stared into it with fierce old eyes like an eagle's. But for the most part it was cold and very lonely; there were sudden savage winds of pain; mist and cloud hid the horizon and the sun. The wife whom he had so stormily loved and deeply tried was dead: killed by the climb, the rarified air of the great height, the loneliness. Almost all acclaimed him now; few followed his vision. Were shams any the less? Were men ignoring mere happiness for the sake of God, and finding joy? Did they act on his "Produce, produce, if it be only a potato!"? Was England founding a new aristocracy of talent; colonizing her possessions with the plus of her population; finding wise governors for her bewildered millions? He was honored as an artist, ignored as a guide. He was alone in the face of death, as he had been alone in the face of life. Emerson had come to him once, a serene voice and noble heart, out of the distance and enigma of America. But who had come since to understand or even to speak?

Such was Carlyle when one Sunday a young man stood at the door of the Chelsea house. The seer looked from haunted, truth-seeing eyes into a face different from all he had known. Here was not the saintly serenity of Emerson's face, but a face of demoniac power, aggressive, confident, yet reverent toward greatness.

"Sir," the youthful visitor said, "you have long been to me a living voice; yet you have been an abstraction. Now I seek to know your living presence as I have known your living influence, in this our brotherhood of woe and duty."

The Sage of Chelsea looked at him from under shaggy brows; then bade him enter. Carlyle spoke with not quite the spate and torrent rush of old days, yet with an animation renewed by this youth so animated by deep ardors and high desires. He had felt the call of Emerson's words? Ah, the good Emerson! So he wanted to write and bring wisdom to men through words of power? He had been a cowboy? He had come from the plains whither once he, Carlyle, had dreamed of immigrating with rifle and spade from an England whose ears he seemed unable to tickle even with artillery? He was a Man of the Deed, no mere prettifier of art, "seeking to perfume dead dogs"? He had read Mill and Shakespeare and *Sartor* under stars mirrored in the Mississippi? The derring-do of Harris touched the seer deeply. He recognized a new avatar from Yankeeland, another of the royal breed of whom Emerson had been the first. Growing stern again—feeling, as prophets must, the weaknesses of the man: his self-assurance, his plangent aggressiveness—he gave advice which he himself had scorned: "Not to proclaim opinions offensive to the majority of men, rashly and defiantly; but rather, in silence, and in study, to wait till one's nonage is past. The best sign," he thundered, "of maturity is moderation!" (Was it moderation that wrote of man's thunder-riven wonder-passage from eternity to eternity?—that chanted the taking of the Bastille in the tongue of Titans?) So the great man talked, rekindling the lava of his heart amid the ashes of the days. Not for years had he felt so portentous an omen; he had not lived in vain if his words had called this youth. But he was old and tired; gloom shadowed hope. He fell silent, listening to this stranger who was not daunted even by genius: good forthright words, these—substance and not shadow, words with blood in them. . . . Emerson, for all his greatness, had been too sweet a saint for a world of brute inertia where dynamite must blast the roads of God. Sun-stuff was more than "light": light came from the burning core, the livid volcano-star where hell's fury suffered that heaven's light might shine. And here was a man who knew the blood, sweat, and tears; the Thor's hammer, Mjollnir, that smote evil giants and serpents. Here was one who had killed to live; who knew that life is no pageant of "clotheshorses and patent digesters," but a "brotherhood of woe and duty." Good! The weary heart warmed; the tired eyes gleamed. Suddenly he rose and walked to his desk; he wrote, and handed the young man what he had written. "Take it to Froude," he said. "The good Froude!" (Was there a touch of wry condescension in the phrase?) "He will help you." The scribbled note read: "I expect more considerable things from this young man than from any I have met since Emerson." Here was passport to immortality!

The sage was tired; Harris, tactful always and only in the presence of genius, withdrew. Carlyle clasped his hand, and bade him "Good speed and God speed!" The door closed, and literal tears sprang into Frank Harris's eyes—the only tears he ever shed, tears for greatness or for the pain of greatness—the sacred tears.

Such was the first of several meetings. None of the others, perhaps, was quite so great. But there were walks and talks with the Scotchman who never seemed quite to have been young, and never quite to have grown old. The terrible torrent of his humor, like the magnificent jests of God overwhelming Job out of the whirlwind, fell in blinding sheets. So much that he had said which none had heeded! His mind had been a great instrument of power, burnished to man's uses, ready to build the road toward the future; yet instead of using him, England had turned aside to horse racing at a perpetual Derby! Harris could understand, for he felt himself also a statesman of the deed. He felt the rugged power behind the voice like a mountain wind; he knew the grandeur and tragedy of this Himalayan man.

Reading Carlyle's words about Harris, many think of the honor they do the younger man. But is not the greater significance the honor they do the older man? To have seen at once in this obscure youth one of God's Spies—is not that final proof that Carlyle was great? Did not Harris come, to eyes that could see, trailing clouds of promise? Did not Carlyle feel, tangible already, the shape of things unseen? With that second sight which is insight, he foreknew "Montes"—that splash of crimson glory; the grave sublimity of "The Magic Glasses"; the profundity of *The Man Shakespeare;* the insights of *Contemporary Portraits.* His words were not only an honor to Harris, but also a glory to Carlyle.

Those walks and talks of the old man who had completed his work and the young man who had not begun his made history. Harris spoke of those pages where Carlyle had painted to the life such contemporaries as Coleridge. "There," he suggested, "rather than in salvage from the dustbins of history, lies the seer's most precious gift. Many are called to write of old, unhappy, far-off things and battles long ago; few are chosen to look about them at the living great and paint them in their habit as they are." Why had Carlyle not done more of that?—a little about Tennyson; more about Coleridge. And there were Browning and many another whom he had known in the flesh and whom only he could recognize and portray. Why write of the dead Frederick and not of the living Ruskin? Leave the past, that one could know only from records, to the pedants! Turn to the present, incarnate in the splendid and dreadful flesh. Carlyle felt the pertinence of this; there was in his eyes nostalgia for the past that might have been. He turned to the younger man: "Do you write them," he said, "do you paint them, these portraits of the great whom you meet still in the flesh. There is work to fill every blue day that shall dawn for you." It was challenge and consecration; it wakened to design what was already desire; from that word *Contemporary Portraits* was born.

Once, passing the place where his wife had died, Carlyle removed his hat and stood bareheaded in the rain, his long gray hair wind-blown, rain-wet. . . .

From these meetings of two men so different in temperament yet so equal in genius, came a portrait in words as great as Whistler's in oils. Harris understood Carlyle as few others have; the bulk of his portrait is sane and glowing truth. The aberrations of Carlyle's sex-life, being controversial, are generally mentioned—a pity, for the rest of the portrait is more important.

Whether Carlyle told Harris that the trouble between him and Jane Carlyle was that their marriage was never consummated—whether Harris is right in his gruesome revelation of Carlyle's supposed impotence—usurps too much attention. Shaw calls it incredible. Even if it were true, it would have violated Carlyle's character to confess it to anyone. Harris, so vehemently sexed, probably read the opposite flaw into a genius that intrigued and yet rebuked him with Puritanism. But though these items (because they are scabrously sensational) are generally cited, they are nonessential: the great revelations are not of Carlyle's supposed impotence, but of his certain power.

Partly through Carlyle, Harris turned toward Germany. In "Sonia," George Lascelles heard Ruskin at Oxford bid his young listeners study social questions on the continent: for "the student, like the apprentice, should have his *Wanderjahre.*" For George Lascelles, substitute Frank Harris; for John Ruskin, Thomas Carlyle.

Harris had also discovered for himself his two great favorites—Goethe and Heine; Heine, lord of humor and master of poetry, the flaming Jew; Goethe, the Olympian, poised above the world's vain "wurrawurra," seeing life as an infinite progression toward an infinite perfection that we forever approach but that we never reach.

And Germany was the young power in Europe. Both socialism and great individuals were there—was there not Wagner, or Bismarck? The great problem for society, Harris thought, was in what Goethe called the battle of the Haves and the Have-Nots; it could be solved only by a social justice that would not be, to individuals, an injustice. How combine the good of the many with the freedom of the few? How bring the thesis of individual liberty, the antithesis of social needs, into the higher synthesis of a true commonwealth? Perhaps Germany was working out the answer. In an anarchic England, money-centered—in a France where the vision of the few was checked by the conservatism of a peasant-centered people full of inertia like their ancient earth—men were not even seeking the answer. By fortunate investment of his Brighton savings in Chilean bonds, which he had bought in decline and held till they rose to new heights, he had funds for travel.

But war broke out between Russia and Turkey, and Harris was desirous of seeing so lethal a phenomenon at first eye. Skobeleff, a genius among generals, was there—a Byron of the steppes who had captured the imagination of Europe. Securing permission from Skobeleff, and a promise from several American papers that his correspondence would be paid for at twenty dollars a column, he sought the battlefield.

By way of Moscow, Harris came to Plevna, where Osman, the Turkish leader, was besieged. He found that genius is hated even among generals, a fact that helps to explain the miscarriage of wars. Skobeleff, the genius, was an aide to mediocrity: Dragomirof was in command. Harris found Skobeleff a fellow of wit and fire, able equally in the lists of war or love (though here the too eager flame had burned itself out). He studied the art of war, the genius of improvisation in battle, as he watched Skobeleff devise a way to evade the deadly rifle fire of the Turks. At the heels of the impetuous general he had his total immersion in fire (he had had only his baptism in Texas) as he stormed into Plevna. He discovered that mediocrity would rather lose a battle than see its subordinate with genius successful: unsupported, Skobeleff had to abandon the town he might have held. It was initiation into life, for war is the knife-edge of politics, naked from the sheath.

Accounts of the battle of Plevna corroborate Harris. Skobeleff, who went through it without a scratch, was a romantic figure: "His extraordinary daring, and amazing freedom from the usual accidents of warfare, inspired his men with the belief that he

was almost a miraculous being; and he increased his popularity
in the ranks by his cheerful and sympathetic manner." [2] The
scene after Skobeleff was driven out of his conquest by lack of
reinforcements is also corroborated. "The broken remnants . . .
were driven back in utter ruin, and General Skobeleff was almost
mad with rage and anguish. 'He was in a fearful state of excitement,' says Mr. MacGahap. 'His uniform was covered with mud
and filth; his sword broken; his Cross of St. George twisted
round on his shoulder; his face black with powder and smoke;
his eyes haggard and bloodshot and his voice quite gone. He
spoke in a hoarse whisper. I never before saw such a picture of
battle as he presented.' At night, the same correspondent saw him
again in his tent: he was then calm and collected. He said, 'I have
done my best; I could do no more. My detachment is half destroyed; my regiments do not exist; I have no officers left; they
sent me no reinforcements, and I have lost three guns.' 'Why did
they refuse you reinforcements?' he was asked. 'Who was to
blame?' 'I blame nobody,' he replied. 'It was the will of God.'" [3]
But Harris knew that it was not the will of God but the malice
of men, the stupidity of superiors.

The description of the battle reveals what Harris endured; for
he too was in the thick of it.

Skobeleff was a brilliant initiator into the art of war. He was
also a Homeric hero: in a later campaign, before the battle of
Senova, he concluded a speech to his men thus: "God asks you
to be heroes! " [4]

Yet for all their fascination, the bright eyes of danger were only
an interlude. Harris was still in his *wanderjahre*; still the apprentice of wisdom. He went to Germany, to become a student in the
University of Heidelberg.

In Germany Frank Harris found thorough scholarship and
reverence for the mind; here was no English cant, sneering at

[2] Cassell's *History of the Russo-Turkish War*, Vol. I, p. 416.
[3] *Ibid.*　　　　[4] *Ibid.*, Vol. II, p. 539.

learning with faint patronage or dilettante disdain. Yet he discovered liabilities underscored in red, such as the pedantic arrogance in even such a scholar as Kuno Fischer, who ranked Goethe first, and then claimed Shakespeare as the second of "Germanic" geniuses. (Was it unconscious inferiority that made Germans claim the superior men of other peoples? These Teutons of the forest, still barbarians, forever sneered at other lands as barbarous, and forever stole their glories—as the Visigoths once looted Rome.) Harris scraped his feet in desecration of the classroom, and dared, when invited, the incredible heresy of contradicting a German professor. To the credit of Kuno Fischer, this aroused his interest more than his anger: what could one expect from a wild American? At least he was interested in ideas, even if, as was to be expected, he got them wrong.

Harris saw his Germans clearly. Through Sonia's eyes he judged them: "The Germans are like their language—large, but ill-formed and awkward; disciplined mediocrities they all seem to me, and the women, hens, 'cluck, cluck, Kaffee klatch.'" He did not like the Germans, though he admired Germany; he preferred the Russians—an elemental people, moving like the tides or the winds, freely lavish like the sun.

Harris's most intimate discovery of German arrogance came when a corps-student jostled him off the sidewalk. He was told that the fellow was seeking merely to *"rempeln"* him, or ask him to fight; so he ran after him and fought him in the American way of squaring off and sending a fist to the jaw. The student fell in a heap; the bystanders sent for the police. Harris was accused of having hit the student with his cane: how else could he have knocked a man senseless? So he gave another quite successful demonstration on the jaw of one of his accusers, then walked away. Next morning six policemen came to hale him before a judge, for *"groben Unfugs auf der Strasse"*: he was sentenced to six weeks in Carcer (the University Prison), then dismissed from the University.

Harris went to Göttingen. He was glad to do so, for it had been the university of two great men—Heine and Bismarck. There he listened to lectures by Lotze, with whom he discussed the gilded mediocrity that is often called the Golden Mean. He studied history and philology. His work here, just as in Lawrence, was eclectic: never, though he studied in many of the world's greatest universities, did he complete a prescribed schedule or take a formal degree. He sought wisdom for its own dear sake, never as a passport to a position. He was the Commando of colleges; the Ishmael of education.

Yet he did not forget Carlyle, or his own destiny. He had begun to write, as a letter to Carlyle, December 12, 1878, proves. "For a long time the choice of a life's calling embarrassed me. After many doubtings and much uncertainty, I have determined to do my work with my pen; as a volunteer in the ranks to fight for what seems to me the best cause. Having enough to live on in a very modest way, which contents me, I need not to be a mercenary soldier. I think that this my resolution does not spring from idle vanity, but has gradually grown, as I have of late become more and more convinced that in this way and no other can I do my work.

"When, in January, 1877, I called upon you, I asked you many questions concerning the writer's art. Yet the faults of bombast and weakness which I then dimly felt, I, now deploring, yet find it not easy to correct. Sometimes, almost despairing, I have thought that perchance they were radical shortcomings inherent in my blood. The Celtic vanity with its characteristic love of loud words (you may remember that I am an Irishman), the besetting sin of self-annunciation, I have struggled by calm reflection and thoughts of higher duties to overcome, as yet with all but too imperfect success. Still I work on at Philology and History, and in my spare time sketch plans and embody thoughts which when finished strike me with an overwhelming sense of my own impotence; then and there I confide them to the fire. For the last three years one work—a novel—has been continually in my thoughts. Sensible, however, of my deficiencies, I have hesitated to tell the story which presses for utterance, and at last, tormented yet enthusiastic, I turn for advice to the Man, who, for some years filling my mental horizon, has done me more good than any other preacher living or dead. . . . In the enclosed 'Skeleton of a Novel' I could not avoid mentioning you, and I have done this freely as if not destined for your eye. Knowing you to be throned above all unrealities, I send you this sketch—seeing some of its faults in a glaring clearness, not because I think it is the best I can do, but because its faults are so naked in their deformity that perchance you will be able to tell me what inner fatuity they spring from, and how best to correct them. Yet I would not send it to you for the faults' sake alone, but because I believe your tolerant sympathy will feel for me, at least, in my aim; and if as I think there be something worthy in the object, your experience and insight weighing and recognizing it will aid me to do the work, while showing me at once the pitfalls and the highway. You will at once see that no *Man* wrote this sketch. The liquor is still fermenting, throwing off many bubbles, and is in a state of much greater commotion than a good liquid could be, yet you will be able to tell me how to help the fermentation so as to bring it to a more speedy termination and you will be able to predict—what, if cleared and settled, the worth of the draught will be. Is there . . . the possibility that a strong generous wine . . . can come out of this muddy liquor? If your answer is favorable, you will comfort me, which help I need; if unfavorable, I must still work, for this is appointed to me.

"I await your answer, I turn to you, because I know no other man to whom I can bow, whose judgment I value. Knowing by your silence of late years, and by what you yourself have told me about your bodily weakness, that we can look for no more from

your pen, I would not trouble you, Sir, if I knew of any other
help; but so it must be. . . .

"With Love, therefore, and Reverence too deep for words,

I subscribe myself,

Frank Harris"

What was this "Skeleton of a Novel"? It must have dealt with
material most ready to his hand: his own life. Was it a version
of his life on the plains? That he read Carlyle there and owed
much to him may explain the words "I could not help mentioning you." Or it may have been a more ambitious autobiographical
novel, in which his visit to Carlyle is more dramatically realized.
Carlyle, either because he did not like it (which is possible) or
because he was old and sad (which is probable), made no reply.
This silence hurt Frank Harris: did it mean that the great beginning was a false springtime? The final effect, however, was good:
the frost forced the young tree to gather its life for richer blossom
and for larger fruit.

Harris saw much in Germany. Berlin he called a "Weltdorf,"
or World-Village; he did not include it among his great cities.
Yet there he heard Bismarck speak. For Bismarck he had reverence: a more extrinsic Carlyle, a hero of action; a man of ruthless
power, used, statesman-like, for good. Harris was a radical conservative, whose sympathy was equally for the inarticulate poor
who might need help and for the articulate genius who might
bring help. He dreamed of becoming a Bismarck of England, a
statesman of genius such as Carlyle might have been. He came to
know Wagner, too—"the little hawk-faced fellow with the plowshare chin." [5] He lodged in Munich in the very house where Wagner had lived; somewhere in Germany he met the master and
listened to his melancholy at the critics' estimate of him, and to
the assurance of his own estimate of himself.

From Germany Harris won wider knowledge of literature—of

[5] Letter to Gerald Cumberland, August 29, 1918. Published in Gerald Cumberland, *Set Down in Malice*. Brentano's, 1919.

Shakespeare, ironically, even more than of Goethe—and experience of what social planning can do for a people. He mastered German so thoroughly that he had to unlearn it before he could attain his own English style. But he tired of the North (as Goethe did) and turned to the South and the sun.

Bernard Shaw said later that, as critic, Harris alone could "bend the bow of Ulysses"; now, symbolically, he was to visit the land of Ulysses—the Greece to which Byron Smith had introduced him. . . .

In *Confessional* Harris writes noble pages about Athens: "Athens, too, we can never forget. In it we live again the youth-tide of humanity. Here we become warriors and artists, poets and philosophers, without straining effort; here our dreams are fulfilled, all our powers realized. On its Acropolis we still see the stately temples, and all around them fair statues, incorporating in human form those ideals of love and wisdom and majesty which still guide our aspirations. Here the old religion of law loses its terrors; the fallen veil reveals a fair humanity, and we can give up our adoration for words and looks of love. In Athens life opens before us, life and the joy of living. We have not forgotten the boy's delight in rivalry and conquest, the keen pleasure of strife for strife's sake, but we have come to recognize that life itself is a perpetual struggle, whether it be the artist's struggle with his material, or the statesman's strife with his surroundings, or the saint's conflict with his own unworthiness. At length we realize that living implies continual overcoming. And so we throw ourselves into the world, and are orators, artists, poets, as the desire moves us, attempting all things, and succeeding in all our endeavors. Behind us, as we pass, we leave eloquent words of wisdom, statues of astonishing perfection, poems of deathless beauty, deeds that can never be forgotten; but, at last, we are brought face to face with the hard lesson that of himself the individual, however gifted and however powerful, is not omnipotent, and it is Rome that teaches us." Such pages prove that Harris did not visit Greece as a space on the map, but as a mood of the spirit.

Frank Harris found not only fragments of marble; the lucid mathematics of the Parthenon; the beautiful drift-stones cast up, half broken, by that great human river that was Greece; the salvage of genius. He also found modern Greeks who reverenced their great past, who kept the classic language alive, who lived the life of the spirit. Learning modern Greek, he found more in the music of Sophocles than he had even when he studied with Smith. The light of the sun fell honey-colored over the blue hills of dream. The Aegean, where the ships had sailed to Salamis, was wine-dark and many-sounding. He was an eavesdropper upon history; a worshipper, afoot and lighthearted, where supreme genius had once dazzled the world. He found no men of whom he might paint contemporary portraits, but he walked awed where the great dead had lived, and heard the whisper of immortal ghosts.

And among the living there was the lovely Eirene. The sister of Damala, husband of Sarah Bernhardt, she taught him secrets of love that no English or American girl knew.

Greece brought him that baptism of the sun which Arles brought to van Gogh. He was drenched in the sun-stuff of Apollo; he knew the golden rain that fell on Danaë. He was bathed and cleansed in light.

One of his adventures was a rediscovery of the great dead. Plutarch had written that at Thebes, when Philip and the youthful Alexander made blitzkrieg out of Macedon, a band of noble youths swore to stop them or to die. They formed their ranks against the tank-like charge of the massive spear-wedge, in a devoted three hundred. But they were steam-rollered by the mountaineers from the north; the long spears broke only after they had gone through ribs and vertebrae. In honor of this gallant death Thebes buried the three hundred in a river-bed where had been their last stand, in a single grave of glory—turning aside the very river to make them a tomb. Harris, stirred by the story, visited the place of their death. In his autobiography he makes himself a hero of archeology, initiating the discovery; in an earlier account (the *Saturday Review*) he says that he arrived just as Schliemann, the famous German archeologist, was about to excavate the grave. The *facts* are probably given by the earlier account; the *truth* is given by both: for the truth is the gallant spirit of the youths, and the pity and glory of their fate, and this not Schliemann but Harris made articulate. Schliemann excavated their bones; Harris, their spirit. The diggers found earth heaped in a suggestive mound near the carved "lion of Chaerea," and disinterred skeletons that added up to three hundred lacking three —and three urns containing ashes, evidently of mortally wounded youths who, dying later, had been cremated and buried in the grave of glory. The bones were horribly broken, showing the havoc that the Macedonian spear made with ribs or spine. A gruesome footnote to glory!—also, a justification of the hero against the debunker: for Plutarch, at whom sceptics sneered, was right. Harris hoped that in the modern world youths as noble may band themselves together—to die if necessary, to live if possible, for ends even more glorious. He knew that the world's need was a new Sacred Band; he wished, himself, to be one of such a Three Hundred.

His wander-years took him to Constantinople. "There is Constantinople, the city of lawless lust and savage cruelty; the stones of it are blood-stained with purposeless murder; the waters flowing by it are scared to haste by the deeds they witness there. Constantinople will be remembered as men remember in their own despite the grimmest tales of giant and ogre over which they shuddered in childhood. Besides, Constantinople is the grave of Athens; in Saint Sophia there still dwells the memory of her loveliness, and the wavelets of the Sweet Waters whisper to each other her *requiem*."[6]

[6] "Great Cities of the World." In *Confessional*. Copyright, Nellie Harris, 1930. P. 94.

Frank Harris noticed that in the churches which the Mohammedans used as mosques, the crescent was falling from the peeling walls and the cross was appearing underneath. He saw symbolically that, fair as is the paganism of the Greeks or the stern purity of Mohammet, the light of Jesus who "speaks for the soul" is greater. "In time I came to see that Saint Sophia was a greater achievement even than the Parthenon, and learned in this way that the loftier spirit usually finds in Time the nobler body." [7]

By way of the Black Sea and the Danube he came to the city of Buda—with Pesht across the great bridge. He reached Vienna, "the rose-red city half as old as time," whose gay, melancholy, light, supple spirit he was always to love. Here he made successful love to a café singer, Marie Kirschner, who was later to become the heroine of his story, "A Mad Love."

Italy called him. He spent some weeks in Florence, Ravenna, and Milan, studying churches and paintings and discovering the scabrous humor of Ariosto and the genius of Dante, that eagle among the poets. Leopardi, however, won his intensest devotion. Harris, like Leopardi, was grave and fundamentally grim; he too had felt the touch of the world's fangs, bared most readily to tear those who (once they are dead) are the world's glory. He saluted the dark poet of "the heart's deep languor and the soul's sad tears."

Two Italian episodes are revealing. Lamperti, one of the world's great teachers of music, hearing Harris sing, wished the resonant American to become his pupil, assuring him that such a voice could rise to grand opera. But Harris felt that he had a higher destiny than the tinseled splendors of the stage. The second episode reveals his artistic intuition—and his canny sense of financial values. In Milan he picked up some Visconti armor of the 14th or 15th century; he bought a "gold inlaid suit complete for 100 pounds," which he sold "five years later in London for 5000 pounds." [8]

[7] *My Life and Loves,* Vol. II, p. 90.
[8] *Ibid.,* p. 94.

Finally he returned to Paris, where during the summer he widened his circle of acquaintance. He met Turgenief, the great Russian in exile, the third after Tolstoi and Dostoevsky. The author of the poignant *Smoke* and of *Fathers and Sons* with its mordant realist, Bazarov, was out walking one day and fell into step with the strolling Harris. They conversed; but Harris, as he said, was utterly unknown—had done nothing. . . . He was diffident; he did not question Turgenief about Tolstoi. It was a meeting of courtesy, not comradeship. Harris was yet a neophyte of great men; an apprentice of portraiture.

Frank Harris also met one his great friends, de Maupassant. Harris was always to use most aptly and to appreciate most highly that form of narrative in which life is seen by a lightning-flash— the short story. In this de Maupassant was a master: he taught Harris much, by precept and example. The excess, the exhausted nerves, the lust-wakened madness of the man, though implicit, became explicit only later: now he was the stocky Frenchman of peasant blood, with a mind like a small intense blacksmith's flame, red under fierce draught. Power—narrow power that would fan itself into expression and exasperation, and burn itself out!

Such were Frank Harris's wander-years. He had gone through Europe like Ulysses, forever roaming with a hungry heart. Literatures, scholars, universities, artists, generals, singers, writers, statesmen, the social and intellectual life of peoples, paintings and statues and fragments of marble stamped with imperishable grace, and (not least) the love of women—all these had made him a man of the world—and a man of more than "the world." He was ready to meet the great of his day; he was growing toward those later and greater initiations into the glory of Shakespeare, into the height of the spirit.

The lad from Galway, the cowboy from Texas, had come far. The rich culture of Europe had entered not only into his mind, but into the rhythm of his blood. He was already a cosmopolite, a citizen of the world.

What was his destiny? Sometimes he hoped to become a Bismarck of England who might remake the map of man; sometimes he realized that he was an artist, who might remake the mood of man. He was sure at least that he belonged, like the Three Hundred of Thebes, to a Sacred Band.

By birth, English was his language and England his home. For him, therefore, England was the place to go; and the heart of England was London. He was never an admirer of Tennyson, but there was a couplet of that honeyed Victorian that he often quoted and always praised: the lines from "Locksley Hall" about the London that flares on the horizon, calling the heart of youth. For there dwelt

Men, my brothers, men the workers, ever reaping something new:
That which they have done but earnest of the things that they shall do.

He loved the lines because he too had once seen the flare of London, and dreamed the known dream that leads to the unknown deed.

Frank Harris came to that center of financial power, of world empire, of science and literature which was the London of 1882. He heard the future where "men his brothers, men the workers" were reaping something new; and, feeling in his heart that Carlyle had seen truly, he knew that all which he had done was but earnest of a greater deed.

Chapter IV

KITE AGAINST THE WIND

(1882-1894)

"LONDON, to me, is like a woman with wet draggled skirts (it's always raining in London), and at first you turn from her in disgust, but soon you discover that she has glorious eyes lighting up her pale wet face . . . . What society can be found comparable to that which throngs the streets of Old London—the London of Shakespeare and Elizabeth, of Cromwell and Milton, of Chatham and Nelson, of Wordsworth and Coleridge, of Carlyle and Browning? Even now, after living but a short time in London, we become aware that the spirits of these men compass us about; this is the very air they breathed, these skies they gazed upon, these ways they trod; and the deeds they did, and the words they spoke, live still and reveal their souls to us with such reality of represent-ment that we can easily conjure up their bodily presence." [1] Thus London to Harris was a city of history and atmosphere—of the humorous tang of Dickens and the tenuous mist-poetry of Whistler. In its sterner aspects, it might be the London of Blake's visions, or the London that Thomson saw as a City of Dreadful Night.

But to the young, eager Harris it was rather an oyster to be

---

[1] "Great Cities of the World." In *Confessional*. Copyright, Nellie Harris, 1930.

opened and eaten; one must add, however, that he hoped to find in it the Pearl of Great Price.

There could hardly have been a more brilliant or a more diffi-cult field. In literature, Carlyle, just dead, had left Olympus va-cant: who could climb to his height? (Frank Harris, in his heart, answered: "Frank Harris!") Dickens was dead, too, and George Eliot; but of the older writers enough were living to daunt the most hopeful—Tennyson, Browning, Arnold. Ruskin was writing of art (and suing Whistler); Whistler was painting nebulous nocturnes and austere studies in Carlyle and motherhood, and flinging verbal paintpots dexterously at the world and Ruskin. Younger comtemporaries made a brilliant galaxy: Rossetti, Swin-burne, Morris; Cunninghame Graham; Aubrey Beardsley (artist of the brothels of the soul) and Max Beerbohm (critic by cari-cature divinely apt); those opposite Irishmen from Dublin and Ulster, Wilde and Shaw; Dowson, with the monotone of his single valid experience, Cynara; Davidson, with his crabbed great-ness, and the violet-eyed Middleton; the great adventurer, Richard Burton. Kipling, Chesterton, Wells, Hardy, Moore, Bennett, Gals-worthy were stars as yet to fall on Piccadilly. And Harris was to play their recording angel—who wrote down what for most of them "the last dawn of reckoning shall read."

The early Victorians had done their work. In the present dec-ades the Aesthetes of the Green Carnation and the Apostles of Social Revolution (or of that brake on revolution, Fabianism) were to move into what they regarded as Bleak House. It was not only William Morris who refurnished the Victorian parlors long hideous with antimacassars, clocks under glass, and stuffed atroci-ties supposed to be chairs and sofas; the young writers were changing the intellectual furniture of Bleak House. The '80's and '90's were a day of spring housecleaning and interior redecorating. Harris took vivid part in this; but if he wished to evict Mrs. Grundy, it was only so that humanity might again dwell in the House Beautiful.

As yet the younger writers had hardly arrived. Certainly Frank Harris had not! How could an outsider from Galway and Lawrence, without friends or money, storm a world capital? His money was almost gone; he had no prestige of birth or friends; his American years would hardly endear him to Londoners, who at best would feel as transient an interest in him as in some red-shirted Joaquin Miller—a sensation easing the tedium of a day; he had no university degree, no substantial work accomplished. What could he do?

One passport might help him: Carlyle's letter of introduction. He hastened to present it, journeying out of London to Froude's home by the sea.

Froude was a first writer of the second rank. Influenced by Carlyle, with less of a volcano for a heart, he had a fine, partly derivative talent. He was a journalist of genius. As biographer of Carlyle, and even more in his own lucid studies in history, he had a niche in the Hall of Fame—and certainly high honor in his own day. "The good Froude," Carlyle had called him.

He was genuinely interested. So Carlyle had been more impressed by Harris than by any other man since Emerson? Such words laid an obligation upon all who heard them, especially upon those who had loved Carlyle: they seemed the codicil of a will, vesting a heritage of help.

As a bookman, who did not know that adventures come to the adventurous, as love to the lover or God to the God-centered, Froude was fascinated by Harris's tales. A cowboy who had met Carlyle? Here was a dainty dish to set before an editor! Harris, appraising his man, expressed himself in a torrent of talk: though obscure, he was not diffident; he knew in whom he had believed —Frank Harris, and all the future latent within his genius. He told of his life on the plains; of reading *Heroes* by the side of Wild Bill Hickok; of rising from his reading to kill a buffalo or a Sioux. Froude had written of the campaigns of Caesar, of killings by the hundreds of thousands; yet he had never shed blood.

Here was a younger man who talked quietly of deeds of derring-do as routine of the trail. Harris's stories fascinated him as the grim but glamorous tales of Othello fascinated Desdemona.

Froude promised to tell his publishers about Harris and to introduce him to the influential of London. In two weeks he would return to London; meanwhile, had Harris any work that he might read? Harris, whose first love was poetry, gave Froude a slim black notebook in which he had written in his "clear, firm, bold copperplate, a few dozen poems, chiefly sonnets." Froude promised to read them and to introduce the writer to his own publishers; so, without having met very deeply, they parted.

In a few weeks, Froude came to London and gave a dinner for the young man with the passport from Carlyle. The mighty men of London were there, whose nod would open doors: Chennery, editor of the London *Times,* that solid and central sheet; Charles Longman, "our best publisher"; Austin Dobson. Froude made a good speech: he told of Carlyle's letter, of Harris, of the poems; in proof of his own approval, he read several. Harris—his twenty-seven-year-old heart elated with assurance of triumph—slipped into the hall to get one of his later sonnets (which he thought his best): surely the company would insist that he himself should read! As he returned, he found the door blocked by the shoulders of a tall man; waiting for entrance, he heard the tall man ask someone what he thought of the poems. The answer, from a hidden man with a thin light voice, was lightning in the face—dazzling, blinding . . . "Good, but not great. . . . Knowledge of verse form; genuine feeling; but no new singing quality, not a new cadence in them. . . ." The executioner with the thin voice was Austin Dobson.

Froude called Harris. He wished to introduce him to Longman. He would himself write an introduction to the volume; Longman would publish it; Harris's career would be launched like a yacht: Froude's hand would christen it and break the bottle of champagne; the yacht would glide out on the Thames of a *Times* review and find the open seas of fame.

But Harris said no. He knew now that he was no poet; he refused the proffered help: who can succor what does not exist? He spoke stammering words: the verses were not good enough; he was not ready to have them published; he asked them back.

Astonished, Froude lifted his eyebrows. He was hurt publicly—with that deep hurt which we never forgive because it comes from those who refuse our help. It was a complete break; even the letter from Carlyle had led to nothing. Harris excused himself and hurried home: he wished to be alone with a dead poet.

In his room he reread the verses. How had he thought them good? Set them beside the best, beside Blake's

> *Let thy west wind sleep on*
> *The lake; speak silence with thy glimmering eyes*
> *And wash the dusk with silver....*

beside Keats'

> *Forever wilt thou love and she be fair....*

beside Shakespeare's

> *After life's fitful fever he sleeps well....*

The artist's lot is hardest: he must compare himself not with contemporary rivals, but with the great of all time. What drastic criticism! He would have relished Chopin's march for the dead, with its wild grace of grief. He saw that his verses were blossoms made of paper, clever but false—not the living blossoms of rose and apple, rich with the sap of earth. He set fire to all but three; tossing all night, he burned the last three in the dawn.

The question remains: was he right? Was Austin Dobson right? Suppose that Keats, heeding his critics, had returned to his pestle and pills? Austin Dobson was only a minor poet; he might have under-seen genius. Harris was never dissuaded from his *prose* by adverse criticism; yet he assented to Dobson's criticism of his verse. And the few poems that have been published here and there show that Dobson was right: there is no "singing quality." Frank Harris could appreciate high poetry; he could even better phrases of the greatest poets; but he was not himself a singer. Compare his verse with his prose.

> *And although they were only hysterical fools*
> *Fit for asylums and for schools . . . .*

The second line is acidly original; the music, however, is rusty metal grating on broken cogs. But his prose!—"The words we use are like little pieces of colored glass: it is almost impossible to arrange them so as to render the white light of truth in perfect purity." "Blessed are the strong: for they are as suns shining."

Thus by his wise integrity, Frank Harris refused the career that was offered him, and won the ill will (who can doubt it?) of Froude. He decided to rise the hard way—and the great way. One of Frank Harris's favorite proverbs was: "Every kite goes up against the wind." If the world's wind was against him, was it not the way to rise?

The Fourth Estate was not the power in Victorian England that it had been in revolutionary France; yet perhaps with a journalist's pen an impecunious, unsponsored young man of talent could open the oyster of the world.

In his journalistic career Harris proceeded soberly and ably, as he had in America: he applied himself to make opportunities; he set himself to exploit the opportunities he made.

He visited the offices of Chapman and Hall, who published books and the *Fortnightly Review*, "the most literary of our journals." (The *Fortnightly Review* was typically British, a journal of grave decorum even in format. It knew nothing of the bounce and besom of American journalism; it was as different from such journalism as Rotten Row was from the prairies where

rode the eagle-helmeted Sioux.) Harris introduced himself, by
Carlyle's letter, to Chapman; Chapman introduced him to T. H.
S. Escott, the acting editor. But Escott—a somewhat pompous but
able mediocrity—had nothing for him, save possibly (in the
future) some translations. Day after day, in spite of rebuffs, Harris
was waiting in the office, till at last Chapman asked him to report
on the manuscripts of two books. It is well to note the persistence
and patience, the steady groundwork, of the young Harris.

Meanwhile, by sober insistence he had won entrance to the office
of R. H. Hutton of the *Spectator*. Here he got a half-grudging
commission to write reviews of a book on Russia and of one by
Freeman on America. He first went to the British Museum and
asked for all of Hutton's books. He soon saw the stature of the
editor—"a very small entity, a gentle-pious spirit, intensely religious." Writing the review with this in mind, he made an immediate impression, which he italicized by referring with beautiful
justice to Cardinal Newman as "the greatest of all the Fathers,
the sweetest of all the Saints."

The review of Freeman was published in the *Spectator* July 7,
1883. Even in this first journalism, Harris spoke with resonance.
He criticized Freeman, or the greater de Tocqueville, with graphic
concreteness. America? To be sure it was tanged and rude: so
was that American plant, the skunk cabbage; but Americans had
a *good-natured* rudeness, and intellectuals must remember that—
far worse a fault!—"flunkeyism is the failing of an aristocracy."
Others might see that "the American hopes all from energy rightly
applied, the Englishman relies upon steady perseverance," but it
was Harris's subtler eye which saw that the American, more than
the Englishman, "has a marked liking for intellectual power."
The review revealed one born to write, who had served his apprenticeship; if his journalism was not yet masterly, it showed
mastery.

Shakespeare once held horses at a theater door; Frank Harris,
like his hero, held the horses of others at the door of literature.

Can we blame him if he sometimes braided a dingy mane into knots, or slipped a burdock burr under the saddle of a spavined gelding?

(According to Einar Lyngklip, Harris supplemented his journalism, which was a precarious livelihood, by working as a clerk in a stock-exchange office, with a broker named Klein. He was so working in February, 1883.)

Out of the gray clouds of this earlier obscurity the dawn came up like thunder.

Harris began to supplement the brilliant but intermittent reviews for the *Spectator,* or his manuscript reading for Chapman, by work as a reporter for the *Evening News,* a paper conservative in politics and policy. As an American, used to bite and zip in journalism, he thought it timid and drab. In politics he was a radical who supposed himself left of center; actually he was not left, right, or center—but a dynamic innovator who would turn the *flux quo* (to him life was never a *status quo*) toward the boldest objectives. The *Evening News* was no platform for such ideas. Yet it violated no principle to report news for its pages. The dilemma of London journalism was the same that challenges writers the world over: how to make a living without losing a life.

Perhaps as compensation for his conservative connections, Harris turned in his leisure time to the revolutionaries of London. These ranged from the doctrinaire, humorless Hyndman—incorruptible work horse of early Communism, who founded the Social Democratic Federation—to the brilliant unpredictable Shaw, who galvanized the Fabian Society. Hyndman was a plodder; with the figure of a grocer, he dressed in an "everlasting silk-faced frock coat" and wore "a long, flowing, dark-brown beard": a man never theatrical and always theoretical, a brave soldier for Man. No general of genius, he was a good drillmaster. In his *Record of an Adventurous Life* he speaks with appreciation of Harris's outdoor oratory, and, with unconscious humor, of his

effect upon the "intellectual development" of some forgotten nobody in the Social Democratic Federation. As an outdoor speaker,
indeed, Harris was a champion terrible among the spears of the
enemy. His voice was an instrument of elemental power; the
cataracts blew their trumpets from the steep. Though like his
Louis Lingg he distrusted all florid rhetoric, knowing that "it's
the shallow water that has the lace foam on it," he was no pedantic
intellectual. His words, like Lingg's, were bombs. He was so bold,
indeed, so plangent in his bitten bronze, that he often frightened
conventional radicals. His speeches were flung dynamite.

The man he rated highest among the radicals was William
Morris—that bridge builder between the medieval past and the
revolutionary future. Morris had begun with strange nostalgia
for the Lost Land of far away and long ago—the trumpets, the
gonfalons, the heraldry, the strange wild loves and cruelties and
honors and killings of the Middle Ages. His poetry of that life-
splashed time seems so like the speech of hypnotic memory that
one wonders if he is writing out of some previous incarnation.
But he turned from this, to bring the integrity of workmanship
and all the love and color of that earlier time into the printing,
the furniture, the daily arts, of England. He was, Harris thought,
"an artist-craftsman as Leonardo was." Finding his task hopeless
until the world had been shattered and remolded, he embraced
revolution; he became a militant speaker, and the most stirring
poet of socialism. He wrote some of the great marching songs of
the new day; men still hear their "sound and rumor" in "the
eventide of fear." Frank Harris loved this quiet, large-eyed, sad
artisan and poet; this rich man who took the side of the poor.

Frank Harris also met a brilliant young mocker of platitudes,
that unsocial socialist, that Major Barbara with the beard—George
Bernard Shaw. His white beard of today was then a red-gold
flame, and his strength was as the strength of ten because he ate
vegetables. Buoyant in an obscurity that he was too big to believe
in—which never came nearer than the reach of his clear, crisp,

provocative voice—he spoke to the future that already existed in the prescience of Marx and the providence of the Life Force. Provocative, witty, in a paradoxical way that seemed flippant only to fools, he danced a verbal ballet of flame. His was the wise banter of the Gods. Harris walked a graver way—as a centurion leading a legion into battle. Shaw's tactics were those of the terrible light cavalry of the Mongols, shooting swift arrows; Harris's were those of the close-locked charge of the Roman legion, eager for the thrust of the short sword.

Frank Harris first listened to Shaw at a socialist gathering in the East End of London. Shaw spoke "under the auspices of the Social Democratic Federation of Hyndman and he spoke as a confirmed Marxian." Very tall—over six feet in height—he seemed to Harris thin and angular, with a long face like a plowshare cutting its way everywhere to bedrock; his fair long hair was rufous, his reddish beard "untrimmed"; his eyes, "gray-blue" and English, added the lilt of Mephistopheles. His clothes were careless tweeds; he wore a Jaeger collar over a conventional tie. His movements were abrupt—jerky even, like those of his changing mind; he gave a sense of perfect unconstraint.

Harris's friendship with Shaw was one of his great friendships. They were the giants of the day, representing as opposite temperaments as the world can offer, yet one in genius. Shaw knew Harris's quality too well to allow aberrations of temperament, a fierce tendency to quarrel, or outlaw intransigence to destroy their unity. In spite of all that Harris might do, Shaw saluted his genius and remained his friend.

Neither Harris nor Shaw could long associate themselves with Hyndman. They were originals, unable to hang their genius obediently in the party line and goose-step like a galvanized corpse. Hyndman sent down a manifesto to be signed; it seemed silly to Harris, so instead of signing he resigned. Flowing beard and fierce mustache were outward and visible signs of inward and invisible differences: Hyndman was enlisted in a regiment of the line; Harris was a guerrilla fighter. But he was a fighter all his life long for those who had only their chains to lose. (Did they have only their chains to lose? Too often they supplemented their chains of economic steel with the brass fetters of prejudice!) It is significant that the one friend among radicals whom he never offended or outgrew was Emma Goldman.

Some radicals, later, wondered whether this man who loved rich food and fine wines, who wanted books and pictures and a bank balance, could be one of them. It is a common *non sequitur*. Jesus encountered it when he had to defend the woman who poured over his feet the box of ointment which might have been sold to feed the poor. Harris's belief was that the Have-Nots must win from the Haves assurance of the daily bread: from that belief he never wavered; to that belief he was never false. But he believed also that man does not die of hunger only, nor live by bread alone; but by wisdom, love, and the art which gives distinction to life and to which life should give honor. Even the poor might, by finding their life, lose it: what good would it do for the prisoners of starvation to attain bourgeois comfort if they became, like the bourgeois, the prisoners of sleep?

While he was still poor, he spent much time with the underprivileged—yet no more than he spent later defending the Boers, the Chicago "anarchists," the victims of the New York Night Court. His radicalism was no stopgap activity, no self-advertisement; he was by nature a fighter for the world's underdogs. He continued to be so when he became an overdog.

Meanwhile he was becoming an overdog in London. Suddenly —no one knew exactly how—he became editor of the *London News*.

The kite had gone up against the wind and was flying high. As usual there were hands to tug at the string and pull the kite down, breezes to tear it to tatters or dash it against a tree. Did any outsider ever enter an old, closely knit social group, there suddenly to expand in power, without malice as to his means? The gossip of London had its explanation.

In the beginning was the gossip, and the gossip became flesh. It was incarnated in *The Adventure of John Johns,* by Frederic Carrel—a book that went through seventeen editions and sold 100,000 copies. The very fact of its popularity shows, as Carlyle says of Beaumarchais' *Mariage de Figaro,* "that it flattered some pruriency of the time. . . . Small substance . . . thin wiredrawn intrigues, thin wiredrawn sentiments and sarcasms; a thing lean, barren; yet which winds and whisks itself, as through a wholly mad universe, adroitly and with a high-sniffing air: wherein each, as was hinted, which is the grand secret, may see some image of himself, and of his own state and ways." The poems of Blake, the prose of Carlyle, the *Contemporary Portraits* of Harris, do not go through seventeen editions in their own day. It is the minor books that have the major success. They say what every raw nonentity wishes to believe. *John Johns* was a sprightly, diverting book; it revealed how London regarded the cowboy who had risen to sensational success. Carrel disavowed any direct portraiture—"any resemblance to persons living or dead is wholly coincidental"; but John Johns was Harris as London wished to see him. In Carrel's book, Harris was, in a sense, recognizable, even true up to a certain low level. It was as if a mosquito that met van Gogh in Arles had written his life.

Harris's parable of Lilliput is apt: "Some little men a finger tall went out one day from the town of Lilliput for a walk. When they returned they said they had met a giant. The People of Lilliput at first refused to believe them: there were not any giants, they said, it's a childish superstition. But all the excursionists stuck to their tale, till at length one Lilliputian asked: 'What was the giant like?'

"'He was clad in leather,' said one excursionist. 'And all over dust,' added another. 'And don't forget,' cried a third, 'that he smelt unpleasantly.' And some began to believe them, for the description was detailed and peculiar and they all agreed on the main points.

"The Lilliputians had not seen above the giant's feet, and they judged the whole by what they saw."

John Johns is a man from "down under"—where the wombat and the kangaroo play. He speaks often of the open spaces where he had his headquarters in the saddle. He is a great actor: his face can express a Gethsemane of woe, a Transfiguration of the Ideal. But this is a pose; inwardly, his emotions are like a cash register adding up personal gains. He is a Robot Superman, beyond good and evil—but never beyond the advantage of John Johns. Penniless, he has arrived from Australia. In London he uses women as rungs of the ladder, climbing on broken hearts. His first position (on a newspaper) is due to his conquest of the wife of an elderly newspaper proprietor; later he marries a widow of wealth and prestige and clambers thus into advancement.

The popularity of the book proved two things: Harris deeply interested London; and London was resolved to interpret him in a certain way. To reduce the supernormal to the subnormal soothes the vanity of the mediocre: hence debunking. It was a left-handed compliment to Harris that 100,000 copies were sold and seventeen editions printed. Similarly Hitchens's *The Green Carnation* succeeded because of popular interest in Oscar Wilde. Nothing in either book would have warranted such a success, except the intrinsic interest in its victim.

Harris may have become editor of the *Evening News* by winning another man's wife. He denied it: he naturally would; London believed it: London naturally would. But whether he did or not, it was at worst merely a contributory cause: no woman, however infatuated or influential, can maneuver an incompetent into high position and keep him there. Her husband will not be blind enough to give such a post to a nobody—nor will a nonentity increase the circulation of the paper from 7000 to 70,000. John

Johns—the superman with the cash-register heart—is a theatrical fantasia. The rise of Thomas the Bootblack by honesty and application is no more melodramatic than the idea that a man can rise to high position merely by a false face, a glib bravado, and the seduction of women.

The theory that Harris succeeded by intrigue recalls a story that he loved to tell. Some friend, he says it was George Moore, asked his recipe for coffee; but in using it, Moore always forgot (says Harris) the first step—to begin with the best coffee!

Harris became editor of the *Evening News* because of promising ability; he remained editor because of his proved competence. He increased the circulation from 7000 to 70,000. He edited the paper for four years. He made such an impression that four years later he was chosen to edit the *Fortnightly Review,* one of the most honorable of British journals. Are such things to be predicated on adultery?

The editorship of the *Evening News* made him a man of mark. He had arrived. He had place among those who controlled London. If he had been willing to play the game and pay the price, he might have safely won wives amid official secrecy and private gossip. To play the game was to uphold the equilibrium of English morality, literature, politics; the price was conformity and compromise. London was not concerned with morals—but with morality. A man might be a sepulchre—if he was only whited. He must never defend Parnell or the Boers; he must praise the "right" artists (tepidly), and attack the "wrong" artists (ferociously); he must never upset the applecart of *laissez faire.* That game Harris could not have played if he had been willing; that price he would never pay.

Now he wished to turn out an influential and successful paper. He swept dust and cobwebs out of editorial and composing rooms; he renovated the policy. He got issues out early; instituted a crisp swift style; fashioned headlines and leaders to attract. He explored byways that seemed to some *risqué.* He wanted to make the *News* a great paper; he succeeded in making it successful.

His journalism was American, sometimes lurid, often sensational, at times salacious or even scandalous. It was effective—as journalism; it was inconsequential as literature. If he had died as editor of the *News* he would have been only another American who made good.

His opinion of English journalism was low. Journalism in many countries, he said, "can still be turned into an art by the gifted and high-minded; but in England thanks in the main to the anonymity of the press . . . the journalist or modern preacher is turned into a venal voice, a soulless Cheapjack paid to puff his master's wares." [2]

He wrote later: "I edited the *Evening News* at first to the top of my thought as a scholar and man of the world of twenty-eight; nobody wanted my opinions, but as I went downward and began to edit it as I felt at twenty, then at eighteen, then at sixteen, I was successful." [3] Evidently he attained "success" only by failure.

Compare him with William Stead. Stead was a born journalist, with a flair for advertisement and the exploitation of human interest; he was able to do what Harris never could: to espouse popular causes, to incite crusades of popular morality, to mingle sensationalism with conventionality. Harris had no abiding interest in journalism; no belief in popular crusades; no intuition for middle-class prejudices. Stead, because he was the lesser man, was the greater journalist. Harris, soon losing his interest, never made the *Evening News* great; Stead swept on to a colossal success that symbolically culminated in his death on the Titanic.

That Harris did well, however, by the world's standards, even if he felt that he had to write down to the level of an adolescent

---

[2] Frank Harris, *Oscar Wilde: His Life and Confessions.* Covici-Friede, 1930. Pp. 41-42.
[3] *My Life and Loves,* Vol. II, pp. 146-47.

public, is clear: for in July, 1886, at the age of only thirty-one, he was made editor of the *Fortnightly Review*. It seemed that, like one of Napoleon's privates, this unknown young man from America carried a marshal's baton in his knapsack.

The *Fortnightly Review* was a literary magazine of honor and influence. It had once been edited by George Henry Lewes, biographer of Goethe and husband of George Eliot; it was now edited by John Morley. Harris, the youngest editor it had ever had, was the greatest it was ever to have.

John Morley was entering politics. He was a liberal, lucid and fair; a thin, scholarly man, his mind like Scotch soil. He was meticulous, exact, and not richly sensitive to the new winds: a professor on Parnassus. He had maintained the tradition of the *Fortnightly* in the classical way, making it an instrument of high thinking and plain writing, like a smaller Matthew Arnold slightly chilblained.

"In popular opinion, his editorship was summed up in the fact that he spelled God with a small 'g.' . . . At this time, Morley must have been about 45 years of age; of spare figure, some five feet ten inches in height; cleanshaven, with large rudder-nose, firm drawn-in lips of habitual prudent self-restraint; thoughtful, cold gray eyes, large forehead—'a bleak face,' I said to myself. Manifestly I was not much to his taste. I was as frank and outspoken as he was reserved, and while he had already climbed a good way up the ladder, I thought nothing of the ladder and despised the climbing. Moreover, his gods were not my gods and he was as unfeignedly proud of his Oxford training as I was contemptuous of all erudition." [4]

Why was a young American chosen to edit this organ of British decorum? The directors knew him as a vigorous, shrewd editor, who had already raised one moribund paper from the grave. The *Fortnightly* was "dying of dignity"—it needed its vitamin B_1. Something about Harris had enabled him, as a boy, to get a job

[4] Frank Harris in *Pearson's Magazine*, May, 1918, p. 33.

under Brooklyn Bridge; something had got him admitted, as a youth of nineteen, to the Bar; something had won him, as a young man, the acclaim of Carlyle. It was evident in his pages or in his presence. He had power of personality that was equivalent to magic. Otherwise would a young American, without fortune, friends, or university degrees, largely unknown and only thirty-one, have been selected to direct the *Fortnightly?*

The format of the *Fortnightly* remained solid and unobtrusive. Frank Harris refrained from the exhibitionism which had helped the *Evening News:* he had here a medium for his highest qualities. He edited the *Fortnightly* with a sober power that was Sophoclean.

An editor may be great in any one of three diverse ways. He may efface himself like the God of the Deists, fashioning his universe like a fine Swiss chronometer and then standing aside to hear it tick and to watch it run. Such an editor is Olympian: he selects his contributors wisely; he chooses their best work and places it in apt relation to the work of others, as a connoisseur hangs pictures in a gallery. He chooses and fuses, he selects and arranges and blends; out of the many colors he makes a spectrum, out of the many sounds a harmony. To be such an editor one must have prestige, a journal of unquestioned excellence, an audience that can appreciate the finest work, and money to pay contributors handsomely. Frank Harris was such an editor when he directed the *Fortnightly*. There is another sort of editor, also great. He is not only persuasive but also pervasive; he is great not only in his deistic transcendence but also in his theistic immanence. He is beyond the magazine, as the God of Deism is beyond the world; he is also immanent, as the God of Theism is immanent. He is brilliant in his selections, as God is brilliant in His creations; he is also evident in personal power, as God is vivid in His immediate presence. Frank Harris was to be this sort of editor when, some years later, he bought the *Saturday Review*. There is still a third way of being a great editor—the way of Pantheism.

Here the editor is himself the stuff and substance as well as the pervading directive *élan*. He writes most of the magazine; he shapes and touches all; he *is* the magazine. Such an editor sometimes does this because he can by temperament do no otherwise; he sometimes does it because, having little money, he has to. The editor who cannot buy the best talent has to make up for it by giving himself. Such an editor Harris became in *Pearson's*. But now in the *Fortnightly* he effaced himself and yet revealed himself by a deistic transcendence.

To the most impatiently brilliant of his friends such editing seemed tame. Whistler, the butterfly with the wasp's sting, gibed: "But no! You've not done it by the way of genius: every month the *Review* appears regularly, just what one looks for, a work of high-class English mediocrity: lamentable you know, quite lamentable." The white lock shook truculently; the wasp wings whirred like metallic gauze.

And if one sought the pervasive atmosphere of a person, the poetry of the artist's mood in Whistler's pictures, he would be disappointed in the *Fortnightly*. Harris was like a window of clear glass through which one looks into a garden—glass so clear that one forgets it and does not realize that to look from it at just that angle is to see the whole garden in terms of art.

Studying the issues, one sees that the editor was moving to the left of center and enriching the Scotch soil of Morley. One of Harris's earliest discoveries among Morley's rejected (but not returned) manuscripts was a paper by an unknown H. G. Wells, "The Rediscovery of the Unique." He sent for Wells, talked with him about future contributions, and published his work. And if he published the recognized Matthew Arnold and the now tolerated Swinburne, he also published Davidson, Wilde, and even Verlaine. Harris in picking men of talent or genius seems to have had "absolute pitch." He could not always command the rarer notes (for there had to be voices before he could acclaim them), but he knew the pitch when he heard the voices. It was

great editing to pick out amid discords and minor tones the clear
resonance of Wells; or to hear above the soberer, safer notes the
Pan's flute of Wilde.

Frank Harris published the scholarship of Dowden; he published also Pater's poetry of criticism. He featured the chaste and
lucid Arnold; also the epicene pagan and verbal assassin of kings,
Swinburne. (Beautiful was the lovely "Kaiser Dead" of Arnold—
that tenderest of dog elegies!) He published scholars and econ-
omists now forgotten; he also published poems of Davidson and
Verlaine that will be forever remembered. He did this sometimes
over the almost literal dead bodies of his directors; and he paid—
as Verlaine attested—more generously than other editors. Harris
wrote: "It had been customary to pay not more than two pounds
for any poem, but I gave Matthew Arnold, and Swinburne too,
25 pounds a page, which came out of my salary." [5] He was bold:
he published the Preface to *Dorian Gray*—which was like erect-
ing a curiously wrought image of metal on a high hill, to challenge the lightning.

Nor did he entirely keep himself out of the magazine. There
were grave editorials; resonant, sun-orbed criticism; trenchant,
deep-voiced stories like "Montes" and "A Modern Idyll." These
were never exhibitionism, never self-exploitation. They were
stories of chiseled art yet pulsing life; they were new and daring;
they got him into trouble with his directors. But for the most part
the supposedly ego-centered and self-mongering Harris disproved
such slanders by his practice: he was a champion of others rather
than a protagonist of his own genius. His concern was to make
the *Fortnightly* a forum for the best that was being said in England—or, if he could, in the world.

It is remarkable that so great a writer could be so great an
editor. A high level of talent is sufficient for good editing; genius
is often a handicap: for genius does not often know, and always
scorns, its public; it is too intense in its own vision to be fair to

[5] *My Life and Loves*, Vol. III, p. 157.

the vision of others; it has its own work, and cannot give itself to further the work of lesser (or even equal) men. To be a great editor requires catholicity, a detachment from one's own atmosphere, an objectivity not too deeply motivated by personal mission or meaning. Harris, for all his personal genius in creation, was one of the great editors of all time.

But no editor is a god on Olympus. Frank Harris had to consider a conservative publisher and a board of cautious Victorian directors. Some contributions—such as Davidson's "Ballad of a Nun"—his directors would not allow him to publish even after he had accepted and paid for them; for others they refused to pay the generous amounts that Harris set. Chapman was increasingly difficult: he was a conservative business man; he hated poetry and "thought it should be paid for at ordinary rates." Harris wrote: "When he found that I was giving my salary in payment to the contributors, I fell in his esteem. To give Swinburne fifty pounds for a poem seemed to him monstrous; and when I bought certain articles dearly, he wouldn't have them at any price. . . . And if he disliked art and literature, he hated the social movement of the time with a hatred peculiarly English; he looked upon a socialist as a sort of low thief, and pictured a communist as one who had his hand in his neighbor's pocket. My defense of Henri and Ravechol shocked him to the soul. And without Chapman's sympathy, I couldn't make of the *Review* what I wanted to make of it. Chapman wouldn't have Davidson's 'Ballad of a Nun'; he cut it out of the number when he saw it in proof though it was paid for; and Bernard Shaw was anathema to him. I was like a boy whose growth was being hindered by too narrow garments." [6] Harris, who loved Browning's "Andrea Del Sarto," often quoted—shrugging his shoulders—"And thus we halfmen struggle. . . ."

Yet in spite of all, what beauty Harris brought into the *Fortnightly!* Here was a sonorous ode by Swinburne; here the wistful

[6] *My Life and Loves,* Vol. III, pp. 162-63.

grace of "Kaiser Dead"; here an immortal sadness of Verlaine's. Here was a beautifully styled review, grave with subtle vision—"Prosper Mérimée" by Pater; and, only a little later, the Preface to *Dorian Gray*. So from month to month there was at least one great thing or one new thing; sometimes a masterpiece that made history. All magazines, fifty years later, are cemeteries: the question of their greatness is answered by the names of the dead there buried. Are they the names of those who cannot die? As we wander past the headstones of the authors in the *Fortnightly*, we come often upon the Immortals. It is a Pantheon or Hall of Fame among magazines.

Frank Harris edited the *Fortnightly* for eight brilliant years— 1886 to 1894. Arthur Waugh, once managing director of the magazine, said: "Never perhaps in its history were the purely literary qualities of the *Review* so various and so high." Harris's place in London during those eight years was that of a great editor; in retrospect he remains one of the greatest editors of all time.

The kite had gone up against the March wind—and it was flying high.

Chapter V

RUFFIAN AT VANITY FAIR

(1886-1894)

As EDITOR of the *Fortnightly Review* Frank Harris was welcomed at the dinner tables and in the drawing rooms of London. Wilde's famous gibe is witty: "Frank Harris has been received in all the great houses of London—once." But Harris visited the great houses for more than eight years; if he went to each only once, there must have been a plethora of great houses!

Harris was received in the great houses not once but many times. He was a fascinating guest. All witnesses, even the hostile, give eager or grudging testimony to the magic of his voice, the excellence of his art. He was a magician of the winged word; a god of speech.

W. L. George said: "One does not meet Frank Harris: one collides with him."

Hesketh Pearson wrote: "Almost, one might say, electric sparks flew out of him in every direction. This has gained him all his enemies, because the majority of people don't like being electrified. It has also gained him his greatest friends, because some people like the human dynamo." [1]

Gerald Cumberland wrote: "In telling a story, Harris is elliptical: a faint gesture serves for a sentence, a momentary silence is

[1] Hesketh Pearson, *Modern Men and Mummers,* pp. 102-32.

an innuendo; a lifting of the eyebrows, a look, a dropping of the voice, a slowness in his speech—all these take the place of words. He is an exquisite actor and he is at his best when he is sinister and menacing. One need scarcely say that the effect of one of his stories, told in private, with only one or two listeners, is extremely powerful, for his personality, so quick to melt and suffuse his speech—coloring it and vitalizing it—is strong and strange and full of tropical richness." [2]

The most diverse witnesses attest the quality of Frank Harris's voice—a basso profundo, a trumpet, an organ thunder. It could arrest the conversation of a hotel dining room, the gossip of a theater between acts; it could halt a runaway horse, it could recall a fleeing army. It was a spate of music, a Niagara of eloquence. W. L. George thought Harris's voice most striking; that it sounded like the rustling leaves of a brass artichoke. Aleister Crowley thought that it was like the voice of Jove—not the Olympian Thunderer, but the Jove of rain, a voice that seemed to sob and tremble. It reminded him of the *lacrimae rerum*. But then, in a swerve of change, it became a voice swift and terrible, like the stroke of a cobra. Michael Monahan likened Harris to a Brobdingnagian talking behind a closed door. Kenneth Hare, hearing Harris's voice, thought of the words of Milton about the far-off curfew

> *Over some wide-watered shore*
> *Swinging low with sullen roar.*

He thought that such a voice made even the kettledrum seem like a skylark's trill. Frank Harris's voice, indeed, was magnificent —like a men's choir singing *Dies Irae* in full-throated Latin.

And Frank Harris's eyes, too; Frank Harris's famous glance! It was a jaguar glance. His eyes seemed balls of onyx. There was a nakedness in his look. It was a look you could lean against.

[2] Gerald Cumberland, *Set Down in Malice*, pp. 32-46.

At times there was in it something nonhuman; was it not both subhuman and superhuman, the glance of an animal or of a god? It transcended reverence, pity, and fear—though all of these at times shone through it; it was a lion's look. It seemed as if the soul behind it was poised to pounce, like a great cat in perfect stance.

And the presence behind the glance gave a sense of certitude. No Hamlet-hesitance here! Physically, like bird or bee, Harris had a sure sense of direction: he was never lost; equally, in the life of the spirit he had a sense of his destiny. It was this splendid certainty that secretly startled men when he entered a room: others paltered and huddled and drifted; but here amid the drift of the world was a man who drove. Every man in a room he entered disliked this certainty; every woman liked it. Harris disturbed or angered the men, for he had what they had lost; he perturbed and fascinated the women, for he had what they instinctively sought in men—and had not found. His entrance was that of a god from an elemental and older earth.

Forcefully, with high disdain, as if biting phrases from burnished bronze, he spoke in measured cadences. His arrogance was Olympian. His talk was of books and men (and women); of strange deaths and fierce loves; of Indians and Presbyterian elders; of saints and harlots; of Jews and Jesus; of brilliant symbols of beauty; of ideas and truths that perish never. Max Beerbohm said that Harris was the finest talker in London—the London of Whistler and Wilde. Such talk had not been heard since Shakespeare, or Johnson, or the torrent-monologues of Carlyle. It was mordant, it was tender; it shot flaming arrows into the bull's-eye of truth, it lifted life into image and symbol; it skinned mediocrity alive, like Apaches torturing a rancher; it brought tears to the heart as it evoked the pathos of human circumstance; it lifted the spirit like a terrible trumpet. It was bawdy and daring; it reverenced the saints of the catholic church of the world's holiest; it was ribald—and it was religious. The torrent of that mighty voice plunged onward with the roar of Niagara; over its plunge shimmered the rainbow.

W. L. George heard Harris tell "The Holy Man" by word of mouth. Harris held him with a grip of the hand and a spell of the eye. George—himself a brilliant writer and raconteur—was compelled, upset, and attracted; he was like the rabbit of legend, lured and held by the eyes of the snake. When the story was over, he woke with a strange start, as from the trance of hypnosis.

As a conversationalist and story-teller in London society, Harris had the power and won the glory.

Meanwhile Frank Harris hoped to become an English Bismarck. He was a "radical Tory." He believed, with Carlyle, that progress comes from the great man; but he also believed that genius must serve society, never be isolated, never aloof. A statesman must be radical in the sense that he goes to the root of things; he should be conservative in the sense that he preserves the best of things. Harris wished to become such a statesman, who by spoken word and accomplished deed might renovate England and renew the world.

There was in England (he thought) a drift in this direction. Lord Randolph Churchill, father of the famous Winston, seemed to give promise of political eminence that would lead to great deeds, until, after a nervous breakdown, he retired from politics to die. At the other extreme from the Tories were the Socialists, or the Labor Party. In the middle were the Liberals—typified in all their "words, words, words," by that Bland Old Man, Gladstone. Did they know what they wanted? Did they want anything —except to let fundmentals alone? Did they know how to create liberty, not *laissez faire?* One heard much talk about it and about, but evermore came out by the same door wherein one went. Their action (if not their oratory) was lukewarm; they led nowhere with a brave drum. Meanwhile there was so much to be *done!*—slums to be cleared, foul stables waiting for cleansing rivers, lands beyond the sea to be colonized, things commonly used (railways, utilities, banks, mines) to be nationalized. Harris saw this so clearly that he did not realize how far from intending it his Tory friends were. To him these things *must* be in the minds of those who aspired to govern England.

He quoted Churchill with approval: the aristocracy and the working class were free of prudery and prejudice; the middle class alone was narrow and dull. The Tories were closer to the Left—to the workers, to the Socialists—than to the inert central smugness of the *bourgeoisie*.

Harris stood for Parliament—and failed. He believed it was because he was too short: leaders of England (he thought) had to possess height. Actually it was because he was never politic enough for politics; his integrity kept him from paying the price of politics. The basic cause of his failure was philosophic, it was rooted in his character; the specific causation was his refusal to join the pack of the world's bloodhounds hunting Parnell. It was magnificent; but it was not politics. He was too single in soul. He might be beyond good and evil on the stock market or in a deal with the ruffians of finance, the pirates of commerce; that was wolf eat wolf. But in politics he sought for principle and statesmanship. What could one do with such a man? Certainly not elevate him to power; he might even do what he said he would! To the *bêtes gris* who are politicians, Harris was a *bête noire*.

But socially he was a delightful black panther. What teeth he had, and what burning supple grace under the sheen of skin! And one can never tell what a panther has done, or will do. Bagheera, the black panther, is a diversion in the parlor or at the dinner table.

Londoners not only entertained Harris, they let him entertain them. The old Duke of Cambridge was his guest at a typical luncheon, and James Russell Lowell, the graceful minor American, then ambassador to England; Beerbohm Tree shared the board with the agitator, John Burns; George Wyndham faced

Alfred Russell Wallace; and Oscar Wilde furnished verbal fireworks.

Much was forgiven him, for he charmed much. Few understood the burning center of his spirit or the perfection of his art; but none could deny his magic. And his position was established by the *Fortnightly*. Also his great work was still latent. It is easier to like a man of promise than a man who has fulfilled it, for genius is as terrible as an army with banners. It is better to see the banners picturesque upon the horizon; to hear—over the hills and far away—the awful trumpet faintly blowing.

London society had a worldly substance veneered with sophistication: there was Bohemianism among journalists, even among aristocrats who prided themselves on freedom from prejudice and Philistine "morality," and among politicians who privately made no pretense of sainthood. Such society, the world over, is intimate to those who have entrance; tolerant so long as its basic invalid "values" are not denied; seemingly frank and superficially free. Allowing latitude (if not longitude), it is not easily shocked. On the surface it seems refreshingly wider than middle-class morality and the nonconformist creeds. Only after a time, only after much tolerance, does it decide that the amusing, talented outsider is an enemy alien. Then it is ruthless.

As Shaw says, Harris failed in London because he told the truth. Society could not believe at first that he was one of God's Spies; but once it was indeed evident that he was that terrible scourge of God, the seer, the prophet, Harris—for all his brilliant charm—was seen as a panther from the jungles of the night. The hunters got their guns and called out the beaters.

But meanwhile he was fascinating to the more brilliant men, and to many women. For women he had the magnetism of virility, and also the charm of a heart that could see and a tongue that could say. Women—starved often for the art of love, and usually for the love of art—found both in Frank Harris.

Yet Harris was too original and bold to be a safe guest. Dining beside a duchess he might resonantly talk of Whitman's "A Woman Waits for Me" till the whole table had to listen. One had to whisper that he had been a cowboy in America; that he had been born in Ireland.

Bernard Shaw, thinking of these days, calls Harris a "ruffian." He says that Harris was a "born outlaw."

One had to be careful of Harris's neighbors at the table—or even whom one invited, for his voice carried far and his personality dominated the room. If you set him next to a bishop, he might chagrin the reverend gentleman by revealing a deeper knowledge of Jesus—and, the next minute, shock him by intoning the most incandescent blasphemies of Swinburne. If, taught by the angry snorts of the retreating bishop, you set Harris next a pretty girl who prided herself on emancipation, he chanted the praises of chastity and won her to St. Theresa till she decided to join a convent, or was shocked at his saintliness, as was the bishop by his blasphemy. He might talk to an innocent young girl about the genius of Rops or the sexual habits of de Maupassant. He might horrify a choleric and chortling general by praising the conscientious objection of Antigone. He might pour the acid of disdain over the scholarly decorum of Edmund Gosse, fussy over the diapers of mediocrity. He practiced a freedom of speech such as can be granted only in the forecastle of a pirate sloop—or in the purlieus of Heaven.

Shaw wrote: "When they escape upstairs . . . they condole with one another. Gosse says, 'My God, what a man!' The bishop says, 'Oh impossible; quite impossible!' " Shaw, confessing that he has himself suffered such terrible broadsides from the pirate ship, goes on: "I have seen and heard you do such; I have been condoled with, and have had to admit that you are a monster, and that clever as you are it is impossible to ask anyone to meet you unless they are prepared to stand anything that the utmost free-masonry of the very freest thought and expression in the boldest circles can venture on. Poor old Adolphe Adam used to turn away from

Beethoven's symphonies, crying *'J'aime la musique qui me berce!'*
You would run after him with a trombone, blaring Beethoven's
most challenging themes into his ears." Shaw did not find this
disagreeable: it was "quite genuine and natural." It was the genius
that comes from God, shocking only to the conventions of feeble
and fallible men. "But . . . Harris with his teeth ever in the plump
calf of propriety" was not one to induce ease in Babylon. The
crux of it was that one could never ask Harris to meet Mrs.
Humphry Ward; and, no matter how Harris might thank God
for that, one could not have a career in London unless one could
be trusted "to take Mrs. Humphry Ward in to dinner and leave
her under the impression that one was either a very respectable
or a very charming man."[3]

The result? People, after Harris's exile, asked what could have
been wrong with him: they suspected him of being "a Jew, or a
financial-blackmailer-journalist, or another Verlaine, or a German
spy, or something. . . ." The reply, says Shaw, is simply that Harris
was "a ruffian." He concludes: "As to myself, of course, I am a
ruffian. Set a ruffian to catch a ruffian. But I am only ruffianly
nor-norwest. Though it be ruffianism, yet there's method in
it. . . ."[4]

The humor of this criticism is that Harris denied it. He was
not a "ruffian"! He was so authentic an original that he had no
intuition of the effect he had upon people; he could not recognize
it when it was pointed out. He was always himself—when the
north wind doth blow, do we marvel that we shall have snow?
He had the insouciance and aplomb of Whitman; neither, by
taking thought, could have subtracted a cubit from his stature.

Fortunately, London society, if not really free, was sophisticated;
for a time he was its lion, for a longer time he remained its black
panther.

---

[3] Quotations from a letter from Shaw to Harris. It is printed in full in *The
Wisdom of Frank Harris,* a booklet published by *Pearson's Magazine,* 1919.
[4] *Ibid.*

Frank Harris wrote, later, "All this while in London I had one passion: the desire to know and measure all the men of ability in art and literature I could meet. I had, however, a myriad pleasures, among which I must put first the love of horses, of riding and driving, I mean. I still kept up another dozen of athletic amusements; I ran and walked regularly, and boxed for at least half an hour each morning, just to keep myself perfectly fit. . . ." [5]

His horses were famous. Ever since his days on the Texas plains he had loved horses: he never forgot Blue Dick. Now in London he was "the only editor who drove fine horses tandem down Fleet Street"; he had, during the decade of 1885-1895, "some of the best driving horses in London." He loved animals and felt that cruelty to them—since they were without speech to complain—was the unpardonable sin. He loved the mastery of power and speed, as of a man calmly seated at the heart of a whirlwind, driving it steadily to his goal. The rush of London air recalled the freedom of the plains, the lost life of the trail.

The authenticity of all this is attested by other witnesses, such as Sir William Rothenstein.

He loved to box more than he loved boxing as a public sport. The "great game" as played in the roped ring for money was, to him, sordid commercialism, rousing the beastliness of men, and serving the avarice of a few manipulators. He tried to stop a fight short of the kill when the crowd, lusting for others' pain, wanted the unlucky fighter to go down under a knockout after his stout heart had kept him fighting till he was a flailed plum. To Frank Harris this was not sportsmanship, but blood lust. He loved the art of boxing more than the battle of sluggers; he learned the art well; found that a blow down was more powerful than a blow up; and trained his body to quick skill.

He ate well and drank well, too. He learned that in the life of the flesh and the luxuries of good living, the English were the first people in the world.

[5] *My Life and Loves,* Vol. III, p. 90.

He lived in London in a great musical decade. Those were the years of Gilbert and Sullivan: he attended their operettas often, he delighted in them; he met both men. He thought Sullivan the greater, "a very great musician who kept his child's heart to the last." There was Dolmetsch, too, the Belgian. He played Bach on the clavichord (made by him as it had been made in earlier days); "to hear him play Bach on the instrument that Bach had written his music for, was an unforgettable experience: it was like hearing a great sonnet of Shakespeare perfectly recited for the first time." [6] Sir Henry Wood was conducting his operas in London. And at Oxford Harris had the highest spiritual experience of these years. The boys of Magdalen College Chapel sang a cantata by Purcell; it brought tears to his eyes; he had "a divine unforgettable hour with those minstrels of God." How could a people that created such music and rendered it so divinely, starve miners and degrade the proletariat and loose war upon the Boers?

There were scientists in London, also—Alfred Russell Wallace and the brilliant lame Lord Kelvin; not only aesthetics, but the *logic* of nature, was served in the London of that splendid time. He loved to quote—

> *What if Art be slowe,*
> *Sweetlie let it growe,*
> *As groweth tender grasse*
> *'Neath God's smalle rain.*
> *But of shoutyng, strivyng, crying, roaryng, fightyng,*
> *Waxeth naught save dust aloft,*
> *Upon the plaine.*

There was so much in London to seek and find! London's intellectual and aesthetic riches intoxicated him. There was drama; there were museums, libraries, picture galleries, architecture; there was the misty poetry of the Thames, as haunting in

[6] *Ibid.,* p. 102.

physical presence as on the canvases of Whistler. And above all there were great men.

Among the older great men he came to know Robert Browning—slightly. The poet of "fifty men and women," the splendid fighter who rejoiced in the adventure of life and of death, the romantic who saw the assurance of God in the crisis of a great hour, was his fellow diner-out in London. More subdued than in the days when he wore lemon-colored gloves as a young man about London, Browning was somewhat deaf and not immediately impressive. Harris felt that he could never reach the secret of Browning's soul. It was one of his few failures. (Perhaps the quiet eyes that saw so deeply into passionate, adventurous souls read more in Harris than Harris guessed; had the meeting come earlier, there might have been another "Waring.") Frank Harris's mistake—which he never recognized because he could not understand that some men find only a single love in a life—was to question Browning as to what woman had inspired "The Last Ride Together." That was enough to explain his failure! Harris was shocked to find Browning set in inconspicuous places, below some general or political vane-of-all-weathers.

Frank Harris met Matthew Arnold—lucid and thin, a lover of "ideal humanity." Harris advised Arnold about audiences in America ("They expect elocution. . . . They will come to see you as a notable, and a few will stay to listen to you as poet . . . ."); and talked with him about Keats—and Mrs. Humphry Ward. He assimilated the best of Arnold, that English Renan; he knew the worst: the gentility that saw underbreeding in Keats' love letters. Yet "I always felt him superior in range and rightness of thought to any of his contemporaries. . . . He had perfect manners, too . . . met everyone on the pure human level, preferred to talk on high themes, yet used to banter charmingly with the barbarians. . . ." [7] The scholar-gypsy—whose tragedy was that as the years went on, the gypsy died, the scholar lived.

[7] These scattered quotations are from *My Life and Loves*.

Greater was the obscure immortal, James Thomson, of the "builded desolation and passionate despair" of the City of Dreadful Night. Harris—the successful editor, the talented outsider who seemed to have the keys of London—sought out the somber magnificent poet of sorrow, the hidden hero who, Meredith said, possessed the highest moral courage he had ever known. Harris pitied the man who stood in the streets of London on feet that peered through broken shoes, and who, defeated by a world that condemned him to poverty and oblivion, was committing suicide by alcohol; but he acclaimed the *poet*. Thomson loomed like a transcription of his own "Melancholia" (which was Dürer's too):

> *Titanic from her high throne in the north,*
> *That city's somber Patroness and Queen,*
> *In bronze sublimity she gazes forth . . . .*

Harris could do nothing for him now. It was too late. "Dead Faith, dead Love, dead Hope" were a trinity in that darkling life. The significant circle of figures upon the clockface had been marred, but still the bodily mechanism went ticking on, turning the useless hands that told no time, till it wore itself out and stopped. But it meant something in those tragic last days for Thomson to know that his secret could be told because at last it had found ears to hear. Harris brought laurel, even though late.

And Frank Harris knew Pater—that lucid sphinx who, inept in speech, could write pages of prose perfect like poetry. He knew the waspish butterfly, Whistler of the white plume; he heard Whistler's famous monologue of wit, and praised it (too highly) as "the best lecture heard in London since Carlyle lectured on Heroes." He came to know George Meredith too.

With Meredith indeed he had one of his great friendships. The Sage of Boxhill who, almost alone of the Victorians, had faith in Nature and dared trust his body to the earth whence grew the rose, was to Harris the sun-clearest of critics, the novelist of wide-vistaed pages, the poet of the great "Modern Love" and "Love in the Valley." The joyous flow—like the Thames sparkling in sun-light—of *Richard Feverel!* The perfect aptness of *The Egoist!* Only once was Harris critical: when Wilde had fallen from his laughing height into the *De Profundis* of Wandsworth Gaol, Meredith would not sign a petition for his release. Harris had trusted him most and asked him first; but Meredith's love of Nature caused him to hate the unnatural, his health made him averse to perversion. He would not sign.

Meredith, in turn, appreciated Harris. "Montes," he wrote, was the work of a master; it was equal to the greatest stories of France; what other hand in England could write such a story? His letters to Harris, almost undecipherable in the firm-bitten strokes of a pen that spoke the energy of the author, are great documents.

"How funny it is," he wrote in one letter, "to see my junior launching on the old tides, amid the rocks and the shoals and the Tipsy Tritons!—and while I feel for and with them! Heed nothing of the outcries. I think you are now near success, and still I count on your strength in thinking it would be better for you to get a pelting.

"I suspect that your discontent with 'The Sheriff' arises from the absence of a woman in the narrative."

Great praise—and sly, wise criticism!

Frank Harris met scientists too: Tyndall, and Huxley (the John Bull of Evolution); greatest of all, Alfred Russell Wallace, codis-coverer of evolution. Wallace, unlike the static Darwin, did not mark time in the mire of a mindless animal mechanism, but marched toward the horizon of the future. Harris could not share his harmonies or gleams from worlds unrealized, for his own mystical nature was undeveloped; but he knew Wallace to be one of the wisest of minds. Far lesser was Herbert Spencer— once supposed to be *the* philosopher of evolution; Harris, even in Spencer's heyday of acclaim, knew better.

Frank Harris met brilliant young men from Oxford and Cambridge, falling stars that flashed a promise, the predestined young men such as Hubert Crackenthorpe, Lionel Johnson—

> *Alone to the Alone I go,*
> *Divine to the Divinity . . . .*

He came to know the minor poet of the single perfection of monotone, the sad singer of "Cynara"—Ernest Dowson, the frail gifted youth who drifted into Hell, "faithful in [his] fashion." Dowson was shy at first, yet quick with impulse; he appealed to the heart as a girl does, with "a child's confidence and a child's hesitancy," and an awkward grace. Gentle and shy, full of "quaint quirks of verse," he was quick-changing as an April day. Once, after months of separation, Harris found his face chiseled by tragic lines. After lunch they walked in Hyde Park; Dowson, challenged to prove that he was a poet in his own right and no moon for Swinburne's sun, quoted the sonorous, haunting rhythms of "Cynara." Here was immortality murmuring within the elaborate-simple enamel of a sea shell! Frank Harris listened with a shaken heart to match the singer's stormy eyes. He had no cowardice in praise. Praise is the due of the poem—as the song of the lark is the due of the sunrise. "Whatever brought you to that height is good: whatever way you trod, blessed. What do the thorns matter? or the bowl; whether of hyssop or of hemlock, who cares? Your name is enskied and sacred, shrined in the hearts of men forever, and I called you a weak dreamer and failure!—You who, before any of us, have won your way into the heaven of renown."

And there was Richard Middleton—a man of brooding reticences out of which summer lightnings leaped; a dark thickset fellow with large violet eyes. Seeking a pagan joy, he found a pagan sadness.

> *Ah, would that my soul had wings,*
> *Or a resting place.*

He only half found the wings; never the resting place. He sought in nature and in love what he was never great enough to reach. Meanwhile he gave the world a few grace notes as the logbook of that stormy voyage which ended in the sudden deliberate scuttling of the pinnace of his life. Lonely and ill in Brussels, he sought respite in the green mist of ether, writing the terrible last word on a postal to a friend, "A broken and a contrite heart Thou wilt not despise."

Dear God, what means a poet more or less?

To Frank Harris a poet meant never less, but more: he had done all he could for Middleton—helped him get his volume published; published, or helped to place, his stories; fed him in his hunger. Aleister Crowley tells of one such instance, which to Harris was not one of mere *charity*. Crowley and Harris were walking together one night, when suddenly Middleton appeared among the crowd—an apparition of the night, half-hidden almost immediately among the other faces and in the darkness. He was a famished poet of promise, big and soft and tame like a lost Newfoundland dog. Harris broke away from Crowley with a leopard's leap; found Middleton amid the crowd; caught him by the arm. Harris forgot his own weariness in his pity for the starved and lonely boy, and carried him off, startled, to have dinner at the Savoy. It bewildered and it angered Frank Harris that the world treated poets like stray dogs.

Frank Harris also knew the austere Scotsman touched with the grace of the Muses—John Davidson, the schoolmaster who reached the slopes of Parnassus. Harris tried to encourage him in the face of a world that flung a meager pension to a poet, like a dry bone to a dog, while judges and cabinet members got too much for their own good; he spoke the words of recognition that a poet must have if he is to live. But the world was too much for Davidson: poverty and obscurity were complicated by cancer; at the edge of a cliff he fired a bullet through his brain and fell into the sea that he had loved. Such a world, hating and destroying its poets, was, Harris felt, literally damned.

Frank Harris met Ruskin, tormented master of prose but not of life. He loved the Gothic cathedral of Ruskin's style: the sweep of architecture, the soaring towers, the rose windows, with only the gargoyles lacking to complete the catholicity. He knew the brackish puritanism of the man—the perversion of a spirit that, in fear of life's stranger realities, could burn the sketches that his own beloved Turner had made of prostitutes in the brothels of London. But in spite of this murder of a man's work, what a hater of social lies Ruskin was; what an artist in prose!

Frank Harris knew Richard Burton, that tougher Elizabethan, contemporary, ironically, of Victoria. He had adventured in most of the wild places of the world. Master of oriental languages and life, he made the first full-blooded, unexpurgated English translation of the *Arabian Nights*. Him, too, England was to ruin: not by crucifying, but by ignoring.

And there was Cunninghame Graham. A hidalgo of the North, he loved and sought the strange places of the earth—Spain, Africa, South America. Lover of savages unspoiled by civilization, of the great spaces of the Pampas or the green hell of the Amazon, of Spanish peasants and Arab horses, he wrote of them with nostalgia. Frank Harris challenged him to a horse race in London: his own English thoroughbred against Graham's South American mustang; and Harris—said Harris—won. (He loved to race—on foot, on horseback; in his stories, at least, he always won.) The fiery grace of Graham, the sardonic Harris, the flying horses, the startled Londoners .... Two wild men of the world, skyrocketing through Hyde Park: Graham, *El Conquistador,* like "a portrait by Zurbarán of some Spanish noble who followed Cortez"; Harris, the cowboy from the plains. Graham, even in England where all wore conventional riding clothes, was clad in breeches and brown boots and sombrero, and mounted on a mustang of many colors. Harris rode a thoroughbred English horse, about

15½ hands high. The two seemed "circus riders," a cockney shouted. They were skyrockets of romance. Harris felt a deep instinctive kinship with Graham, for they were fellow outlaws, both more eager for the vital experience of life than for even the most vivid transcript of it.

In those London days, Frank Harris also met, in his own inimitable friendly way, many whose claim was no greatness of their own, but a mutual interest in writing. Harris was generous of his time and energy; he, the social "ruffian," the scourge of blatant mediocrity, would listen with gracious kindness to unknown and sometimes inarticulate candidates for literature. Such an evening is finely painted in a sonnet by John Armstrong Chaloner, printed in 1913 by the Palmetto Press, Roanoke Rapids, North Carolina.

TO FRANK HARRIS
Of London

That night in fair Park Lane I *tortured* thee—
Sat in thine house and read from sun to sun
Whilst through the windows came from Piccadilly
The distance-soften'd midnight traffic's hum—
Should wipe out many sins on that dread day
When thou dost stand before the bar of God!
For the unselfish—the *heroic* way
You listened as I through my story plod!
Thine eyes grew red—from agony, not tears;
Thy breath came thick and fast from sheer fatigue,
But from thy fluent lips shot forth no jeers:
Thou steadfast stood'st as one o' the Theban League!
'Twas story—first and last—I e'er did write!
Undying gratitude doth these lines indite.

It is a sincere feather from a moulting bird of song.

And Frank Harris met "important" men as well as great men. The fine chill Balfour—lacking temperament, lacking blood—

with his brittle political *savoir faire* and cold grace; Asquith and Curzon and Randolph Churchill; Winston Churchill, too, and Lloyd George; George Moore, with his face rufous like underdone pork: these he met, saw or saw through, praised and appraised, and fixed like flies or butterflies in amber. He was the unknown Recording Angel in London. From the Ragnarok of Carlyle to the "Recessional" of Kipling, from the grim blasphemies of a de Maupassant to the lambent ballet of Shaw, from the surging granite of Rodin to the bronze of Gaudier-Brzeska—he was God's Spy of the great.

Meanwhile, as Frank Harris observed and recorded the dramatic tensions and heroic creations of others, passion and first marriage both wakened and marred his own life.

His letter to Kate Stephens describes his marriage best. Looking backward, he wrote there of his love in words that carry conviction in their throb and pang. Its objectivity makes it more convincing, as its date (July 4, 1915) sets it earlier, than the longer account in *My Life and Loves*.

He wrote: "Let me tell you about that marriage. I was in love with an American girl, came to passion through pity, grew to devotion; all I gave but earnest of what I could give. She had been loved, been badly treated, revenged on my passion her doubt of man, her disdain of men. I got to know an English woman of great position who was extraordinarily sympathetic. She wanted to know why I did not go into Parliament: gave dinners, introduced me to the real leaders of the Conservative Party, fired my ambition in this direction, and made the way straight before me. One night the American had taken her mother to Maryland without notice to me, and I felt indignant. I told my English friend all about it. She simply said: 'The girl doesn't love you. Why should you waste a thought on her?' Like a fool I confessed: 'I can't help it: she paints the sky for me.' The English woman answered, 'Put away childish things: you ought to be the English Bismarck in a dozen years.' 'How?' I asked. She said, 'Marry some one who's proud of you and can help you, and you'll do the rest.' 'Would anyone marry me when I love someone else?' 'You think you love her,' she replied, 'but it's not real love—desire merely.'

"A week later I married her and found the most perfect and sympathetic friend was turned by marriage into a madly jealous woman in a night. At the end of a week in Paris, of scenes and reproaches and tears, I knew I had made a child's blunder! I traveled for six months and then returned to London with ambition dead in me and hope dying, to live the life of a man about town in the smart set. In a year the Prince had taken me up and asked me everywhere: in two I was dying of self-contempt. The American had come back and we lived together, each feeling that both were responsible for the fiasco.

"At length I broke loose: left the great house a poorer man than I had gone into it; bought the *Saturday Review* on credit and made it the greatest paper they've ever seen in London. . . . Four years later I sold it for forty thousand pounds profit and went to France to live and write. The American married a rich man on his deathbed, and when he died wanted to come back to me; but I had begun the writer's career and would not change it to become the bellows and the fan to cool a harlot's lust—the phrase is Shakespeare's . . . ."

Such is Frank Harris's own account of his love and his first marriage.

The American was Laura Clapton. "She was rather tall, some five feet five, and walked singularly well, reminding me of Basque and Spanish girls I had seen who swam rather than walked, a consequence, I found out, of taking short even steps from the hip. . . . Long hazel eyes of the best; broad forehead, rather round face, good lips, firm though small chin, a lovely girl, I decided, with a mane of chestnut hair brightened with strands of gold." [8] Laura was of mixed ancestry; her untidy conventional mother gave her a strain of careful meanness; her Irish, Micawber-like

[8] *My Life and Loves*, Vol. II, p. 129.

father gave her boldness, flair, and beauty. Trained for the stage, she was actress in her life as well—a life narrowed by sore needs and bitter pride. To Frank Harris she was a distraction and eventually a defeat. She was the prototype of the Dark Lady in Shakespeare's life as Harris read it. He could not forget her; he never forgave her.

In speaking of Shakespeare's love, Harris says: "I cannot help thinking that the first reason for her infidelity was his own unfaith. . . . If we know anything about Shakespeare at all, we know that he was always a loose liver. It is curious, too, that he never suggests the man's prior fault as excusing or explaining a mistress's slips. . . . Mary Fitton was probably as true to Shakespeare as he deserved. . . .

"Let us take upon us the mystery of things for once, and be God's Spies and discover the heart of the secret. Had Shakespeare, instead of telling Mary Fitton how he desired her, told her how beautiful she was; had he given her tenderness as well as passion, and honeyed flatteries rather than jealous reproaches, he might have kept her true to the end. It was just his weakness, his terrible greedy sensuality, that blinded him and prevented him using his attaching, soul-subduing qualities. . . . He did not love her unselfishly enough to win her or lightly enough to accept her infidelities. . . .

"The woman a man loves with such passion must be his ideal, must correspond most intimately to all his desires—conscious and unconscious—as coin to die; she is his complement; and to condemn her is self-condemnation." [9]

It is great criticism of Shakespeare—and of Harris.

What troubled Frank Harris most in Laura was a vague, insistent sense that even in her most passionate intimacies she held something in reserve:

> *There was a door to which there was no key;*
> *There was a veil through which I might not see.*

[9] *The Women of Shakespeare.* Kennerley, 1912. P. 286, *passim.*

The fault was mutual. Dominated by her mother, Laura was ambitious and irked by poverty. She could not see Harris, the artist who was God's Spy: his art was "interesting"; its worth lay in its price and its fame. He was, she told him, "sure to become a great writer." But it was his success, not his quality, of which she was thinking. There was verve in her, however, that delighted him more than her bodily charm. The fault lay in him also. He did not seek to awaken the divine Isis within her, to lead her with him to the mystery of things, to take her spiritual breath away as he took her bodily breath. No woman loves a man who does not satisfy her flesh; but no woman loves a man unless he also satisfies her soul. She must be ravished by body and mind; Frank Harris never made Laura awake to his insights or aware of his vision. Thus his love was a beautiful fragment, not a statue. It taught him much: without it, would he have understood the passion of Shakespeare? But in itself it was tragic.

His subsequent first marriage was, as he says, "a child's blunder." It was recoil and rebound; the minus for the plus; a frustrate healing for a frustrate love: he had found in passion less than half of what love must be; now he sought, without passion, for the other half—solace, understanding, friendship. But that is impossible without passion, as passion is impossible without understanding. Van Gogh, taking Sien to live with him, was making an opposite but no more unworldly mistake. Yet such mistakes, motivated in depths below the reason, are deeply significant. Harris himself wrote of similar things: "He had yet to learn that just as oil only smooths the surface of the waves, so reason has merely a superficial effect upon character." [10]

Frank Harris married a widow of wealth and intellectual charm, a Mrs. Clayton, who lived in Park Lane. A friend of the Prince of Wales, she had been introduced to Harris by the Duke of Cambridge. Sir Henry Johnston, in his *Memoirs,* describes them as "not a happily matched pair, though the wife struck me

---

[10] "Gulmore the Boss." In *Elder Conklin.*

as a nice, kindly woman." She was older than Harris; her maiden name had been Edith Mary Remington. (Harris often quoted with relish Shakespeare's advice that a man should marry a woman younger than himself.)

Frank Harris and Edith Mary Remington were taken in a net of irony. She loved him, for she felt his power and wished to sway and guide it into the decorous paths which alone he could never find, and without which he could never succeed. She loved him, for she was reaching out toward her own fading youth, hoping to rekindle it from this torch of vigor. She sought beauty by cosmetics, by clothes. She was resolute for his love because she must have known by gossip and have learned by experience that he was insatiable and hardly to be held by the most dexterous of women. The years with Frank Harris were difficult: they ravaged her nerves and ravished her beauty. If she had only known, it would not have been hard to hold all of Harris that she had ever had; but she needed poise above the jealous heart. Nothing cooled Frank Harris's passion more than temper and spasms of upbraiding: he could not be held by one who tried to hold him. He had known many women, he was a connoisseur of love; she was too cultured for the ardor of a Sophie, too English for the esoteric lore of an Eirene. Only with her mind could she have held him —by wisdom and noble friendship; but she destroyed these by her jealousy.

Frank Harris was wrong in being surprised by the change in her. He was less of a man of the world than he supposed; he was too single in purpose and too intense to understand the weakness, the complex simplicity, of those who were not, like him, super-human, or preterhuman, or inhuman. He was surprised—and hurt; when he was hurt he withdrew into himself: he seldom forgave, he never again respected, the weaker nature. He did not hate: his feeling was worse, as if a pagan god looked coldly on human clay. All by which she had won him ended and vanished: it suffered a sea-change of tears. She was just another woman;

her friendship and her wisdom were gone, like a quiet lovely house before a flood. He looked on her coldly; he saw the lines showing in the delicate skin, the pallor of the eyes too blanched with tears. He was bound to a woman who had lost joy, yet who insisted on joy as her right, who upbraided him if he even seemed to seek it elsewhere. If a girl or a woman wrote him—as many did and always would—it was a cause for tears if she could not read the notes, for temper if she did. She opened his letters, and revealed her treachery by spasms of reproach. What life was this for a man of his freedom and width of need?

Another cause of conflict was the fact that he had been a poor man who had begun to make money; she, a rich woman who, having money, had bestowed riches. She had condescended to the poor adventurer; she expected appreciation—and gratitude. She could not forget her gift, even though outwardly she ignored it; she knew that she had brought him much, and she felt a right of eminent domain. She had given him too much to forgive him much. He, proud, independent, dominantly masculine, avid in appetite and ambition, scorning money as such and yet hungry for the life that money can make possible, used her resources freely—and hated her for giving and himself for taking. That she thought he owed her a debt of love because she had given him a richer life than he otherwise would have had, rankled and irked. He could not forgive her that she had given him so much. It would have been better if she had been some poor waif of piquant beauty and need, and he had lifted her into light and ease. She felt that she was Pygmalion; but Frank Harris would be marble for no woman's art.

She was decorous, gently nurtured, free only by sophistication. He offended the gentility of her mind, even while he fascinated her; she was a delicate daughter of Nineveh, he a prophet from the desert. Their life together was irony for both, yet its tragedy was the fault of neither. The best they could have done would have been to live and overlive, as on the outward plane (and only there) they did; for to the world they seemed charming host and hostess. But there was a grimmer mordancy, a bite of bitterer contradiction, a touch of the strident, in Frank Harris.

Sir Sidney Low tells of the marriage. Mrs. Harris, he writes, belonged to "one of the best 'County Families,' with some fortune of her own." Harris, he thought, was not handsome; yet he had a magnet-charm for women, with his virility, powerful voice, "dominating egoism," and "round lion eyes" like those of only two other human faces, Kitchener's and Stanley's. Thanks to his marriage, Harris had "established himself in what seemed a secure niche in the London social edifice." He had a delightful "little house" in Park Lane; there he entertained "a great many of the people best worth knowing." A royal duke took tea; peers balanced poets; the dull talk of politicians was spiced by the epigrams of Oscar Wilde. Harris, as host, enlivened all by "fiery thrusts of savage criticism and biting satire." [11]

Thus Frank Harris's life lay broken between the "terrible greedy sensuality" of his unsatisfactory passion, and the unreal comradeship of his unsatisfactory first marriage. For a while he grew bitter and worldly; drank too much and ate too much; moved in the Smart Set. His sense of defeat was an asp in his heart.

But he had work to do. If life seemed to return to chaos, the artist must be God's artisan forever recreating it into cosmos. His very tragedy drove him to creation. As he wrote in "The Sheriff and His Partner," "I often think it's the work chooses us, and we've just got to get down and do it."

In getting down to the work which was his to do, Harris turned to his American experiences. His life in Galway had been too immature; his London life was still too recent. But his American life was significant, and neither too close nor too far away: he could recollect it in tranquility.

---

[11] Sir Sidney Low, "Impressions of a Vivid Personality—the Man and the Writer." London *Observer*, August 30, 1931.

But meanwhile he had assimilated the culture of Europe; he had been matured by books and men; he knew the technique of the masters. France especially, and French artists like de Maupassant, had given him a sense of chiseled words, of life stripped to form. He united the material of America with the technique of France.

His first stories were published, significantly, in a French magazine. He sent "A Modern Idyll" and "Montes the Matador" to Ferdinand Brunetière, the celebrated editor of the *Revue de Deux Mondes,* who replied: "It is the first time I received two masterpieces in one letter."

The first of these American stories to be written was "The Sheriff and His Partner" (1891). Immediately "A Modern Idyll" followed; then, in 1892, "Elder Conklin," "Eatin' Crow," and "The Best Man in Garotte." "Gulmore the Boss" was written in 1893. Collected, they formed the volume: *Elder Conklin.*

Elder Conklin, published in 1894, fortified the position that Harris had won. The same magazines that had rejected the stories separately, reviewed them favorably as a volume. Professor Dowden reviewed them with lucid praise; he wrote of their "muscular athletic style, in which every word is plain and every word tells." [12] Coventry Patmore, the poet, was even more affirmative. In the same issue of the same magazine he wrote: "Kipling never did anything better than the two short stories, 'Eatin' Crow' and 'The Best Man in Garotte.' The interest is human and heroic, and the execution perfect. . . ."

Patmore's praise is justified but overpitched. One can think of stories of Kipling's that transcend these particular two, for example, "Without Benefit of Clergy" and "The Man Who Would Be King." *Elder Conklin* is Harris's slightest volume of stories; yet it is technically fine, and in content significant. At first it seems quiet, the transcription of life called "realism" which hundreds of lesser talents were to do in years to come. But the stories

[12] The *New Review,* December, 1894.

are like sunlight which at first we regard as a photographic agent, but which, we eventually realize, is the light by which we see the intense canvases of a Rousseau. The book is salty with a salient irony; it is strong with overtones of courage and passion.

"Elder Conklin," the title story, shows the breadth of Harris's understanding. It is the story of a man of some fifty-odd years—hard, resolute, grizzled, shrewd: a Yankee in Kansas, who serves God with bleak integrity; loves his daughter with a terrible tenderness that will drive him to cheat for her sake; and stands unshaken and alone—shotgun in hand—before a lieutenant and a squad of cavalry, with General Custer in the background. The Elder is no hypocrite, even though he salts the pasture of the cattle he is selling, so that on the way to town they will drink until each gains some sixty-five pounds. It is part of the battle which is life, and it is for Loo's sake. The Elder's prayer is magnificent. Speaking to the stern God of his religion, alone in the night, he reveals the grim tenderness and tension of his heart. Loo is so young and pretty, so like a flower! If there has been sin and fault, let its punishment fall not upon her but upon him.

There is dainty realization of Loo—the proud, untutored, lovedesirous girl of Kansas, who wants to win the fastidious Bancroft, the scholar from Harvard; but who loses him through her innocence and directness. So she elopes at last with the middle-aged lawyer whom she does not love, to spite the pedant whom she does. There is Bancroft from Boston, who loses the one love of his life because he puts convention before nature. Harris, the "ruffian" of Shaw's wit, is here the artist of delicate rectitude. Meticulous in truth, he is never a propagandist or himself a protagonist; human in pity and in understanding, he never blurs the single white light which is the truth of the multicolored spectrum.

"A Modern Idyll" is the story of a popular clergyman, a preacher of great gifts and good, who has fallen in love with the charming, half-demure, Eve-coy wife of his deacon. He is mad with passion; she holds him off—and leads him on. A call comes from a great Chicago church. The salary is $10,000—twice his present salary; the opportunities are vastly wider. He makes his remaining contingent on her acquiescence. Meanwhile he wrestles with himself and the will of God: if he stays, he may never have such a call again; if he goes, how can he preach a great sermon of farewell when all his parishioners will know that $10,000 has bought him? He is an artist; that final sermon means much. Meanwhile the tangle of his passion has enmeshed him; he thinks that God wishes him to stay and give up his illicit love; he half decides to—yet knows that he cannot cut it out of his heart. He makes up his mind to stay; uplifted by his renunciation, he preaches such a sermon as he never has preached before: a master-piece, it affects his congregation like a symphony. That afternoon, the deacons, led by the husband of the woman he loves, come to give him $2500 which they have raised, as earnest of an annual increase to a salary of $7500. Hardheaded men of the world, they have decided that he must be a saint to renounce the call. His re-calcitrant love is with them—the first to greet him, the last to leave him. When he passionately presses her for an answer, she coyly says, "You're just too silly for anything." And she gives him her lips.

"The Sheriff and His Partner" is full of a hard western reti-cence of courage, shot through with the flame of guns. There is no bravado, only a puckered silence like thin ice over death. The quiet-spoken sheriff, the people of the town who insist that before a man speaks of what should be done he should put up an "ante" of proven courage, the sheriff's partner, a slow-spoken, quick-shooting man from Missouri who goes to die on a dare and kills before he is killed, are graphic engraving of the West.

"Eatin' Crow" is the story of one of the brave born fools of the world who, learning one extreme, ignore the other. Charley Muirhead, on first coming from New England, had allowed him-self to be made the butt of ridicule. His tormenter in the first camp was a little Irishman whom he could easily have broken in two. Instead he "ate crow." His degradation made him leave and start life anew; even, in his shame, to give up forever his girl back East. Now, unknown and able to make a new start, he pursues opposite tactics: no longer will he "eat crow," but ram word or deed down the throat of anyone who insults him. He does so successfully—once.

They warn him: "'If a man was steel, and the best and quickest on the draw ever seen, I guess they'd bury him if he played your way.'

"'They may bury me,' retorted Charley bitterly, 'but I've eaten my share of crow. Can't go back East now with the taste of it in my mouth. I'd rather they buried me.'

"And they did bury him—about a fortnight after."

"Gulmore the Boss" is a larger canvas, with more nuances of civilized implication. It is based partly on the character of Byron Smith, though not on anything that happened literally in Lawrence. Gulmore is a shrewd political manipulator; a Tammany leader in a western town. The true villain is Hutchings, the lawyer, who for political prestige and a chance to go to Washington and the glamours of Congress, sells his party, his friend, his soul. The foil for the Boss and his political jujitsu is Roberts, the professor. "Square shoulders and attenuated figure—a mixture of energy and nervous force without muscular strength; a tyrannous forehead overshadowing lambent hazel eyes; a cordial frankness of manner with a thinker's tricks of gesture, his nervous fingers emphasizing the words." Roberts fights in his scholar's way a gallant but losing battle: a dirty fight as the Boss fights it, with no holds barred. Roberts is accused of being an atheist because he praises Buddha and Socrates in the same sentence with Christ. He is dismissed from the university by his colleagues of the third sex and a college president who is a chameleon of the spirit. But he triumphs, for he wins Hutchings' daughter away from her father and secures a position at Yale. It is no more a mere story of the West than Antigone is a mere story of Athens.

"The Best Man in Garotte" is full of the dynamite latent in the hearts of lonely, lustful men. It gives a snapshot of the famous Wild Bill Hickok, disguised as "Bill Hitchcock": "He was tall and broad-shouldered; his face long, with well-cut features; a brown mustache drooped negligently over his mouth; his heavy eyelids were usually half closed, but when in moments of excitement they were suddenly updrawn, one was startled by a naked hardness of gray-green eyes." The story tells of a moment of tension when the heat in men's souls was smouldering with latent lightnings. The best man in Garotte is Lawyer Rabley, who because of his fairness and popularity has been made a judge. He is loved for his charm and wit, especially for his stories. On this day of the gathered thunderheads of anger, he enters the bar at an untimely time. He crowds Hitchcock the killer. Hitchcock picks up his glass and dashes it in the Judge's face. The Judge mops his face free of the dregs and starts toward Hitchcock, only to meet the muzzle of a Navy Colt. But the others have Hitchcock covered; they warn him that, if he shoots the Judge, they will blast his life. Dave Crocker, their spokesman, says that it must be a fair fight and asks the Judge to choose his champion, since he is no shot, and Hitchcock is a marvel on the draw. The Judge affirms his own right to his own danger. To make all fair in spite of him, the bystanders place two guns—one loaded, one empty—under a hat in the next room. The duelists draw lots. Though his friends wish to give the Judge first choice anyway, he refuses. Hitchcock, seizing a gun, snaps it at the Judge's head—harmlessly. The Judge, raising the other revolver, suddenly drops it and runs from the room and the town. In astonishment and "half contemptuous sympathy" the rough men of Garotte force the wolf-like Hitchcock, snarling over bared fangs, to crawl on his belly out of the bar. But Judge Rabley never comes back. "Men said his nerves had 'give out.'"

To read *Elder Conklin* is to ride into the lost West. Here is frontier America as it was in its crudity and courage, its beauty and pain. Harris has lifted the ill-luck of many roaring camps, and the quieter landscapes of Kansas, into art. For Americans it is a heritage that will rank as history with art for its antiseptic against time. Here, preserved in amber, is the West.

If Frank Harris is right in believing that even a dramatic creator like Shakespeare reveals himself in his characters, it is equally true of Harris. Here we see *him:* catholic, just, sympathetic with all sorts and conditions of men—Puritan, political boss, scholar, minister, proud lovely girl; a man, also, of courage and action. *Elder Conklin* is a man's book.

The years from 1886 to 1894 were a period of success in Frank Harris's life, a blue day of sun and summer, yet what the weather-wise call a "weather breeder." He occupied his place of highest dignity, if not of greatest brilliance, as editor of the *Fortnightly;* he was the friend of men and women distinguished in art, science, literature, politics; he held a place of honor amid the important and the great. He found passionate love which failed him in one way, and conventional marriage which failed him in another. He began his career as writer. His place was high, his promise seemed higher; few could foresee that he was born for the highest destiny—and therefore for the sternest fate.

Meanwhile the world seemed his oyster. Few suspected that within the oyster of the world he sought the Pearl of Great Price.

Chapter VI

PITY AND TERROR

(1884-1900)

As FRANK HARRIS moved through London he met most of the great men of the day—among them the most delightful companion of all, whom, in some limbo of eternity, he said he would most love to hold in timeless talk. That sunniest comrade of wit was Oscar Wilde. And this comrade of comedy was to be his hero of tragedy. That tragedy Frank Harris was to record with the grave beauty of pity and terror.

In his *Ballad of Reading Gaol,* Wilde, forgetting himself, watches the "man who had to swing," in his gray prison clothes like ape or clown, till the terror of his own fate is made all the greater because he forgets it in pity for the graver fate of another. So the life of Frank Harris is lifted to a higher intensity of terror and a higher integrity of pity because he was the most passionate spectator and the most articulate spokesman of the tragedy of Wilde. (Peace to the fiery Robert Sherard and no pistols for two!) During the enactment of that tragedy, Harris was a Greek chorus, exhorting Wilde in vain, explaining the action to shuddering friends, chanting overtones of pity. He would have been more if Wilde had let him: a participant, with horses at the door and steam yacht on the Thames, ready to enter as *deus ex machina* in romantic fiery rescue. After the tragedy, he was its greatest dramatist.

Wilde and Harris had curious similarities and obvious differences.

Both brought Celtic blood to the wider opportunities of England; both went to America, where they absorbed something of that newer continent. (Both even met Walt Whitman.) Both were outsiders in London, winning their way by the brilliance of their talents. Both were iconoclasts of the decorums of Victoria and the taboos of Mrs. Grundy. Both were raconteurs and superlative conversationalists; both were artists of the written word.

But there the similarities ended. Wilde was fastidious, perverse in sex, a playboy, a man whose keenest criticism remained kindly, an aesthete whose sparkling wit seldom turned to satire about the society of which he felt himself a part, a man of humor who loved to bask in the sun of favor, one whose appetite for pleasure was paramount. He was the "amiable, esurient Oscar," easily daunted by the ferocity of the world—a figure destined for sunny gardens, like some statue of a Greek god (grown corpulent with excess of good living). Harris, on the other hand, was fierce and trenchant, lavish but natural in sex, unable to pose; a man whose wit was grave and sardonic, who loved humor in others but seldom used it, whose perverse nature was to be the opposite in all things to all men, who in spite of ambition must be ever the lone wolf baying at all the sheep dogs of the world. He was combative, aggressive, a treader of the grapes of wrath, full of a high disdain and a dauntless energy against all that the world could say or do—a figure destined for the wind-swept sky, like the wild hawk. Each complemented the other. Wilde was half frightened and wholly shocked by this Captain Kidd loose in London, yet vitally attracted by Harris's vigor and art. Harris, at first contemptuous of the "oily and fat" Wilde with his mincing ways, was more and more fascinated by the wit, the humor, the spontaneous flow of brilliant talk, the generous riches of Wilde's heart. Each found in the other the things he himself lacked.

Harris met Wilde about 1884. He saw him "continually, now

at the theater, now in some society drawing room; most often, I think, at Mrs. Jeune's (afterward Lady St. Helier). His appearance was not in his favor; there was something oily and fat about him that repelled me. . . . The snatches of his monologues which I caught from time to time seemed to consist chiefly of epigrams almost mechanically constructed of proverbs and familiar sayings turned upside down." [1] Harris noticed physical mannerisms such as "pulling his jowl with his right hand as he spoke," and that his jowl was "already fat and paunchy." Yet he continues: "I don't remember what we talked about, but I noticed almost immediately that his gray eyes were finely expressive; in turn vivacious, laughing, sympathetic; always beautiful. The carven mouth, too, with its heavy, chiseled, purple-tinged lips, had a certain attraction and significance in spite of a black front tooth which shocked me when he laughed. He was over six feet in height and both broad and thickset; he looked like a Roman emperor of the decadence." To Harris with his lack of height, the greater physical stature of Wilde made him indeed seem a stooped and lazily looming emperor.

They saw much of each other. They were not, like Wilde and Whistler, too much alike to be happy together. (It is biological relatives who are keenest rivals for earth and air.) Harris, like Wilde at the customs in America, was quick to declare his genius; but it was a different genius. He and Wilde could shine without detracting from each other's light, like sun and moon. Harris could publish things of Wilde's, and spread his praises by tongue and pen; he could set Wilde an example of serving art at the expense of pleasure; he could encourage the lazier Oscar (lover of talk, laggard to write) to set his gems in gold. Wilde, on the other hand, quickened Harris by stimulating his desire to emulate; by giving his graver mind a constant sun bath in wit; by his love of beauty, fructifying like spring.

Their intercourse was not mutual praise. It had to be, between

[1] *Oscar Wilde: His Life and Confessions,* pp. 63 ff.

such men, clash and stimulus—the meeting of two master swordsmen, who, though they practiced with masks and buttoned ra-
piers, contended for the precedence of crying: "A hit, a hit!"

Wilde's most trenchant wit lay in such rapier thrusts. "Yes,
Frank, you have been invited to all the great houses of London—
once." In more petulant moments he abandoned wit: "Frank Harris has no feelings. It is the secret of his success, just as the fact
that he thinks other people have none is the secret of the failure
that lies in wait for him somewhere on the way to Life." When
he was fairest he wrote: "You are a man of dominant personality: your intellect is exigent, more so than of any man I ever
knew: your demands on life are enormous: you require response,
or you annihilate: the pleasure of being with you is in the clash
of personality, the intellectual battle, the war of ideas. To survive,
one must have a strong brain, an assertive ego, a dynamic character. In your luncheon parties, in the old days, the remains of
the guests were taken away with the debris of the feast. I have
often lunched with you in Park Lane and found myself the only
survivor."

Einar Lyngklip records a revealing episode. Wilde and Harris
once visited a dog show together. "It seems that on one platform
set apart from the rest a shaggy mongrel had been put on exhibi-
tion with all the thoroughbreds, perhaps for contrast by some
practical joker.

"Wilde was delighted and wanted to stop and look at him.

" 'Look, Frank! The only dog at the show that is like no other
dog here. And like no other that you've ever seen anywhere in all
the world!'

"Suddenly taking Frank's arm and turning him round so as to
look more directly at him, he exclaimed excitedly: 'Why, he is
like you! He even looks like you, Frank!'

"The sensitive Harris, always touchy about his personal appearance which he always profoundly resented, took it as anything but a compliment, and apparently quite plainly showed he

had been hurt, for Oscar immediately went to great lengths to explain, adding:

" 'That's how I meant it, Frank. Like him you are set apart and alone. Like him you could find no twin anywhere in the world. You are a new combination of the elements. Life has tried a new mixture in you. Like him, also, you might be the founder of a new line. Every new line is founded by a hybrid. By a mongrel. By a sport.' "

Harris, for his part, was a stern critic of Wilde. He knew the lack of natural magic and original insight in Wilde's first poems: they were not the native wood-notes of a Blake or even a Housman —but, as Shaw said, a *"Pastiche* of Morris, Swinburne, and Rossetti." Harris knew, also, the superficial brilliance of Wilde's lectures in America, derivative in doctrine and even phrase from Pater, Ruskin, Whistler. Wilde was more like a canary singing in a cage than an eagle on his roads of storm.

Harris found Wilde's destiny in his talk—as of a spendthrift of wit, tossing epigrams carefully yet carelessly about the parlors of London. Oscar darted like a hummingbird on swift rainbow wings to the heart of wisdom's flower.

Thus, when they were speaking of a young man named Raffalovitch, Harris said: "He came to London apparently to found a *salon.*"

"And he very nearly succeeded," replied Oscar, smiling, "he established a saloon."

"No afterthought, no art, can give any idea of the astounding richness of his verbal humor. One day, walking down by the Houses of Parliament, we came on a meeting of the unemployed who were reinforced by some bands of suffragettes. 'Characteristic,' I said in my usual serious way, 'one of these days the unemployed will make themselves heard here in Westminster. We are witnessing the beginnings of a social revolution.'

" 'You call it characteristic,' said Oscar. 'I think it characteristic, too, my dear Frank, to find the unenjoyed united in protest with the unemployed.' " [2]

Harris found Wilde greatest in his comedies of manners—the wittiest, he said, since Congreve and Sheridan: comedies of divine talk become the staccato idle brilliance of a wit that blew epigrams like thistledown through sunny air.

Harris watched Wilde, however, with a growing ill ease. Words of gossip and scandal were seeping underground like contaminated waters. (It was part of his character that he never heard them about himself.) Oscar was growing brazen rather than brilliant; he was led toward doom by a half-laughing, half-frightened insolence. He coarsened; he was growing worldly, even sordid; sometimes as they dined, a boy, strolling past, would look at Wilde and laugh strangely; another sought to blackmail him with a letter.

There was Alfred Douglas, too—an enigmatic figure. Harris, since he loved Wilde, hardly liked this youth who incited the worst in his friend. Beautiful, though a *boy;* fierce in arrogance like his terrible father, the Marquis of Queensbury; petulant, aristocratic, he seemed a symbol of perversity. Who could have supposed that it was Douglas who had heard the tempting call of Wilde? Harris, believing in the innocence of his friend, wrongly supposed that Douglas was the villain of the play. Because of this he was to find his book blocked by the quite natural lawsuits of the young Lord.

Yet Harris—always fair in art, even when hostile in life— thought Douglas more naturally a singer than Wilde. Wilde's great poems were the gifts of pain. With fine intuition for high poetry, Harris praised the sextet of Douglas's sonnet on death:

> *For in the smoke of that last holocaust,*
> *When to the regions of unsounded air*

[2] *My Life and Loves,* Vol. III, pp. 135-36.

That which is deathless still aspires and tends,
Whither, my helpless soul, shall we be tossed?
To what disaster of malign despair,
Or terror of unfathomable ends?

Meanwhile Harris and Douglas—both men of pride and courage —both egotists because each had a self worth affirming—clashed almost until the end, and at best agreed only on an unworking truce.

In one way, Harris thought, Wilde's ruin was caused by Douglas, who hated his father so much that, in an attempt to hurt him, he submitted Wilde as guinea pig for a court trial. Thus Lord Alfred Douglas, who had unjustly been judged the more guilty participant in illicit love, was really guilty of a very licit hate!

Harris believed Wilde innocent until Oscar confessed his guilt. This was natural, for Harris had always disdained the inbred love of the single sex; as Shaw says, Harris "was not the least perverted sexually: on the contrary, though he was conscientiously shameless where normal sexual adventures were concerned, he was, outside the straight line of sex, a prude." [3] Harris never suspected Wilde's guilt because he himself never experienced the temptation. Oscar had seemed to him, in spite of something half feminine and wholly unwholesome, too great a lover of beauty for perversion. (He seems never to have noticed that in praising girls Wilde called them "boyish.") But though he hated the vice, he loved the victim.

Harris had long suspected, among men, a smouldering hatred of Wilde, like fire that has eaten underground and burns through peat—a hatred which came from more than a distaste for strange sins. Jealousy among journalists, hatred for genius by mediocrity, a dislike for ideas by the middle class, gathered in a convergence which Wilde's perversion focused into flame like a burning glass. Harris's sense of this constitutes his greatest contribution to the

[3] G. Bernard Shaw, Preface to Harris's *Oscar Wilde*.

drama. To Harris, the casual excuse was the perversion, the causal motivation was the world's hatred of the artist.

The world's rebuttal remains stubborn, however, and is underlined by Shaw. In his Preface to the latest edition of Harris's *Wilde,* Shaw writes: "Alphonse Daudet, asked by Mr. Sherard to intercede for Wilde, replied, 'You see, Mr. Sherard, you are not a parent.' Daudet knew what he was talking about, which is more than can be said for either Harris or Mr. Sherard, or indeed any of the literary enthusiasts who are so wrapped up in their vision of Oscar as a saint, a martyr, and a hero, that policemen and parents are ignored by them as vulgar and irreverent intruders." Even the Soviet Union, says Shaw, starting with no prejudice and no laws against homosexuality, had finally to resort to the severest penalties to curb the pernicious offense. Wilde, after all, was punished as a pederast—though the punishment may have been augmented because he was a poet. Wilde's vice was perverse; it is unfortunately true that the world had cause. Wilde's genius was genuine, and had much to do with the world's hate. Thus Harris has much to justify his verdict; but his case is made more difficult, and the world is half absolved, by the circumstances of the evil.

The strength of Harris's case is the fact that genius is always the bull's-eye of the world's hate. Who can be sure, therefore, of what is casual and what is causal in the world's treatment of genius? But the affair is contaminated and made impure, both from Wilde's side and from the world's side, until one cannot give an unequivocal verdict. Harris has made the best possible speech for the defense.

As to the outcome of the trial, Harris proved himself a seer. Shaw is witness to his clairvoyant Cassandra prophecy. After the trial had proved the prophecy, the question was: should Wilde wait for sentence, or, as the police perhaps expected and desired, should he flee to France?

Harris's advice was to flee the country, and not endure the injustice of a "justice" savage with sadism, malignant with malice.

Harris had the fastest horses in London, fiery at his door. He would drive at a gallop to the river; knock anyone down who tried to interfere; and whisk Wilde beyond the law. The technique carries the signature of Harris in every detail. (One is reminded of Tom Sawyer, that other great romantic and lover of "evasions.") Harris did not reckon with his man, however: one can bend circumstances but not improvise character. Nor would it have been best; had Wilde escaped, he would have written more brilliant and brittle comedies of manners, or drunk himself to death in a mist of talk. What would have become of the *Ballad of Reading Gaol,* of *De Profundis?* Without the expiation, could one agree with Harris's interpretation of Wilde as a genius crucified? What evidence of Christ had the sensual, arrogant pagan yet given? The pity that would have saved the man from crucifixion would have deprived him also of the stone that is rolled away.

But what drama!—the fierce and fiery Frank; the slack and wilted Oscar, a mountain of passivity, a drooping emperor. Oscar, the sun-natured, the pleasure-loving, cowered now: he could endure pain and even turn it into dark music, but he could not fight. Why should Frank incite and urge him past his destiny? He was a Pagan in the sun, a Christian in the dark; never a Titan hurling mountains. His soul was flabby like his flesh. His spirit was gathering itself for the final bravery of which alone he was capable—the dignity of the lute that, if the wind shatters it, still draws music from its fate. Could Frank not understand? Even when he spoke of the world-weary and the passion-worn his words had the sound of a trumpet. Oscar was tired; his hands were slack and nerveless; he needed all his strength to suffer and endure. His soul was a Sargasso Sea, a tideless water, a Nirvana of the drifting weed. Frank, that blue Gulf Stream of life and light, went flowing by and called him to come; but he could not. "Go," he said. "Go, Frank; let me die my own death."

The lion eyes devoured him with scorn, then softened into tenderness. *"The crucifixion of the guilty is still more awe-inspiring than the crucifixion of the innocent: what do we men know of innocence?"* The words shaped themselves in Frank's heart: all things turned there to phrases fashioned like the bronze of Rodin. He felt the manacles of mist that bound the flabby giant; no, Oscar would never fight! All his arrogance was gone, his lust for good living, his pagan pride. The obverse of his paganism was the strange defeat-Christianity that Christians never knew. Sensuous still, his religion was a thing of incense and atmosphere and chants in the darkness, with pale candles. Frank never shared it: he was a Christian of the sun.

Yet how thoughtful this Oscar who could not save himself, who would not let others save him! His one fear was lest he had lost a friend. "You are not angry with me, Frank?" He would almost violate his nature in order not to hurt a friend. One wanted to shake him: one ended by shaking his hand. One wanted to waken him, by cold water or a blow, from his somnambulation to the pit: yet one loved him for his childlikeness. Virtue, even though it was but a miasma of virtue, went out of him. Even in this bedraggled hour he was great.

Even Christ could not save the Thief upon the Right: for the soul is free. Harris shrugged his shoulders and set himself to save what he could from the wreckage of the trial. He advised Oscar how he might yet win; but he knew that Oscar had chosen defeat. He was talking, he knew, to the dead!

After the tension of such a *cas célèbre,* when there is much to be said and little to be done, it is easy to seem brave. Today we see Wilde fairly and talk about his perversion and punishment without prejudice or peril. It was not so then. The case was as bitter as the Dreyfus affair. Those who spoke in favor of Wilde were in peril of losing their positions and were certain to lose their reputations. Among the few who stood staunch was Frank Harris—no fair-weather friend, but a comrade in chaos.

He wrote an article in Wilde's defense which the printers of the *Saturday Review* refused to set up. Knowing the temper of the time, who can doubt that they would refuse? Knowing the temper of Harris at all times, who can doubt that he wrote it?

He circulated a petition among writers for the release of Wilde. When the Chicago "anarchists" were on trial, Shaw had circulated a memorial asking for their reprieve; but among the literati of London, "all heroic rebels and sceptics on paper," only Wilde had signed. Shaw says that the "utterly disinterested act" won Oscar "his distinguished consideration." [4] Wilde's brave act was not imitated now save by Tyrell in Dublin. Harris did not approach Hardy first. If he had, the champion of Tess against the President of the Immortals would have signed, and others might have followed. But Harris, more intimate with Meredith, hoped more from his sun-clear greatness; Meredith, however, turned scornfully from perversity and unnatural vice. Discouraged by the defection of his chosen champion, Harris desisted.

Yet by his own efforts Harris had the governor of the prison, whose machine-cruelty throbs through the *Ballad of Reading Gaol,* changed for a milder warden. This respite kept Wilde alive to write *Reading Gaol* and *De Profundis;* thus Harris saved Wilde's life—and, more important, his earthly immortality.

And Frank Harris would not be silent. Walter, the editor of the London *Times* (the Englishman's intellectual hearth and home), said to him: "I wonder that you are going about with him [Wilde]; you are getting a bad name through it." Harris replied, "Really, I never heard that his disease was catching. Genius is not infectious!" Walter seemed irritated, even shocked—"a little pettish . . . not to say petty." But Harris's unshakable word was: "I shall always defend my friends." [5]

Let the cock crow thrice: still this stauncher Peter would not deny his friend.

"I was dining with Oscar Wilde as my guest at the Café Dur-

[4] The account of this, and the quotations, are from Shaw's Preface to the latest edition of Harris's *Oscar Wilde.*
[5] *My Life and Loves,* Vol. III, p. 151.

and, one night in Paris, when a certain English lord whom I knew came over to me with a smiling face; as soon as he saw my companion he stopped and exclaimed 'Good God!' and turned abruptly to the door and went out. I happened to be going up in the lift at the Ritz Hotel a day or two later when he came into the lift at the second floor; at once he greeted me, saying: 'I am so sorry for the other day, Harris, but when I saw who you were with, I couldn't possibly speak to you: fancy going about with that man in public.'

" 'I know,' I said, 'there are not many immortals, I don't wonder you don't want to know them; but why not forget me, too; it would be better, don't you think?' and I turned away and began talking to the lift man." [6]

Meanwhile he tried to encourage Wilde. "Think of a London fog," he said. "It prevents them from seeing clearly; don't bother about them: didn't Shakespeare call it 'this all-hating world'?"

This stalwart loyalty, eloquent with a gifted tongue, did little good to Wilde and much harm to Harris; it endeared him to Heaven, but earned him the hate of earth.

Frank Harris did not exploit the tragedy of Wilde. He visited the exile in France when there was only hatred from the world and expense from Wilde; he helped support Oscar by outright gifts, often lavish; he bought the plot of *Mr. and Mrs. Daventry* when it was only in embryo.

The purchase of this plot is a vexed issue; at the time, it was vexing to Harris. Wilde, in his half careless, half responsible way, sold it to several people, and when it was produced with a sort of flashy success tried to claim it as his own. The evidence is conclusive that Harris bought it in good faith and wrote his own play. Shaw's comment is final: if Oscar had really written it, it would have been a masterpiece and would have become a classic. Since Harris wrote it—it was only another play. "As to a line of this play having been done by Oscar, either Mr. Sherard does not

[6] *Ibid.*, p. 169.

know chalk from cheese, which seems improbable, or else he has never seen a line of *Daventry* or seen it acted." [7] Harris had no talent for the theater; his genius was too intensely personal, even in so objective a form as the story. The play must have been a mere germ when Oscar sold it; one recognized nothing of him in its construction or dialogue. Its flash of success was due to the gossip that connected it with Wilde, a success of scandal. Its substance, apart from the shadow of Wilde's name, was all Harris's.

Harris bought it with the best intentions. He understood and forgave the motivation of need and pique that caused Wilde, in his petulant decadence, to claim it for his own.

Harris did his utmost to recall Wilde to aspiration and endeavor, but vainly. Oscar was stridently ironic about the moral Americanism of his insistent friend. He said once that Harris was upstairs thinking about Shakespeare at the top of his voice. Wilde would not rise to the lure. He felt that Harris wanted him to remain always at an intellectual pressure that was dangerous to his exhausted brain; he felt that he needed a safety valve of idleness; and to excuse himself from such intensity, he decided simply to reveal that he had softening of the brain and could not be perpetually a genius.

Wilde was weak in body; weaker in spirit. The motto of the artist, Harris believed, was *noblesse oblige;* it was his own creed and conduct. He disliked the slack, unbuttoned way in which Wilde abandoned himself and seemed to hug his death.

Also Harris hated Wilde's vice, and argued with power against the delusion that the love of man for man can ever equal in ecstasy and beauty the love of man for woman.

After Wilde died, the greatest service was to his memory. Wilde might have said:

> *O God!—Horatio, what a wounded name,*
> *Things standing thus unknown, shall live behind me!*

[7] Shaw, *op. cit.*

And,

> . . . *in this harsh world draw thy breath in pain,*
> *To tell my story.* . . .

And Harris might have answered:

> *And let me speak to the yet unknowing world.*

He did speak—in the book which Shaw called "the best literary portrait of Wilde in existence"; and since he spoke, the world is no longer the "unknowing world." Shaw says: "Nothing was too fine for him [Harris] and nothing too coarse. He was on your level instantly whether you were a master of literature or a hobo; and nothing can persuade me that he did not get out of Oscar all there was to be got."

Both these great writers loved art; both sought an art undiluted by utility or propaganda; both held bad art an abomination. Wilde, however, was more precious, more fastidious; he dwelt in the province of tone and atmosphere. He saw art as self-sufficient, self-sustaining, self-contained: a fourth dimension that seemed a single dimension. Harris, like Whitman and Balzac, saw substance as well as style, and sought to be not only a lord of language but a master of life. Art, to Wilde, was a divine plaything: "All art is quite useless." Art was an embalming fluid that turned beauty into a perfection of death. Harris, on the other hand, wished to raise life into art by infusing it with the greater energy of an nth power, by a transfusion from the blood of God. Art to him must not be utilitarian—or futilitarian. It must be life raised to the infinite of clarity, energy, significance—life immense in passion, pulse, and power.

Frank Harris never wrote, as Wilde did, of "making beautiful colored musical things." He wrote to Arnold Bennett: "I want the realism; but I want also to see the soul conquering its surroundings, putting the obstructions under its feet; heaping up the funeral pyre, if you will, from which the spirit may take flight." He wrote to Gerald Cumberland: "The question for you is, have I quickened you? Encouraged you to be a brave soldier in the Liberation War of Humanity? Did virtue come out of me?"

Compare *The Picture of Dorian Gray* with the flung dynamite of *The Bomb*. Compare *Salome*—that white bird over shadowy waters, that chaste crescent of a young moon walking cold above the pits of death—with the depth and truth-seeking of "The Magic Glasses." Wilde was God's lapidary, chiseling this gem or that jewel to perfect form, and picking out the blinding silver or the deep gold most fitted for its perfect setting. But Frank Harris saw a story or biography as a living flower or tree.

In life, too, they were dissimilar. Wilde sought pleasure first: he wished to hold sorrow, like the night, at the other side of the world. Joshua of the aesthetes, he said to the sun, "Stand still!"— not that he might win at Ajalon, but that he might pleasure himself in the gardens of Babylon. Harris sought pleasure as an integral part of life. He also knew, with Carlyle, "the brotherhood of woe and duty"; with Jesus and Goethe, he saw that grief is the seal of greatness. He was no isolationist of literature. Art was the quintessence of reality; the greatest art came from the greatest life. "Style," he said, "is the way great men talk."

Wilde in his latest and greatest work came nearest to Harris— in the *Ballad of Reading Gaol,* in *De Profundis*. Harris, on the other hand, in all his best stories and portraits attains that integrity of technique which Wilde sought—and much more.

But with all their differences in art and life, Wilde and Harris were two of the few great friends that the world has known. They were, as Wilde says in his ballad, "like two doomed ships that met in storm." Wilde was a pleasure yacht, sailing out in clear sun over sparkling waves, that went down slowly after sudden unexpected storm wherein the lightning struck it; Harris was a cruiser, whose heart carried the blood-red fury of the guns, sailing on through many battles, until at last—battered, old, yet undefeated—it sank quietly at anchor.

Chapter VII

THUS WE HALFMEN STRUGGLE

(1894-1898)

FRANK HARRIS had risen high; but it is the tree of fullest stature upon the mountain that provokes the lightning.

He had outlived his novelty in London. As Shaw, his most philosophical critic, says: "He remained ridiculously incapable of the tactful dissimulation, hypocrisy, and polite mendacity which are needed to consolidate a position in the London governing-class society to which he had effected an entrance. . . . Harris, instead of consolidating that position, shattered it almost every time he opened his mouth. . . . In short, if there ever was a martyr to truth, that martyr was St. Francis Harris." [1]

Shaw wrote to Guido Bruno, "As to Frank Harris, nothing short of his being born again will ever make him an elder of the conventional flock. The instinct that teaches the conventional people to flee from him is quite a sound one: he is their enemy; and being a man of infinite scorn, he never loses the opportunity of wiping his feet on them. It is astonishing how successful he is in imposing himself and compelling attention and interest. You must be content with that: it is the idlest dream to suppose that you can write him up by the methods of the publicity man. It was easy to do that with Mr. Edison, who never hurt anyone's

[1] Shaw, Preface to Harris's *Wilde*.

131

feelings . . . but if they set up an image of an officially recognized Harris tomorrow, Harris himself, after contemplating it for a moment in by no means speechless contempt, would double it up by an emphatic kick in the stomach." [2]

Such a man could not expect the world to praise him for wiping his boots on it, or to acclaim him for a "kick in the stomach"!

Harris's position as editor of the *Fortnightly* grew increasingly difficult. He refused to be at ease in Babylon. He would not let ill enough alone. He would not let sleeping jackasses lie. His comments on men, manners, and morals were frank and mordant; his friends were poets like Dowson and Verlaine, or witty laughers like Wilde, or barb-tongued Arabs of art like Whistler; he himself loved art too intelligently and purely. In politics he was "impossible": he defended Parnell, declaring that he would not "march to victory with the petticoat of Kitty O'Shea for his flag." He wrote a story praising Sonia, who slew a Czar. The wonder is not that he finally failed, but that he succeeded so long. The world's definition of genius might well be: "An infinite capacity for giving pain." And the world is sure sooner or later to inflict on the genius pain of a different sort in retaliation for the pain he causes.

His directors, Chapman and Hall, were excellent men. The *Fortnightly* had a long history of liberalism; but it had been a graceful freedom that wore the hallmark not of genius but of talent. Now Harris introduced new and disturbing writers; he published his own stories, indicating directions and continents not yet charted on the map. He seemed to his directors an *enfant terrible*. There were temper and tempest at board meetings. Acrimony, debate, censure, and ultimatums were the disorder of the day. Sometimes Harris had to choose between giving way or resigning; if he had his way, the directors wished he *would* resign. Whether he lost or won, he was acidly articulate.

The directors of the *Fortnightly* finally dismissed him. The

[2] G. Bernard Shaw, letter to Guido Bruno.

casual reason was an ode by Swinburne, praising tyrannicide; but Swinburne had long committed such verbal mayhem; the bombs of his rhetoric hurt nobody: they were more a convention than a conviction. The ode was only an excuse: the reason was Harris's bold originality.

This dismissal (1894) shocked Harris. He could not comprehend the world's mediocrity, for he would not and could not condescend to the world's level: he gave men the courtesy of his own greatness. In spite of what he thought he knew about the world, mediocrity seemed to him abnormal; he could not really believe that the world existed without benefit of genius.

His chagrin, by his own account, made him so ill that he felt the chill and ghostly wind from beyond the world. The shock and his consequent illness were like an experience of partial death: afterward he was like a man who has risen from the grave.

There was a tendency in Harris which explains his loss of the *Fortnightly,* and also the many enemies he made. That tendency was an aggressive integrity. There are many examples of this.

H. G. Wells—his literary discovery, and long his friend—used to visit him; Frank would mimic a certain Cockney speech (later outgrown) which Wells unconsciously used. Mrs. Harris warned Frank, but expostulated in vain: he would have his cruel fun. Wells, white with fury, finally ceased to come: another enemy— and one who with the years would grow in power. Wells scarcely mentions Harris in his autobiography, and then with venom.

Harris himself gives instances of the same arrogance. Once he was talking to Joseph Chamberlain—a man of prestige, whom the politic of the earth would have conciliated. Harris writes: "One day I waited for him in his dining room where there were several Leighton pictures and he introduced them to me pompously as 'All by Leighton, the President, you know, of our Academy.' I nodded and Chamberlain went on: 'I gave 2000 pounds for that one.' 'Really?' I gasped. 'Yes,' he replied, 'what do you think it's worth?' I could not help it; I replied: 'I don't know the value of the frame.'" [3]

Again, Harris met Alfred Austin, a man of importance if no significance, whose selection as laureate Harris thought "a disgraceful outrage on English poetry." "I had met Austin often, and thought him a mere journalist and place-hunter without talent or personality; but this evening when we met at Wolseley's he treated me with marked condescension: 'I've known Mr. Harris,' he said, 'when he was merely editor of the *Evening News*.' His tone was so high and mighty that I replied: 'I hear now that you write poetry as well as prose: which do you intend to use in the future?'

" 'Oh now,' he replied, 'I must write a certain amount of poetry.'

" 'Why?' I asked, pretending ignorance.

" 'Oh, to keep the wolf from the door,' he replied, smiling.

" 'I see,' I retorted, 'I see, very good: you read your poetry to the wolf—eh?' Austin used to avoid me afterward; but the word pleased me infinitely, perhaps because I am seldom witty." [4]

The same wit angered Gladstone, the darling of the Liberals, a figure that every Polonius would bid him placate. When a friend suggested, after Chamberlain had cast Harris off because of his views on free trade, that he should see Gladstone, Harris himself destroyed the meeting. Gladstone, after dinner, went off to play "Beggar My Neighbor" with an Eton boy. On his return he said that he had got much out of the game: "The boy taught me that four knaves can beat the whole pack." Harris could not resist the temptation: "I should have thought," he said, "that your experience, Sir, would have shown you that one knave was able to do that." Gladstone glowered at him, saying nothing; he took the jest as a personal affront. Thus Harris stepped from the frying pan of Chamberlain into the fire of Gladstone. Was there a place anywhere for so frank a Harris?

Worse still was his jest to Prince Edward. Edward had been

[3] *My Life and Loves*, Vol. II, p. 231.   [4] *Ibid.*, p. 265.

well disposed; they had met at Monte Carlo; Harris had placed money for him, been lucky, and won. Harris had a free and witty tongue, knew wine and Réjane, and was amusing: all these the Prince loved. But once at Monte Carlo Frank was talking to Madame Tosti when the Prince crossed the floor to speak with them. Harris felt—perhaps wrongly—that the Prince meant to be rude; so he copied Beau Brummell's famous word to King George: "Now I leave you," he said, "to your stout friend." The Prince was furious. What demon of the perverse was in Harris thus to alienate the potent of the world?

He had his own explanation. He was, he said, humble toward the truly great, proud toward the truly little. "This sharp-tongued impatience was allied to a genuine reverence for greatness of mind or character; but again the reverence brought with it an illimitable disdain for the second-rate or merely popular. I was more than amiable to Huxley or Wallace, to Davidson or Dowson, and correspondingly contemptuous of the numerous mediocrities who are the heroes of the popular press. So I got a reputation for extraordinary conceit and bad manners." [5] Since genius is the exception and mediocrity the rule, Harris won the few by reverence and angered the majority by his seeming arrogance. No one likes to have his mediocrity painted with acid till it turns blue! This, as well as his graver truth-telling, incensed men against Harris. In the literary ring, like his own Montes, he played not only the final grave role of matador—but also the lighter role of picador, infuriating the heavy-headed bulls with the dainty prick of deftly placed darts, by the swift playful toss of a red cloak.

But soon Frank Harris found a new journal to edit, more brilliant even than the *Fortnightly*. Here he was freer, for he was not only editor but owner; he bought the *Saturday Review,* September, 1894, by borrowing much of the money on the security of shares in the magazine. This paper also was dying of dignity; he gave it a blood transfusion of genius.

[5] *Ibid.,* Vol. III, p. 37.

Harris's editorship of the *Saturday Review* was superlative. He was not hindered by youth or hampered by decorum. Even in format the new vehicle was more sprightly—not a gray-covered bulk, but a large-page weekly without a cover, like the brilliant *G. K.'s Weekly* of London's later years. The *Saturday Review* brought England new waters of life, that the tree of English literature might not wither and that it might "bring forth fruit in its season."

Harris was a literary dowser who went about with his hazel wand, looking for hidden waters. He discovered the springs that were to refresh men for the next twenty years and more. His twig discovered Shaw, Wells, Max Beerbohm, Cunninghame Graham, Joseph Conrad, D. S. McColl (later head of the Tait Gallery), Dr. Chalmers Mitchell (later head of the Zoological Society), and many others. He picked in 1894 most or all of the men who for the next twenty years were to form public opinion in Great Brittain. He set Shaw to writing dramatic criticism—which no one ever had the wit to do before; thus he found a brilliant reviewer, and helped God make a dramatist. (Shaw at the time was an obscure young vegetarian of one novel and a hardly noticed play, who criticized music to the perturbation of a Wagner-fearing public.) Harris set Wells to reviewing novels. Thus Wells discovered Joseph Conrad, in his sympathetic and brilliant review of *Almayer's Folly*—and, in such triumphs, began to discover himself. Even the hostile *New Statesman,* excited by the First World War, and wrongly convinced that Harris was pro-German, later affirmed the genius of his editing. It declared that he had made the *Saturday Review* the most vital and stimulating journal in the English language. It said that, with the intuition of the born editor, he had built up the most brilliant literary staff in London.

Having gathered such a staff, Harris gave them the liberty of talent. He told them to avoid being ferociously negative and bloodily critical, like the *Quarterly Review*-ers who slaughtered Keats, and to find and defend genius. The *Saturday Review* had been a firing squad for talent: a review had been an execution. Harris believed, on the contrary, that a great editor is not a fault-finder, but a star-finder. A magazine should be an observatory, the editor's mind a telescope; he should sweep the spaces of the night, to find and proclaim unknown stars.

The 1890's—called the Yellow Nineties because of the *Yellow Book,* and the general prevalence of that color which Wilde hailed as the symbol of strange emotions—were a period of renaissance. The first grave ardor of Victorian literature, culminating in Tennyson, Dickens, and Carlyle, had ended. A new world was seeking a new voice. Aestheticism, with its Swinburne and Pater and Whistler and Wilde, moved in one direction; the literature of social revolt and reconstruction, with its Shaw and Wells, led in another; between, there was a welter of directions— the imperialism of Henley and Kipling, the romance of Stevenson and Conrad. The time had the unity of a bomb: the fragments flew to left and right, but a single dynamite was at the heart of the explosion.

Frank Harris and the *Saturday Review* stood central. There the best of every phase and direction of the 1890's found place and voice and unity, for Harris was not eclectic, but catholic. He gave unity to the work of artists as various as Rothenstein, Beerbohm, Beardsley, Rossetti, and Watts; to the work of writers as various as Harold Frederic, Davidson, Graham, Hardy, and Kipling. Arthur Symons, a critic of delicate insight and a style as lucidly right as Ming china, balanced the provocative Shaw, a breaker of china—even Ming. The *Yellow Book,* a sensation in jaundice at the time, seems today mere period costuming, quaint, eccentric; the later Pre-Raphaelite excess and green-carnation playboyism seem the stained-glass attitudes of a Bunthorne; Fabianism seems albino and statistical, a brake on revolution. But Harris looms ever larger. Without giving himself to any fashion, clique, or program, he selected the best work of the best men in all groups. He was sunlight-giving, life-giving; around his sun a solar system could revolve: a nebulous Neptune, a workaday earth, a cameo moon, a giant Saturn with his rings. He gave his own light and warmth to all. Amid green carnations, *Yellow Books,* half-mountebank *"je ne sais quoi* young men," revolutionaries dying into the fossil statisticians of Fabianism, singers of the sword and chanters of the "White Man's Burden"—amid all these he stood aloof and ironic and yet sympathetic, publishing the best and establishing the true meaning of the time. He himself was no neutral, but a bold intelligence who realized that energy and imagination lie at the root of all ideas.

The *Saturday Review* gave dynamic and direction to English literature. Without the reviews of Shaw, Ibsen would hardly have come into the full stream of English consciousness; nor would Shakespeare have been lifted into living light. Poetry would not have found so full a field if Harris had not been there to appraise it as critic and to publish it as editor. The novel would have been a different and lesser thing without the reviews of Wells.

The *Saturday Review* is still brilliantly alive today. One finds in its pages of yesterday the best of Shaw, before he became Sir Oracle. His review of *Romeo and Juliet* at the Lyceum, in the issue of September 28, 1895, is a masterpiece of wisdom and wit. "The scenery is excellent. Mr. William Harford's 'public place in Verona' has only one defect, and that a very English one. The sky is too cold, and the cypresses too pale: better have painted them with dabs of warm brown on an actually gold sky in the beautiful old fashion, than have risked the Constablesque suggestion, faint as it is, of English raininess and chill. . . ." In criticizing the characters as Shakespeare meant them, Shaw is brilliant. "Tybalt is such an unmercifully bad part that one can hardly demand anything from its representation except that he should brush his hair when he comes to his uncle's ball (a condition which he invariably repudiates) and that he should be so consummate a swordsman as to make it safe for Romeo to fall on him with complete abandonment and annihilate him. . . . This is one of the great sensations of the play: unless an actor is capable of a really terrible explosion of rage, he had better let Romeo alone." Of the supple delicacy of Mrs. Patrick Campbell he says: "I am convinced that Mrs. Patrick Campbell could thread a needle with her toes at the first attempt as rapidly, as smoothly, as prettily, and with as much attention to spare for doing anything else at the same time as she can play an arpeggio." About the quality of Shakespeare there are great sentences. "Romeo has lines that tighten the heart or catch you up into the heights, alternately with heartless fustian and silly ingenuities that make you curse Shakespeare's stage-struckness and his youthful inability to keep his brain quiet. It needs a great flowing tide of passion, an irresistibly impetuous march of music, to carry us over these. . . ." Such criticism was then as beneficial as today it remains delightful.

Harris also recognized creation. In the *Saturday Review* for July 10, 1897, he published a masterpiece by Davidson.

THE BADGE OF MEN

"In shuttered rooms let others grieve,
*   And coffin thought in speech of lead;*
I'll tie my heart upon my sleeve:
*   It is the Badge of Men," he said.*

His friends forsook him: "Who is he!"
*   Even beggars passed him with a grin:*
Physicians called it lunacy;
*   And priests the unpardonable sin.*

He strove, he struck for standing ground:
*   They beat him humbled from the field;*
For though his sword was keen, he found
*   His mangled heart a feeble shield.*

He slunk away and sadly sought
*   The wilderness—false friend of woe.*

"Man is the enemy," he thought;
   But nature proved a fiercer foe.

The vampire sucked, the vulture tore,
   And the old dragon left its den,
Agape to taste the thing he wore—
   The ragged, bleeding Badge of Men.

"Against the Fates there stands no charm,
   For every force takes its own part:
I'll wear a buckler on my arm,
   And in my bosom hide my heart!"

But in his bosom prisoned fast
   It pained him more than when it beat
Upon his sleeve; and so he cast
   His troubles to the ghouls to eat.

Back to the city there and then
   He ran; and saw through all disguise,
On every sleeve the Badge of Men:
   For truth appears to cruel eyes.

Straight with his sword he laid about
   And hacked and pierced their hearts, until
The beaten, terror-stricken rout
   Begged on their knees to know his will.

He said, "I neither love nor hate;
   I would command in everything."
They answered him, "Heartless and great!
   Your slaves are we: be you our king!"

The poem gives the psychological history of modernism to the
time it was written, and, prophetically, up to the Second World
War—from Rimbaud to Hitler.

In editorial policy Harris was provocative and trenchant. The older *Saturday Review* had been conservative in a predictable Tory way; Harris sought to make it radical in the sense that it went down to the roots of things, conservative in the sense that it preserved the best of things. He was no Shaw, accepting overnight the total greatness of Ibsen and hailing him as master of Shakespeare: one must go back to the *roots* of literature if one would be a radical. He was no Kipling, accepting overnight a pattern of imperialism and hailing the acquisition of other lands as an advance of the English spirit: one must conserve the eternal England of Milton and Shelley, of justice and liberty, if one would be a conservative. So Harris "took an independent line," as the *New Statesman* said, and opposed aggression on the Indian frontier, or Boer-baiting in South Africa. To the critics of the Right he said: "If this be radicalism, make the most of it!" To the critics of the Left he said: "If this be tradition, make the best of it!"

Harris opposed the Germany of Wilhelm. At a time when conventional Englishmen admired the militarism of the Kaiser, Harris called him "William the Witless." Germany under Bismarck had been wise even when ruthless; Germany under Wilhelm was blatant even when it inherited momentum from Bismarck. Wilhelm had dismissed the master whose hand had been strong on the rudder; now he imperiled Europe with his "colossal vanity and reckless impertinence," by steering toward the rocks of war. The prescience of Harris was graphic enough to lead the Kaiser to list him, later, as one evidence of England's long hostility. Harris, however, was no warmonger. Is the man who points to an idiot playing with matches guilty himself of arson? He criticized a Germany untrue to its best; he criticized an England untrue to its best. "The sword of England's power," he said, "is too heavy for the feeble hands that hold it."

Arthur Symons called Frank Harris the most brilliant editor he ever met. Indeed, as Einar Lyngklip says, "No young upstart —certainly no cowboy from the colonies—ever before took the driver's seat in so handsome a vehicle as the *Saturday Review*, already old and 'dying of dignity,' and drove it to a new age and a lasting dignity that it had never dreamed of. No other young man took to the highroad so confidently in so old and brittle a rig, after calling in and harnessing to it a triple-brace of colts and wild jackasses, and rode regally to his destination. Frank did! And what is more, all the old men now acknowledge what the young men then knew—that the colts and jackasses he had called were all thoroughbreds."

Yet with all his brilliant editing, Harris found time for his own work. In the *Review* he published those tentative essays which were to become *The Man Shakespeare*. The first one appeared in the issue of March, 1898, under the title: "The True Shakespeare, an Essay in Realistic Criticism." They were to grow during ten years until they emerged in what Francis Hackett calls "that marvelous jeweled book."

During the same period, the other giant of the day, Shaw, was hailing Ibsen: "Greater than Shakespeare?" was his question. Though appreciative of Shakespeare, he regarded him as irreligious—going no higher than the sound of church bells and the flight of angels; he had no conception (Shaw thought) of the *élan vital*. Harris was wiser. He knew that Shakespeare took on himself the mystery of things, seeing beyond this muddy vesture of decay and our mortal coil the seeds of time and the ripeness that is all. As he differed from Shaw in his deeper appreciation of Shakespeare, he differed from Wells in his deeper appreciation of Jesus. Harris was never a "modern," for to make modernism a criterion is to destroy truth with time. Everything is modern— once. The true criterion is not the accidental place on the time line, but the height on the line of eternity that is at right angles to any time. Therefore he found his greatest artists and men among those who, never having been merely modern, could never be ancient. Shakespeare and Jesus were his greatest among the sons of men. It is significant that at the very time when Shaw was

turning to Ibsen, Harris was returning to Shakespeare; that while
Wells chased falling stars over the bowl of night, Harris found the
fixed star of Bethlehem.

Whether or not the pen is mightier than the sword, the sword
often disturbs the pen. Frank Harris knew that war is the knife-
edge of politics drawn from the sheath, often determinant of
human destiny. He had long had an interest in South Africa; he
knew many of the men—Rhodes and some of the Boers—who
were leaders in that troubled land. In January, 1896, when the
Jameson Raid took place, he sailed for Africa.

Frank Harris opposed empire in India and Africa, though he
sought intenser colonization of the colonies, and peaceful penetra-
tion in Africa. His sympathies were pro-Boer because he sought
the true advantage of England. He knew the Boers—their solid
homely strength, their integrity (mitigated by lack of political
intelligence or by knowledge of the world), their desire to be let
alone. He knew that some Englishmen in South Africa had a
flashy desire for quick wealth, a willingness to let greed incite
war, a lack of knowledge and imagination so great that they supposed the Boers would not fight. These men influenced the English ruling class. And that ruling class revealed here again the
same fallacy of soul which led them to ignore poets like Thomson
and prophets like Carlyle.

In Africa he interviewed the leaders of the Boers. He angered
some by his impartial criticism of their folly in not winning the
Dutch in Cape Colony to the common cause by giving them
"preferential duties in favor of the products of the Cape farmer."
He warned Kruger against such mistakes. Kruger, however,
"closed the drifts to their produce . . . he had no plan at all, no
foresight. . . ." He was "more hatefully short-sighted even than
Chamberlain." [6] The Boers trusted to lethargy and phlegm till the
crisis came, then fought defensively instead of initiating an inspired offensive strategy. Oom Paul Kruger, a man of solid worth

[6] Frank Harris, *How to Beat the Boer*, pp. 10-11.

and integrity, lacked the supple wit and wide vision of a statesman. He was an Old Testament captain of fighting men, not a prophet—neither a Jeremiah who sees the danger, nor an Isaiah who sees the ideal.

Harris compared Lord Milner and Oom Paul. "Milner, tall, thin, with shaven stony face, calm, direct regard and immaculate attire, the type of clean intelligent efficiency; and Oom Paul, huddled in his armchair, looking like a sick gorilla with a fringe of thick, dirty hair under his heavy animal face, and small hot eyes glinting out under the bushy brows: the one man ignorant to the point of believing the world to be flat, the other intelligent and equipped with all the learning of the schools, and yet Kruger a great heart and a great man, and Milner small and thin, proud of easily holding his emotions in leash to his reason. I dreaded the clash, for behind Milner was all the power of Britian, and yet Kruger was right: 'We Boers hold South Africa; you can't get rid of us; it is foolish to bully your bedfellow.' " [7]

Harris's articles in the *Saturday Review,* sent from Africa, increased the pulse rate of its readers. Formerly the *Review* had been Tory to the bone, even its literary iconoclasm and political departures had not convinced most of its readers that it could possibly mean what it indubitably did. Now, however, its editor was a Don Quixote, charging not only the windmill but the wind. Yet it had large circulation and intellectual authority.

Before returning to England, Harris traveled in Africa.

He tells of "that long ride up Table Mountain with Cecil Rhodes. I see him standing—a greater Cortez with his back to the Pacific, staring toward Cairo, six thousand miles away, dreaming of the immense central plateau, three times as large as the United States, as one empire." [8]

Frank Harris loved the great central plateau, "where the air is light and dry, like champagne, and mere breathing's a joy;

[7] *My Life and Loves,* Vol. III, p. 311.
[8] *Ibid.,* p. 275.

where the blessed sun reigns all through the long day, and the earth grows odorous under the hot embrace, and the sweat dries on the naked back in selvages of salt like the ripples on a sandy beach, while the night is cool and refreshing as the yellow moon comes up over the black forest and turns the camp into fairyland, while sweet airs breathe sleep on the weary limbs.

"And the freedom of it! Not the freedom of London: freedom to do as others do, dress as others do, and speak as others speak, parroting phrases that were half lies when first coined, and smearing unctuous sentimentalities on dagger-points; no, not that! Africa's freedom is of the wild and waste places of the earth, where one can be a man and can think his own thoughts and speak truth and live truth and stretch yokeless neck and free arms in God's sunlight." [9]

He visited the Zambesi, which he wished to compare with Niagara. "The solitude, the scenery, the great river and the falls, the wild animals of all sorts, and above all the sense of living in the world as it was a hundred thousand years ago, made this experience the chief event in my life, separating the future from the past and giving me a new starting point." [10]

One night he was wakened out of the sleep that had soaked him as sea water soaks a sponge, to see the flap of his tent moving in the ghostly dimness of the lesser dark outside. Sleepily he watched it, till at last he realized that a full-grown lion was playfully sporting with the canvas only two feet from him. He reached for his Westley Richards rifle, and then wondered why he should kill the playful cat. The delay saved his life, for as he waited he heard "a long rumbling sort of moan to the left," and he dimly saw a lioness. The two stared into the denser darkness of the tent; Harris waited, rifle ready. There was a sound somewhere in the camp; the lioness turned, then the lion. Both faded like statues of shadow dissolving, and left him unable to sleep. When

[9] *Ibid.*
[10] *Ibid.*

the long arrows of the light brought day, his bearers stared in amazement and fear at the tracks of two adult lions.

Harris was attacked by malaria and abandoned by his bearers. With a knife and a revolver and twenty cartridges for his rifle, and five cans of sardines and one of soup, he had to reach civilization. The trek was a terrible ordeal; but he survived. At the other end of delirium he came out in a Portuguese settlement; he was sick, however, for a long time. Pieces of the lining of his stomach came off; he was never completely well again; only the discovery of the stomach pump saved him. He was always his own best doctor, studying the laws of the body as he studied all skills and wisdoms, and learning much that the doctors did not even dream.

He carried away from Africa a sense of elemental power—and darkness.

On his return to England, late in 1896, he found the powers of this world and the darkness of their designs already sinister. It seemed to him that certain powerful men in Africa and in England were resolved upon war with the Boers; and in England, as from Africa, he was equally resolute to oppose their desire.

Harris's articles from Africa—uncompromising, drastic, incisive —had made a sensation among readers of the *Saturday Review,* and a wide impression upon England. Cecil Rhodes was too canny a man to ignore so powerful a voice, especially when (briefly, in 1898) Harris went once more to Africa and returned to England to urge peace even more resolutely. Rhodes knew that war was coming; he wished no intellectual Chetnik in his rear.

He sent Lord Hardwicke to ask Harris if he would sell the *Saturday Review.* Harris had done well financially, and had no need to sell; he was, however, weary of journalism and eager to do literary work of his own. He had repaid what he had borrowed; he had raised the prestige of the paper till it was outstanding in the English-speaking world. Now, half reluctant, half desirous, he left the sale to fate: he put the price so exorbitantly high—30,000 pounds for ten or twelve thousand shares—that he thought Hardwicke would not meet it. Hardwicke, however, was willing to pay the price. Harris asked whether this was done with the desire to oust him as editor, or whether he was to be retained? Hardwicke said that Harris should remain as editor.

Some months later, however, Hardwicke came to inform Harris that the policy of the *Review* in relation to South Africa must change, or else Harris must resign. But Harris still held five hundred shares, which made it impossible to discharge him as editor. Hardwicke, a few weeks later, returned to ask if Harris would sell the five hundred shares that gave him position and control. Harris, leaving it again to fate, asked the astonishing price of ten thousand pounds. Hardwicke immediately gave him a check for that amount. The first sale of stock, and the final sale of the controlling shares, occurred sometime in 1898.

Frank Harris knew that he could do nothing now but resign: he would not change the policy of the paper; he could not change his own ideas. Perhaps, on the whole, he was relieved; the stress had been intense, and had long kept him from doing his own work as a writer—particularly from completing his book on Shakespeare. Now, free from journalism, he might engage in eternalism.

An editoral in the *Saturday Review* of November 26, 1898, announced that Frank Harris had resigned as editor. The cause was said to be ill health.

The *Saturday Review* was Frank Harris's last *great* editorial position, on that side of the Atlantic, though he was to be an editor many times again. Thereafter his great work in England was to be creation: he had been a star-finder; now he was to be himself a star.

The sale was a mistake. Harris had made an enemy of all the forces of the *status quo*: during the Boer War, and thereafter until his death, money and politics and conservative society in England were against him. And in selling the *Saturday Review* he was like Frey, the young God of Asgard, who sold his sword to Skir-

nir—so that he did not have it when the trumpets blew for Ragnarok.

Frank Harris did not sell his pen when he sold the paper. After
war was declared he criticized the stupidity with which England
tried to muddle through, in a great pamphlet comparable to Swift
and Carlyle. It was a little booklet, now out of print and almost
inaccessible, called *How to Beat the Boer*.[11]

How to Beat the Boer is brilliant military thinking. Its premise
is that English generalship is as inept in fighting the war as English politicians were in causing it. War was unnecessary: England,
by fairness and good government, was winning control of Africa.
The English language, the financial power of England, would
have gradually triumphed. Oom Paul Kruger, meanwhile, had
been aiding England in his own despite. The flashy folly of the
Jameson Raid, the forcing of the sluggish phlegm of the Boers
into war, were worse than crimes: they were blunders. Now
England showed the same incompetence in her generalship as she
had shown in her statesmanship. How then, since it was now
necessary, was England to beat the Boers?

Harris imagines several of the great dead talking together, and
one of the unknown dead—Aylward, a Fenian. Washington, Dr.
Johnson, Carlyle, Parnell, and Randolph Churchill debate in
Limbo. Dr. Johnson still staunchly believes in the justice of England, yet sternly criticizes the "art of war" as England practices
it. Carlyle sees in the muddle new basis for his hatred of sham,
new proof of the need for great men. Parnell, expecting England
to be defeated, rejoices that a free people are giving the imperialists
the beating they deserve. Churchill deplores the course of Chamberlain which has caused the war, and the ineptitude of his management now that war has come; but he believes that the dogged
will and overwhelming might of England will somehow—he does
not know how—win. Washington, courteously silent till his advice
is asked, says that the moral element is the most important ele-

[11] London, William Heinemann, 1900.

ment in war; and that the English have been demoralized by defeats, the Boers heartened by victories.

Parnell leads the group to Aylward, recently dead, who can tell them something more contemporary about the war in Africa. Aylward is bitter at Kruger for his muddling of the former peace; at England for her muddling of the peace that was and the war that is. He loves England. "A traitor," he says, "is one who dares fight for the weak against the strong, for the oppressed against the oppressor, at twice the usual risk." For all her blunders, England is great and might yet win the war—and even the peace. How?

Aylward is elder brother of General de Gaulle. He says, "I find that from the beginning there have always been two opposing theories of war. One theory, which I will call the barbaric, believes in numbers; the other prefers quality to quantity. The Greeks took the true view, and the defeat at Thermopylae brought about the downfall of the Persian Empire. The few against the many, and the few triumphed!" So it has always been when quality met mere quantity: at Crécy, Poictiers, and Agincourt; at Saratoga, and with Jackson at New Orleans. Where there was brilliant sudden victory (as distinguished from indecisive huggermugger of equally brutish masses), there was an elite corps. The English, dominated by fourth-form mentality and by a blind pugnacity that believes in bulldog courage and bayonet fighting, trust in quantity. Consequently they have some 150,000 men immobilized and badly mauled by some 40,000 invisible riflemen using Mausers from vley or *kopje*. What should the English do? Give up the idea of victory by brute weight, of throwing men at the enemy only to throw them away. *Fire power—quality of fire power!* is victory. Raise an elite corps of five thousand men, chosen for superior marksmanship. Let them be perfected in marksmanship under the conditions of deceptive light in Africa where fiercer suns distort distances. Let these five thousand, in careful waves of cover-keeping marksmen, one wave protecting its forerunner with its fire, advance till they dominate a trench or ridge. Give them superior rifles: let the craftsmanship of English gunsmiths (the best in the world!) provide instruments superior to the Mausers. Let them have telescope sights, and stocks fitted individually to shoulders. Abolish drill, red tape, silly patterns of order. Prove that Englishmen can shoot and wage war; then the brave but undisciplined Boers, without long tradition as an army, with little political cohesion, will wilt.

The Boers at present are "unconsciously the exponents of modern scientific warfare. The Boer ideal is to expose himself as little as possible while killing his adversary with a rifle bullet. That is, his defense is as perfect as his attack. And the English papers, in exactly the brainless spirit of the common soldiers, are perpetually occupied in ridiculing the Boers' defense. Would they sneer at a boxer who guarded himself—these representatives of intelligence!"

This, of course, is the pattern suggested in modern times by the brilliant General de Gaulle: a professional army, small, specially trained, mobile, aggressive, swift in initiative, able to use its weapons to superior effect. Quality—quality of men and fire power, of equipment, of training for a specific end of obliteration—is the genius of war. Translate the x and y of general truth into the terms of tanks and airplanes, and you get Harris's theory today.

Carlyle, in rebuttal, urges that genius in command is also needed. He says, "I put no faith in an anarchic horde of marksmen. Cromwell and Napoleon made their armies; it is genius that organizes victory."

To this Aylward answers: "How could I underrate genius! Give brains in the captain, and even now our British soldiers on the Tugela would overwhelm the Boers. Genius is the nth power of the mathematician that raises the value of the force under it to any extent.... But nearly all generals in all armies are mediocrities. ..." Why? "First of all, let us remember that it is a fact. Again and again men like Washington, Cromwell, and Clive have come from the outside, and without any military training have beaten the best generals of the day. This could not happen, and does not happen, in the case of any other profession founded on realities. Our best surgeons may be at the moment excellent or merely average, but no one believes that there is a single layman in the world who, without study or practice, could trepan a man or take a stone from the bladder as well as the worst of them. Our pugilists, too, may be merely average, but no outsider without practice or training would be likely to stand a chance with the ordinary professional.

"The explanation is simple. When a man of genius chances to appear in any other trade or profession, he cuts out a way for himself and makes his own place: insubordination is the birthmark of ability. But discipline is the fetish of the soldier, and the able man who finds it hard to follow the fool, will get no advancement in any army." (De Gaulle and Gamelin, General Mitchell and his superiors!) "Consequently the best regular captains are scholarly mediocrities like Moltke, who carry on war according to approved principles, and in seventy years make no innovations."

How, then, get good generals? "It is in times of revolution that genius comes most easily to the front. Why? Simply because men are in earnest then and correspondingly impatient of fools and failures." And though evidently the English government is not in earnest—else it would have disgraced Methuen after Modder, and cashiered Buller after Colenso—the "English people is in earnest, and may yet make its will felt." Then mediocrity will be swept into oblivion, and genius at last have its day. But this will come slowly; perhaps it will be impossible during the war. Meanwhile the five thousand with superior equipment, fire power, and marksmanship, will, even under ordinary leadership, win the war without the butchery certain to accompany assault by brute mass.

Churchill agrees enthusiastically: he has no doubt that, if England needs such a corps, England will get it. But Carlyle—chastened by the wisdom of sad seniority—fears that the need for "a few good men with the best weapons" (which Cromwell also advocated) will not be met. His words conclude the phamplet: "I wonder what will be the end of it all, I wonder—!"

The bold uncommonsense of Harris's thinking is eternally pertinent. Had it been applied, England would not have been bludgeoned from defeat to defeat in the Boer War, till she paid even in victory a terrific toll. Its application after a diluted fashion by the use of Australians and Canadians who could take cover and shoot straight, was part of the eventual victory. In its criticism of conventional generalship, and in its vision of quality, fire power, and specific training of an elite corps, it is the program of victory.

How to Beat the Boer, unfortunately unheeded, did not win the war for England; angrily noticed, it helped alienate England from Harris. Now at last it should come into its own as a classic of war.

Meanwhile Frank Harris had married again. In London he met an Irish girl some twenty years younger than he—Helen O'Hara, or "Nellie" as he affectionately called her. She was a girl of dazzling beauty, like a gem in a setting of red gold. She had an Irish temper and a caustic wit; she was quite European and a woman of the world. She was vivacious, with eyes of amber, red-gold hair that would have charmed Rossetti, and a skin of rare alabaster whiteness warm with life. Harris called her his best critic: her word about a portrait or story (he said) was final. In his autobiography he writes: "Then I may tell in a fifth volume . . . how I found a pearl among women and learned from her what affection really means, the treasures of tenderness, sweet-thoughted wisdom and self-abnegation that constitute the woman's soul. Virgil may lead Dante through Hell and Purgatory: it is Beatrice alone who can show him Paradise and guide him to the divine." [12]

Bernard Shaw had high regard for her; he wrote: "He [Frank]

[12] *My Life and Loves,* Vol. I, p. 3 of the "Afterword."

was no solitary prophet, either: he could inspire and hold the devotion of his wife, who was much younger than he, and knew quite well what she was sacrificing for him." [13]

Nellie Harris was a Catholic, and disagreed with some of Frank's ideas; but she never disagreed with his genius. Nor was she a puritan toward his love of good living. She laughed at his love of wines—and shared it; long after his death, she said with dancing eyes: "Frank always said water was a very good thing to wash in!"

They were together for some thirty years; after his death she revered him as the master of her life; during the enmity and increasing difficulties that shadowed their last ten years together, and during the poverty and oblivion of the years since his death when the world treated him like a man of ill-fame, she did not waver in her faith in the man or his work.

Characteristically, Harris loved to embroider this romance with a fringe of fancy. He told Art Young that he had met Nellie in an art gallery in Paris, and that, as he told her, he had carried the most beautiful of the pictures away. What woman would not thrill to a man whose heart could weave his wooing into so lovely a tapestry?

Actually they met in London. Frank Harris knew her only ten days before he married her: there is a *blitzliebe* as well as a *blitzkrieg*. One biographer states that this first ceremony occurred in 1898.[14] Mrs. Harris denies that this is so, but does not specify the correct date. She says that she ran away with Frank after knowing him ten days. According to her account, they went to Scotland where they were married through a Scotch ceremony: that is, by registry. She was a Roman Catholic; therefore such a ceremony meant little to her. Frank Harris knew her feeling about the matter. So, on the death of his first (divorced) wife, Edith, Frank and Nellie Harris were married in the American church, Boule-

[13] G. Bernard Shaw's Postscript to Harris's *Bernard Shaw*.
[14] A. I. Tobin and Elmer Gertz, *Frank Harris: A Study in Black and White*, pp. 138 ff.

vard Victor Hugo, Nice.[15] The marriage ceremony in Nice occurred in 1926.

Of that marriage in Scotland a daughter was born. Former biographers have stated that she died some two years later, and that her death was due to vaccination. Mrs. Harris gives definitive rebuttal of both statements: her daughter did not die of the results of vaccination, and died when five months old.

[15] Letter from Mrs. Harris.

Chapter VIII

GOD'S SPY

(1894-1913)

FRANK HARRIS loved Shakespeare's words in *King Lear*: the words in which Lear, passing through madness to transcendent sanity, wishes to take upon himself "the mystery of things" as if he were one of God's Spies. He quoted them often; he explained them in a passage of his finest prose. "Whoever will be one of God's Spies, as Shakespeare called them, must spend years by himself in some solitude or desert or city, resolutely stripping himself of the time-garment of his own paltry ego, alone with the stars and the night-winds, giving himself to thoughts that torture, to a wrestling with the Angel that baffles and exhausts. But at length the travail of his soul is rewarded; suddenly, without warning, the Spirit that made the world uses him as a mouthpiece and speaks through him. In an ecstasy of humility and pride—'a reed shaken by the wind'—he receives the message. Years later, when he gives the gospel to the world, he finds that men mock and jeer at him, tell him he is crazy, or, worse still, declare that they know the fellow, and ascribe to him their own lusts and knaveries. No one will believe in him or will listen, and when he realizes his own lone-liness his heart turns to water, and he himself begins to doubt his inspiration. Then, in his misery and despair, comes one man who accepts his message as authentic-true, one man who shows in the very words of his praise that he has seen the Beatific Vision,

155

has listened to the Divine Voice. At once the prophet is saved: the sun irradiates his icy dungeon; the desert blossoms like the rose; his solitude sings with choirs invisible. Such a disciple is spoken of ever afterward as the beloved and set apart from all others." Now, free from his editorship, Frank Harris was able to give himself to the mystery of things and become God's Spy.[1]

Frank Harris's first book after *Elder Conklin* was *Montes the Matador* (1900). It contained the story that most people know best. It won him the acclaim of Meredith: "If there's a hand in England that can do better, I do not know it."

Arnold Bennett called "Montes" "the best short story in English." Diego Rivera said, "There are greater bulls and bull-fighters in 'Montes' than in all Spain." Kitchin said, "Juan Belmonte, famous matador, praised 'Montes' in Seville." And "Montes" is indeed a splash of splendid crimson, a blood-red star.

Its basis lay in Harris's life. It gave voice to his life among cattle on the Texas plains. There he had come to know how individual they are, like men: here the slow, gentle bull; there the swift honest killer; yonder the unpredictable son of treachery—all instinct with character. In deeper ways the story comes out of his life. His Montes is a master, a genius with the sword; Harris was a master, a genius with the word. Montes, like Harris, is too great for general acclaim: even when he wins the plaudits of the crowd, the cheers are ignorant; men notice the flashy tricks, not the quiet grave perfection. Early in his life he has given up the plaudits of men that mean so little; he nourishes his lonely heart with the flame of his genius and the few great words of the few great critics. Like Harris he is short, and (he thinks) ugly. He is in love with a worldly girl who does not love him, and who betrays him for a tall handsome fellow—a fool with a face. (It is Harris's relation with Laura—the pang of bitterness, the sense of betrayal.) Montes, like Harris, is a man of the deed, a killer whose nature is single as a knife.

[1] *My Life and Loves*, Vol. III, p. 377.

The story throbs with the artist's pride in his skill, the lover's passion, the killer's hate. Clemencia, for all her beauty, is a woman of the world—the fool of a face; like Laura she is incapable of understanding masterwork; she judges by the world's applause, not the artist's secret-open perfection. She is silly, vain; set in her folly, stubborn in her vanity. She wishes Montes always to play flashy tricks, even with the bulls which are too clever and quick (his instinct tells him) to tease. She insists that he shall, until in trying to please her he attempts the impossible and is almost killed by the red knife of a horn. Lamed by the thrust, he is less lovable in her eyes than before, and less a genius (because he has failed, because she knows his secret!) although he gave himself as a hostage to death for the sake of her whim. He knows her folly, her vain light cruelty over which lies only a veneer of grace; yet he obeys his heart in spite of his head. Her mother is like Laura's: she hates Montes; she incites Clemencia to betray him. His friend, Juan, is a flashy mediocrity; fundamentally envious and vile, lecherous and treacherous: a false friend, a feckless matador. (Juan is much like the "friends" whose mediocrity turned against Harris so often.) Juan, pretending friendship, wins Clemencia; the two sport behind Montes' back, and make sport of him in their talk. The scalding passion of the story is not Anglo-Saxon but Spanish: Harris's spirit was more crimson even than a Spaniard's with his *Carmen*. Latin, too, is the cold hate, the passion of the killer, the lust for blood hot on the hands: few other English writers have been able so to feel it. Montes, discovering his betrayal and their treachery, plots the killing of Juan; he plays on his vanity, and, to Clemencia's delight, arranges for him to be a matador one Sunday at the ring. He picks a bull—a Judas, tricky, wild, fierce, with thunder-swollen throat and horns keen for the kill. He tells the nervous Juan, "I shall be as true to you as you have been to me!"—and stands aside. "And I moved to the right hand and looked at the bull. It was a good one; I couldn't have picked a better. In his eyes I saw courage that would never yield and hate that would strike in the death throe, and I exulted and held his eyes with mine, and promised him revenge. While he bowed his horns to the *muleta* he still looked at me and I at him; and as I felt that Juan had leveled his sword and was on the point of striking, I raised my head with a sweep to the side, as if I had been the bull, and as I swung, so the brave bull swung too. And then—then all the ring swam round with me, and yet I had heard the shouting and seen the spectators spring to their feet. . . ."

He faces Clemencia, crazy with grief, staring, her eyes dried by their own tears. She sees in his face the glory of his hate, the passion of the kill. He answers her, laughing, "You mistake. You killed him. You made him an *espada*—you!" She tries to speak, but only falls on the floor in a swoon. Next morning she dies in premature childbirth.

Now old, lonely, bitter, but still fierce in pride, Montes has only one remorse: "I let the bull kill him. I should have torn his throat out with my own hands."

The story is the slash of an eagle's talons at the mediocrity of human circumstances; it strikes like an eagle poised on wings of love and death.

In this volume there is the story called "Sonia." Shaw called it "a shot at a star which hit the bull's-eye"; and "Sonia" is indeed one of the great revolutionary stories of the world.

It is Harris's version of a historical character, Sophia Perovskaya, a girl of the Russian aristocracy who joined the revolutionaries and engineered the assassination of Czar Alexander. She was hanged for her superb crime; comforting her lover at the foot of the gallows, she died as proudly as she had lived.

Sonia in Harris's story is "like a flame of extraordinary steadiness and height." She is a creature of the spirit, who burns her way through the world like lightning, flaming white from her sheath of flesh. Her soul is swift to answer the trumpet of God; her feet are jubilant. She hates stagnation, sloth, mediocrity: "As if material success and contentment were not proof of spiritual failure!" Seeing the stain of the world's pettiness, and man's cruelty, and the clotted insolence and deceit, she cries, "Will no one free us from the lies and liars?" She is resolute against compromise or cowardice: "You are you, and I am I. In either case, the tree has got its full height now and cannot be bent or altered." She believes in free will, action, audacity: "The world to me is fluid, men and women malleable, everything noble and possible." Knowing that she goes to her death, she rejoices—for it is a consecration of life; she writes her lover: "I could not have lived a great life [without a great death], the slow hours would have broken me."

Sonia can be calmly happy, as well: if life were grandly simple, elemental like earth and air, there would be no need of revolt; does one hurl lightnings against the sun? "There is the great earth naked and fruitful, where men labor, where they are born and live and die, and over them the heaven is arched." She is all woman, too, passionate for love; she gives her body because she has given her soul. Her English lover says, "The slim body fluttered in my hands as a bird flutters, and then was still." Her eyes were "flowers beaten by heavy rain."

Her lover, George Lascelles, is a young Englishman who met her in Germany and now follows her to Russia. He loves her and admires her spirit; as an Englishman, however, he seeks the slow action of parliaments, the gentle amelioration of the intolerable. She is furious at this paste of clay in the body of flame. She says, "Every time I talk with you I go away with my soul fainting and weak." Yet he loves her, she loves him; he kisses her "with my heart now, and not my lips alone." And at last, knowing the end near, she gives herself to him in supreme surrender, and wins the ultimate of love from the hands of death.

Coolest of all, she gives the signal by waving her handkerchief and generals the perfect assassination. As the Czar, spared by the first bomb, sees his Cossacks and coachmen dying, he exclaims: "Thank God!" But the second terrorist, whom Sonia has aptly placed, hurls a second bomb that mortally wounds their regal target. The third, pitying the crawling Czar, helps him into the carriage to die. Sonia, imperturbable and implacable, has triumphed. She herself is taken; writes her last letter of love; and dies as she has lived. The slow hours do not break her; like the lightning, she lives by her death.

W. L. George is reported to have said that he considered Harris the greatest short-story writer of the past century, even the greatest that England has ever produced. George, who was almost or quite as much at home in French literature as in English, thought that Harris's stories might have been written in French. This, to George, seemed the highest possible compliment.

Harris had, indeed, the technique of France. His stories are as supple and lean as de Maupassant's. Yet they add to the French technique a richness of poetic feeling, a wealth of philosophy. De Maupassant, for all his French freedom, has little passion above a bleak animal lust; none of the ache and ecstasy of Sonia. Also he has little ability to rise above the brute existence of facts into the meaning which is truth. He is content to record, and like Hardy to exaggerate, the rule of chance, the supremacy of accident. Accident, to him, rules, and ruins by ruling. The destiny of character, the truth that creates the fact, are beyond his sight: they demand insight. He is a brilliant animal—seldom, in the full sense, a man. But to Frank Harris, the fact is only the focus for the passion that fulfills and transcends it; the philosophy, both in individual character and in life, is more important than the accident.

Harris had his philosophy of art. "Realism is like water mixed with some potent spirit, such as whisky or absinthe, while Romance is pure wine. The intoxicating element in both is spirit, the desire of love or life, the struggle for a woman or for bread, a high ambition or a great renunciation.

"The best stories are those of a writer's own time, mirroring the very form and color of the day, in its most passionate or dramatic or pathetic moments: Realistic in form, Romantic in spirit is, I think, the best formula; *Don Quixote,* for example; but the opposite can be very good. *The Cloister and the Hearth,* for instance, one would say, is romantic in form and realistic in content, and yet there is no finer English story." [2]

He sums up his technique in the third volume of his autobiography. "My practice taught me that the most important thing in a story is the speed of narration; no one wants the reader to skip passages or to feel that this or that part is too long. Most writers think that they can avoid being tedious by jumping from one part of the story to another; but this habit is apt to distract attention. The true art consists in so graduating the speed of the narration that the reader feels he is being carried along faster and faster to an inevitable conclusion, much as if he were caught in the rapids of Niagara. . . . And in order to be able to graduate his speed, the introduction of the characters should be deliberate and slow in proportion to the length of the story. For as soon as the characters are all known to the readers and the trend of the story is indicated, then the pace should begin to quicken and . . . the speed should increase and should be felt to be increasing, so that skipping or tedium should be absolutely impossible. I can understand using telegraphese at the end of a story to prevent any suspicion of dragging." [3]

Frank Harris's stories are greater than his novels; and even in the novel, as in *The Bomb,* his greatness is not a slow spacious amplitude like that of Tolstoi or Balzac, but a series of smiting explosions, each like that of Lingg's potent bomb. Harris believed the short story a higher form of art than the novel. He sought a crisis of life, incarnate in perfect form: life seen by a lightning flash.

Beyond the form, however, a great short story must keep the integrity of life. Even Flaubert, said Harris, describing Madame

[2] *My Life and Loves,* Vol. III.   [3] *Ibid.,* pp. 360-61.

Bovary visiting her lover while still tense from a quarrel with her husband, is led astray from life: he stops to describe the corset laces she is undoing, "little golden snakes"; he is seduced from the purity of passion by the lure of the image.

Beyond form and fact, the story should not *under*-write life. If Christ gave his body for bread and his blood for wine, must not the artist do the same? His emotion must be passion; it must be basic and elemental, never albino and cerebral. No wiredrawn subtleties of a Henry James! A story may be—at its greatest it must be—a symbol; a part that contains the whole. A masterpiece means more than it says. It is a well that, whether shallow or deep, reflects the fern, the face looking into it, the moment of the passing sun. The greatest story in the world, Harris said, is that of Jesus about the woman taken in adultery.

Past the world-painting of a Balzac, past the word-painting of a Gautier, Harris used art as a vehicle for philosophic vision. He raised the world from sight into insight. If his technique came from the French masters, he transcended their technique with something both American and English—rich-blooded life; and with something that belonged to the good Greeks and the good Hebrews—meaning. He owed his art not only to the French, but also to Sophocles and the anonymous author of the Book of Job. Of his stories one can say, as he said of Thomson, "Such words sink deep into the heart as meteors into the earth, dropped from some higher sphere."

"Sonia" was prelude to the bomb heard round the world.

The last two decades of the nineteenth century were stormy in the history of American labor. The rugged individualism of the American temperament was supercharged by the lonely ruthlessness of the pioneer; after the Civil War, the spirit of the pioneers was turned into a mood of grab and get and "the devil take the hindmost." Men's hearts were stormy; the frontier's tradition of violence turned easily into direct action. Capitalism was merciless and avid; labor fiercely bold in rebuttal.

At the McCormick reaper works in Chicago a strike broke out in May, 1886. At one meeting of the strikers which was brutally suppressed by the police, a bomb of terrific power was tossed. No one then knew and no one now knows the source: the police claimed that it was hurled by "anarchists"; the workers claimed that it was thrown by an *agent provocateur*. Seven policemen were killed; sixty people, mostly strikers, were injured.

The country was whipped into a fury against "the anarchists"; it understood neither the workers' provocation nor their probable innocence.

In such an atmosphere a trial was a travesty. The accused labor leaders, several of them Social Democrats who were against any form of direct action, were put on trial for their lives: August Spies, Michael Schwab, Samuel Fielden, Albert R. Parsons, Adolph Fischer, George Engel, Oscar W. Neebe, and Louis Lingg. Four were hanged; several received life sentences; Lingg committed suicide in jail. Six years later Governor Altgeld—Lindsay's "eagle forgotten"—pardoned the survivors and denounced the trial. Meanwhile in Waldheim the marble stood over the dead who could speak no more.

But could they speak no more? They were vocal in the hearts of thousands, and the "Last Words" of Albert Richard Parsons still glow.

> *Come not to my grave with your mournings,*
> *With your lamentations and tears,*
> *With your sad feelings and fears!*
> *When my lips are dumb*
> *Do not thus come.*
>
> *Bring no long train of carriages,*
> *No horses crowned with waving plumes,*
> *Which the gaunt glory of death illumes;*
> *But with my hands upon my breast*
> *Let me rest.*

Insult not my dust with your pity,
Ye who're left on this desolate shore
Still to live and lose and deplore.
'Tis I should, as I do,
Pity you.

For me no more are the hardships,
The bitterness, heartaches, and strife,
The sadness and sorrows of life,
But the glory divine—
This is mine.

Poor creatures! Afraid of the darkness,
Who groan at the anguish to come.
How silent I go to my home!
Cease your sorrowful bell—
I am well.[4]

And in England Frank Harris was to be their Homer.

Harris did not write *The Bomb* until 1908. He was, at the time of the Haymarket Trial, editor of the *Evening News*. That conservative paper shared the common view of the distance-distorted violence in Chicago. Yet Harris, by his experience of the world and by his temperament and philosophy, must have been on the side of the accused. The accounts that reached England were ambiguous and prejudiced; he was no man, however, to be deceived or deflected. Shaw certainly was not, for he circulated a petition in behalf of the "Anarchists," which Oscar Wilde alone would sign. (He does not say whether at the time he knew or approached Frank Harris.) If Shaw knew the truth, could Harris—the mordant and fierce, who also was vocal among the radicals of London—fail to know it? Yet he seems to have done little openly to defend the Haymarket victims. There is at least one

[4] *An Anthology of Revolutionary Poetry.* Edited by Marcus Graham. 1929. P. 108.

article that is temperate in justice and wise in understanding; perhaps that is the most that the young editor of a conservative paper could do. That is, however, scant defense; it is also not in character, for Harris elsewhere neither counted the cost nor conserved the dynamite. There is a curious parallel between Harris and Zola: Zola, too, was at first complacent about the Dreyfus affair; Zola, too, was awakened and stirred till he became the foremost champion of Dreyfus, hurling his *J'Accuse!*

As Harris learned more of the affair and brooded over it he was deeply stirred. In 1907 he visited America for the sole purpose of studying the trial. In Chicago he relived the events; he read the newspaper files; he talked with all and sundry who remembered the explosion and the trial. He fused all his research and anger into one white-hot act, writing *The Bomb* as fast as a secretary could take his dictation.

In the last interview any journalist ever had with him before his death, he related with vigor and pungency the way in which he wrote *The Bomb*. Speaking to Raymond Toole Stott, correspondent for the London paper, *Everyman,* Harris said: "Writing comes easier as one grows older. That's my experience anyway. The only thing that worries me is writer's cramp. I can't write for days sometimes. I suppose I overdid it in my youth. That is what induced me to try dictating. It is less of a strain. I found it rather difficult at first, but nowadays I dictate the greater part of my work. . . ."

To the reporter's question, "Are you a quick writer?" Harris replied, "It depends on what I'm doing. I dictated three quarters of *The Bomb* in one night. I started dictating at 7:30 in the evening, and finished at 6:30 the following morning. Incidentally, I didn't see my typist again for three days."[5] Since *The Bomb* contains 329 pages, it must have been a prostrating ordeal!

The Bomb is Harris's best novel. The reason is a fused intensity that kept it at the incandescence of a short story for the length of

[5] "Frank Harris's Last Interview." *Everyman,* December 10, 1931.

a novel. One should read *The Bomb* at a single sitting—though the experience is as exhausting as a mountain climb.

The Bomb begins with the portrayal of Rudolph Schnaubelt, a young German whose family and schooling in Europe are remotely similar to those of Harris. Like Harris he comes to America at an early age; like Harris he works in the caissons under Brooklyn Bridge (factually impossible, since the work under water had ended before the date of his arrival). Like Harris, too, Rudolph soon tires of New York and goes West.

In Chicago he meets Spies, editor of the *Arbeiter Zeitung,* and Engel, who works in a toy shop. Engel is a sweet-natured man, full of pity for the foreign workers who come only to find themselves pigeons to be plucked, and whose chronic semi-employment is a "sediment of misery." Rudolph meets other leaders—some narrow in their stereotyped conception of the Class Struggle, but all burningly human in their hatred of the violence of the police. He meets victims, too: men who have lost their eyes or hands in their work, whose very bones have rotted within their flesh at the touch of phosphorous, and who have no insurance, no compensation, no care.

Rudolph meets Elsie Lehman, and his love deepens into an underplot of passion. (A convenient point of attack!—political animosity could camouflage itself as objection to a too bold love story. The very printers, Harris says, protested and forced him to add fig leaves before they would set up the book.)

Rudolph's greatest discovery is Louis Lingg. Lingg is a creation out of Harris himself, as Eve was made from Adam's rib; he is a projection of Harris into a historical character. Lingg is a Bismarck of labor. He has contempt for utopians and rhetoricians. "It's the shallow water that has the lace foam on it." He can talk, but prefers to act. When a policeman is about to split the skull of a thirteen-year-old boy, Lingg's fist fells the man like an ox under the axe.

Lingg's logic is objective as an adding machine. Yet there is in him also a fury like fire in the hands of a hurricane.

He sees that our civilization is not complex enough: it tends to hold up only one prize as worth a man's endeavor—riches. Even those destined by nature for art or science or leisured living in humble ways are infected with the perversion of money. They are taught to look down upon themselves if they do not fret with the unhappy pursuit of the single objective. Life must be made too rich for riches!

He sees the sophistry of Nietzsche's idea that laws are made by the sickly-weak for defense against the healthy-strong. Laws are made by the strong in order that they may hold in peace what they have won by war.

Lingg's greatest quality is consecration to the deed. The police are growing vicious: they cease to club, and begin to shoot; yet Parsons and Spies—beautiful souls!—only protest. A deed is necessary; so Lingg, an excellent chemist, fashions a bomb.

Lingg's philosophy is: "Oh, there needs no saviour of men from among the gods, but a saviour of God, of the divine, among men."

The McCormick strike occurs. At meetings of peaceful strikers the police begin to shoot. The Haymarket meeting is called in protest; Lingg will act if the police interfere. Rudolph (by his own choice) is to throw the first bomb, and then, Lingg insists, to escape to Europe. Lingg is to throw the second, from which there can be no escape; or, if arrested, to make the trial a platform.

The Haymarket meeting begins. Speakers harrangue; the police charge—the old, old pattern established on the agony of thousands of cracked skulls. Rudolph stiffens with hatred; as shots begin, he hurls the bomb in cold fury. He is half crushed and deafened by the roar of his own deed. As he rises, Lingg tells him not to look—but he does. "The street was one shambles; in the very center of it a great pit yawned, and round it men lying, or pieces of men, in every direction, and close to me, near the sidewalk as I passed, a leg and foot torn off, and near by two huge pieces of bleeding red meat, skewered together with a thigh bone. My soul sickened; my senses left me; but Lingg held me up with super-human strength, and drew me along." Lingg says, "Strange, you neurotic people; you do everything perfectly, splendidly, and then break down like women."

Schnaubelt escapes to Europe; Lingg stays to face the world's fury.

Many are arrested, among them Lingg after a terrific fight. His power compels admiration; he is accepted as the leader of leaders. The trial begins in an atmosphere of hatred; there are prejudice and planted evidence; there are constancy and courage among the accused; there is proof that none of them threw the bomb. Yet the verdict is "Guilty!"

The eight speak, but Lingg acts. He has another bomb smuggled into his cell; sending his kindly jailer out on a pretense, he uses it on himself. The explosion is catastrophic. "The entire lower jaw was gone, and part of the upper. Ragged strips of flesh hung down before his eyes. His chest seemed to be stripped of flesh to the very bones. The eyes were closed, and the right hand convulsively clutched the jailer's coat. But not a groan escaped him."

The mangled superman survives for some time, even speaks through the ruin of his jaws. Never does he groan; never does he complain; never does he weaken.

Nietzsche wrote about the Superman: Harris created him. There is nothing elsewhere in literature since Milton's Satan or Turgenief's Bazarov to equal Lingg in heroic stature. Unmoved by fear or pity, he goes to his end like some force of nature in the hands of a mathematical poet. He is the tidal wave that creates a new continent, the lightning hurled against the Cities of the Plain. Inhuman because superhuman, he is a wiser Siegfried of the Deed, hurling his heroism against the littleness of man.

Arnold Bennett called *The Bomb* "the finest of realistic novels." Bernard Shaw called Harris "the Homer of Anarchism." Its finest memorial, indeed, is Shaw's: "He [Harris] has lifted the Chicago anarchists out of their infamy and shown that, compared with the Capitalism that killed them, they were heroes and martyrs. He has done this with the most unusual power of conviction. The story, as he tells it, inevitably and irresistibly displaces all the vulgar, mean, purblind, spiteful versions. There is a precise realism and an unsmiling, measured, determined sincerity which gives a strange dignity to the work of one whose fixed and ungovernable impulse it is to kick conventional dignity whenever he sees it." [6]

There was natural attack from the Right. There was also attack from the Left—notably from the widow of Albert Parsons—because Harris has the bomb hurled by one of the labor group. Harris, however, absolves Parsons and the humanitarians: he makes the bomb the individual deed of one superman. He gives voice to the quiet clay in Waldheim, as Plato gave voice to the Socrates who drank the hemlock; he writes the superb *Apology* of these modern heretics—explosive, red-flaming.

Walt Whitman would have loved the book. He would have said: "Whoso touches this book touches a deed! Comrade, I salute you from the Open Road—you who obey little and resist much—you who are the spokesman of dauntless rebels the world over!"

The Bomb revealed a master who had reached maturity, yet greater things were to come—*The Man Shakespeare, The Women of Shakespeare,* and *Unpath'd Waters.*

From boyhood Harris had read Shakespeare: first for the stories, then for the characters. In young manhood he had been challenged by Kuno Fischer: was Shakespeare a "German," and second to Goethe? Driven by his militant mind, Harris returned to the plays to see why Shakespeare was one to "steer humanity." Through his years of growth, Harris had been testing himself

---

[6] G. Bernard Shaw, Preface to *The Dark Lady of the Sonnets.* Dodd, Mead & Co.

against Shakespeare, and Shakespeare against the world. Rereading all that had been written about Shakespeare, he found it "tons of talk." The Ph.D.'s had turned the living grain into the shredded wheat of footnotes.

The fallacy of commentators (he thought) had been to see Shakespeare as an "objective" creator of "characters" who were dramatic, that is, who were synthetic. The truth was otherwise. Shakespeare was autobiographical, lyrical; like all creators, he was realizing—himself. His greatest character is Hamlet? But is there merely one Hamlet? Consider Romeo. He is Hamlet in earlier youth: a melancholy dreamer, contemplative, rich in philosophy and poetry, weak in action. He is, as he himself says in the crisis that demands decision, "Fortune's fool." Hamlet-like he cannot decide to be or not to be; Hamlet-like, his action is a spasm of fury, exploding in murderous violence to little avail. And Macbeth? He is supposed to be a man of ambition, of action; but what a man! He sees visions of the weird women on the very verge of battle; he, the captain used to the shedding of blood, hesitates like Hamlet, asking whether to grasp or not to grasp the airy dagger that he sees—or does not see—before him. He has to be driven to murder's red frenzy. In his crises of action he pauses to savor his emotions like a poet, or to bewilder himself with rainbowed fog like a parlor philosopher. There is in him no Louis Lingg. He laments at the end "troops of friends," and the things a poet would miss; he sees life not in terms of battle, but of drama ("a poor player that struts his little hour"); he lapses into nihilism like an introverted Buddha, talking of the sere and yellow leaf; he thinks of life in literary terms, "a tale told by an idiot" that reaches "the last syllable of recorded time." Where is the mosstrooper, the Cromwell-hearted captain, the lord of tumult and shouting? Here is a dreamer, a seer of visions: the play presents a poet having nightmares. Action, ambition? There is neither. When he does act, it is in a spasm of panic, like Hamlet;

both men act as dreamers do when they are forced by fear or fury into a violence they abhor.

Other characters, Lear, even Antony, are similar. Through all the greatest plays looms a single character, varying in situation, varying in angles of emphasis, but always congruous and lyrical. Shakespeare was painting *himself,* first and last; he is the basis of all the great plays. In his more leisured comedies where the world is as we like it, he is Orsino, the "taffeta Duke," with his desire for music, "the food of love," which almost immediately becomes "not so sweet now as it was before"; Orsino who loves love and beauty, who speaks philosophy in the web of poetry, and who suffers from a strange haunting melancholy compounded of infinite simples. Jacques, in *As You Like It,* is Shakespeare thrust into the heat and fury of action for which he is not fitted—"the melancholy Jacques," the witty critic of the march of man, the crowd-shunning and nature-loving fellow to whom "all the world's a stage," the seeker for someone with philosophy in him, a man who must have been hurt by women because he mistrusts them with so wincing a poignance.

The other great masculine character, Falstaff, is (Harris thinks) an amalgam: partly Shakespeare's own rich earthy sensuous humor, partly some man of the time, probably Chettle.

There are prevailing counterparts for the men: the women they love. They are stronger than the men in will and desire; they do not palter and falter or hesitate between the yes and the no. Juliet wills, plans, forces even the contemplative Romeo to act; Lady Macbeth and the Queen in *Hamlet* choose evil with a royal will. Shakespeare was obsessed by women. Even in *Lear* there is a strange eroticism: the evil daughters are, in fact, more lewd and wanton than cruel. Lear, his madness laying his subconscious bare, speaks his own fierce lust—though he is old. He sees lust as the essential corrosion. Lear, strangely, in a play of age and disillusion, is lewd with lust. And the tawny gypsy, Cleopatra? The plays tell of Shakespeare's own lust and love, his own tragic experience with women. His own drama was passion—passion that met defeat, that was betrayed, that wrecked his heart. The sonnets tell the same story. Shakespeare speaks of a "dark lady," the same who in *Romeo and Juliet* is the love-mocking Rosalind with her dark eyes. Harris, following Thomas Tyler, identifies the dark lady with Mistress Mary Fitton, a lady-in-waiting at Elizabeth's court. The name matters little; the thesis is greater than the name. (Watts-Dunton, querulously commenting on the theory in private, to a friend, used to say: "Don't tell Harris, but Mary Fitton was a *blonde!*") The dark lady, with her hair blacker than a raven's wing and her eyes pitchballs in a white face, was the central and consuming passion of Shakespeare's life; he loved her and sent his friend, Lord Herbert, to woo her for him; Herbert, an arrogant young aristocrat, seduced her or was seduced by her. Shakespeare lost his love, and his friend. Though later he himself possessed her, he could never forget or forgive her wantonness (which was lifelong), nor his friend's betrayal. The plays of jealousy, of the torture of love and hate, of the desire for revenge which his gentle nature could not enact, and of the verge of the abyss where one stares into the void of madness came out of the sense-troubled, emotion-tangled drama of Shakespeare and Mary Fitton. She lends her good qualities, while the poet was young and still believed in her, to Juliet (though Rosalind has her eyes); she becomes supreme in the tawny gypsy who loves Antony and betrays him and has "immortal longings" that lead her to the asp. She wrecked Shakespeare's mortal life; she gave him immortality.

Incidentally Harris clears vexed issues. English prudery had avoided open mention of Shakespeare's supposed homosexuality; and, avoiding it, seemed to corroborate it. Harris sweeps the scandal away forever. The language of the sonnets about the male friend is the gorgeous rhetoric of compliment, natural in the day and only different in its greater power of poetry. It was conventional compliment, motivated at worst by sycophancy. But when Shakespeare speaks of his dark lady the language changes: it is not rhetoric but poetry, the very lava of passion. Moreover, in all his plays Shakespeare is hotly desirous of *women,* and able to endow them with glow and lure; he feels intensely the polarity of sex. There was in him no pathetic error of vice: he was the virile male seeking the vivid female.

Shakespeare realized *himself* in his plays. They are his autobiography. Beginning with his hopeful love for the dark lady (with scalding hate for his older wife—scold and termagant, because of whom he is ever warning men to marry women younger than themselves); progressing through the storm of his broken passion and breaking heart; reaching by supreme virtue the final victory of the *Tempest* where he is Prospero: in all this and these, he gives us his own life. From outer defeat he wins inner victory.

> *The rarer action is*
> *In virtue than in vengeance . . . .*

Even in *Lear* he can say:

> *Men must endure*
> *Their going hence even as their coming hither:*
> *Ripeness is all.*

There, too, he makes poor mad Lear triumph at the edge of death. And in *Antony and Cleopatra,* the defeated Antony is a "lord of infinite virtue" who remains "uncaught by the world's great snare."

Harris sees Shakespeare as one overengined by a "beating mind" in a body too frail. (He makes one sad mistake when he sees Shakespeare's physique as similar to the reedy Swinburne's. Such energy and humor as Shakespeare's could never have been housed in such a body as that of Algernon Charles!) Shakespeare, Harris said, was richly sensuous but exhausted by sensuality; almost oversexed yet unsatisfied by gratification; lordly in language, gentle and sweet, fair even to his enemies, snobbish, spendthrift, loving the use rather than the possession of money, lacking the hard courage of the Puritan or the hot arrogance of the Cavalier, unable to understand a democrat like Cade or a saint like Joan; less in character than Jesus (else he would have died not in private obscurity but on a public cross); but of infinite virtue in his search for light and for spiritual and artistic power; wise in all contemplative areas, and rich in senses and in heart. He forced the best out of himself even when worn by his wrestle with the world. He is England's eminence.

The only great criticism of this great book comes in Shaw's Preface to *The Dark Lady of the Sonnets*. Shaw says that Harris's book brought him delight, all the greater because the conventional idea is that a gentle dignity is necessary for one who writes of Shakespeare. But Harris is the contrary and opposite: his very existence insults the pallid ideal; his eye and voice and shoulder discourage the albino amenities. He is extraordinarily qualified by scope of understanding and sympathy that ranges "from the ribaldry of a buccaneer to the shyest tendernesses of the most sensitive poetry, to be all things to all men . . . ," and yet it is his "proud humor" to be "to every man, provided the man is eminent and pretentious, the champion of his enemies. . . ." [7] Yet because of these qualifications Harris has written the best book on the highest subject.

Shaw stands this side of idolatry. He finds a lack of humor in Harris, so that he sees Shakespeare too much in terms of terror and pity: genius has a resilient vitality that laughs at woes which break normal men. Shakespeare had the resilience, the gaiety, the antiseptic salt of humor, to heal the wounds the world dealt. Like Richard he can say,

I myself
Find in myself no pity for myself.

[7] Preface to *The Dark Lady of the Sonnets*.

Shaw cannot see the "broken heart" in Shakespeare's later works —the "Hark, hark, the lark," or Cloten's comment about Imogen: "It is a vice in her ears which horse-hairs and cats' guts, and the voice of the unpaved eunuch to boot can never mend." Shaw even suggests that since the dark lady had to stand up to this, she may have been the one to pity!

Shaw believes that Shakespeare transcended love. All "the bite, the impetus, the strength" must not be left out; nor the grim delight in looking terrible truths in the face. That these are omitted, and that Shakespeare is therefore presented as "Fortune's fool," seems the fallacy in Harris's play: *Shakespeare and His Love.* But in *The Man Shakespeare* this is not so, for there Harris himself is present—deep-voiced, masculine, mordant.

One may supplement this by pointing out that Harris the fighter was unable or unwilling to recognize the fighter in Shakespeare. But certainly the fighter is there. No merely gentle spirit ever wrote:

> *In peace there's nothing so becomes a man*
> *As modest stillness and humility:*
> *But when the blast of war blows in our ears,*
> *Then imitate the action of the tiger;*
> *Stiffen the sinews, summon up the blood,*
> *Disguise fair nature with hard-favored rage:*
> *Then lend the eye a terrible aspect, . . .*
> *Now set the teeth and stretch the nostril wide;*
> *Hold hard the breath, and bend up every spirit*
> *To his full height!* [8]

Also the splendid beating clangor of the developing combat between Edmund and Edgar in *Lear* could not have been written by a poet allergic to action. There was the same tough substratum in Shakespeare as in Harris himself. Perhaps because he wished to see in Shakespeare those aspects which were complementary

---

[8] *King Henry V*, Act III, Scene 1.

and not complimentary, he emphasized the gentle heart at the expense of the militant spirit.

(In Harris's interpretation of Jesus it is the same: the "bite, the impetus, the strength" are minimized; the gentle, almost feminine love is maximized.)

But Harris's portrait of Shakespeare rises to pages of grandly somber prose, as majestic as the music of Bach. He hails Shakespeare as Shakespeare hailed Antony:

> A rarer spirit never
> Did steer humanity; but you, gods, will give us
> Some faults to make us men.

The book ends in grave organ music.

The Man Shakespeare may owe more to Brandes or Dowden than Harris realized. What of that? Harris, whether he got all his ideas from his own mind or some of them from sources he ignored, has synthesized the total into a great book. To read *The Man Shakespeare* is an experience so tremendous that one may liken it to birth or to a conversion like that on the road to Damascus, which changed Saul into Paul. It is the blinding Light, before which one did not see; after it, one should change his name. We come to the tomb of Shakespeare where the professors had laid him with gentle dirges and feeble rushlights; and we find the stone rolled away and the grave open.

Arnold Bennett wrote: "A masterpiece on Shakespeare has at last been written. It has destroyed nearly all previous Shakespearean criticism, and it will be the parent of nearly all Shakespearean criticism of the future."

The book transcends the brilliant partial insights of the only other two great Shakespearean critics, Coleridge and Goethe. They seem, in comparison, writers of splendid intuitive fragments, amateurs of genius. They give a finger or a forehead; Harris gives the complete statue.

Harris wrote a play, *Shakespeare and His Love,* in which he tries to show Shakespeare and Mary Fitton. It is a minor play. Harris was never dramatic. His greatest stories are those in which facets of himself are the protagonists. Strangely, perhaps as a compensation, he was resolved to see Jesus and Shakespeare as opposites of himself: quiet, contemplative, gentle. But as long as Harris quotes from the Gospels or the plays, or as long as he writes lyrically and so is present himself, we find the strength of Jesus or Shakespeare. Harris's lyrical projection of himself supplies what, intellectually, he denies them. But in the play Harris is abstracted and absent; or present only as a prompter, off stage. His absence makes Shakespeare anemic—the world's victim, never the spirit's victor. Shakespeare is world-worn and passion-weary in the play; he is a nightingale singing in a moonlit resignation. Where is the humor that laughed at the drunken fish of a Caliban? This Shakespeare is as melancholy as Keats, as brain-fogged as Coleridge!

The later *Women of Shakespeare* is great. We enter the hearts of the women who are in Shakespeare's plays because they were in his life: the shrewish termagant, Anne Hathaway, from whom he was wisely renegade; the bold, wanton, witty Mary Fitton; his wise, well-loved mother; his beloved, palely realized daughter (Miranda).

Frank Harris is England's greatest Shakespearean scholar because he is the philosopher of Shakespeare, the poet of Shakespeare. He is the seer of criticism. He does what time alone can never do for any great man, but only what the peer that time at last brings can do. He is the burning glass of criticism, centering the diffused sunrays into fire. He is the greater Horatio for this Hamlet:

> *What is it you would see?*
> *If aught of woe or wonder, cease your search.*

We may cease our search, for here at last is Shakespeare.

Among the evidences of the genius of God's Spy, the latest

was not the least. In 1913 *Unpath'd Waters* was published by Lane in England and by Kennerley in America. It is his greatest volume of stories.

The volume ranges from the stock market up to Jesus; from the chiseled irony of "An English Saint" to the transcendent mysticism of "The Magic Glasses." It is solidly based upon knowledge of the ways of the world; yet it soars with tracery of towers and glow of rose windows, like a cathedral.

The story most often noticed is "An English Saint," for it is in the modern fashion, deftly lucid with a faint scepticism lightly brushed in. It is a water color of irony.

Gerald Lawrence, the palely handsome son of a tailor, is the center. He does little except to look handsome. (Harris once said of Kitchener: "No man can be so great a soldier as Kitchener looks.") Gerald has the beauty of a minor Greek god, mitigated by the frail pallor of an ascetic. Docile, feminine, he seems to have the sap of a white birch instead of blood. At Oxford (which he chooses because it is more aristocratic than Cambridge) he makes little impression on the master of his college, who dismisses him as "an amiable idiot." Gerald, however, falls into the hands of an artist in men, Mrs. Leighton, a young widow, rich and at spiritual loose ends. Fascinated by his beauty, she decides to use it. He must be a religious genius, she decides; so she flatters and veneers him, placing him in the right situations and attitudes. She teaches him the "aesthetic value of austerity"; she buys him relics and knickknacks from France and Italy; she praises his honey-colored hair and makes him wear it long. She teaches him reticence, made rich with unspoken thought. She makes him a symbol of the affectation of piety then becoming fashionable at Oxford. She makes him half legendary while still alive: his classmates take to calling him "the Saint." He blushes as he murmurs, "My Master's business." He discovers rapture in the cloistered passivity and aesthetic austerity of a saintly pose. His will-to-power finds its outlet in pallor.

Invited, through Mrs. Leighton's strategy, to dinner at the master's house, he silences the master's praise of militant organization, by saying: " 'Forgive them for they know not what they do' has not yet been organized, or there would be no prisons."

Accepted as a saint, he is offered a vicarage in Surrey with an income of 600 pounds a year. He decides, rather, to spend several years in the East End of London as a Saint Francis of Aestheticism. In his inexperience of life, he falls in love with a pretty girl who comes to sing and dance at the settlement. He runs away with her to Paris for a hectic honeymoon that exhausts him. Mrs. Leighton and his father rescue him, and Mrs. Leighton marries him to save him from his memories. She engineers his debut as a London preacher. The sermon is in praise of abstinence; its chaste pallor and his seem to be full of wan beauty.

Amid the blatant materialism of London such preaching makes a sensation if not an effect; he is raised to Canon of Westminster. Since he preaches only some three times a year (because of a weak heart) his sermons become social affairs.

He eats no meat. He drinks only water. He becomes increasingly known as "the Saint," but his life burns frail and thin—a white flame above a silver candlestick.

He preaches one final sermon to the elite of London, with a vague power, like music speaking without concepts. "I will gladly spend and be spent for you. . . ." His voice has a dying fall, and his head droops on the desk. They carry him to the sacristy; he half recovers, apologizes for his weakness, falls into another syncope, and dies. Even the Archbishop, a worldly man and doubting Thomas of the Church, admits that perhaps "he's as near a saint as we're likely to see."

More pungent is "Mr. Jacobs' Philosophy," a lyric of the brutality of money, the genius of finance. Mr. Jacobs is a Jew who happens to love money and who gets it. Sentimentalizers of the Jew object because the money-lover is not a Gentile; but the sun illumines both Jesus and Jacob.

"The Miracle of the Stigmata" develops a favorite idea of Harris's: that Jesus did not die upon the cross, but, with the connivance of Pilate, was taken down before he died. The resurrected Jesus is living as an obscure man, Joshua, married to Judith. Paul comes preaching; Judith is won to his message: it is all about Jesus and his Gospel—a fighting Gospel, full of clangor and besom. Joshua questions it: did Jesus preach such fiery exclusiveness, such arrogance? Judith does not like this dilution of Paul; abandoning Joshua, she seeks the fiercer apostle. Joshua says, "Jesus wanted nothing but love. . . . He may have been mistaken. . . . He trusted God, cried to Him in his extremity, hoping for instant help—in vain. He was forsaken, cruelly forsaken, and all his life's work undone. But he was not wrong, surely, in preaching love to man—love that is the life of the soul."

Judith breaks in, suspicious. Did Joshua, then, know Jesus in Jerusalem?

Joshua replies hurriedly that he knew his teaching; surely, he urges, Judith would not leave him for the teaching of a stranger? "Ah, Judith, why add to that mist of human tears that already veils the beauty of the world?"

But Judith will add her own brackish drop. Paul tells us, she says, to break all ties for the highest tie. Joshua winces; she asks if he is ill.

At last Judith, because of his disbelief in the Jesus of Paul, goes to dwell with her mother, Tabitha, across the road. Joshua asks in his loneliness, "But why this cup, O Lord, why?"

Some months later, Paul returns from a preachng tour. Shortly thereafter, it is noted that Joshua has not opened his door for two days. His wife finds him fallen by his bench, dead. As the women lay him out, Tabitha cries, "What are those marks on his hands?"—for each palm is drawn into "a puckered white cicatrix." Judith answers that they were caused by an accident that happened in Jerusalem. But they find scars on his feet, a scar in his side—the marks of the stigmata! They run to tell Paul, who cries: "A miracle!"

Paul breaks into eloquence: even an unbeliever in life has borne witness in his death. God has written upon his doubt, as on a palimpsest, the verdict of the cross. All Caesarea is converted through the miracle of the stigmata that has been wrought on the body of the "last unbeliever in Caesarea."

The story, beautifully told, accents an aspect of Jesus. Yet Jesus is too gentle: a man broken by the world's malevolence. A Jesus whose resurrection was only a weak obscurity of love in the defeated flesh, his faith lost in the passivity of quietism, is a diluted Jesus. Yet the story realizes a partial Jesus who, in loving tenderness, would not add to that mist of tears which obscures the beauty of the world.

"The Holy Man" is great. It concerns a Russian Bishop, the youngest dignitary of the Greek Church, who is a man of piety. Traveling over his diocese and visiting remote villages on the Caspian, he comes to a little village where a hundred simple fishermen dwell. He asks for a church: there is none. But the town has a Holy Man. He is not paid, for he will take nothing; he works in his little garden and his home stands in a square of cabbages. He is about sixty, dressed half like a peasant, half like a fisherman. His hair and beard are silver against the tan of his skin; his blue eyes are steady like a calm sea. He has never heard the term "Christian." He asks what "religion" is. But he is eager to hear of Christ; his eyes light up as he listens. "What a beautiful story!" he exclaims. The Bishop murmurs the Lord's Prayer; the Holy Man repeats it. But when he reaches "Forgive us our debts . . ." he insists on saying: "Give and forgive." And he says, "For Thine is the kingdom and the power and the *beauty*." Again and again he repeats the prayer in ecstasy of adoration: how can he ever thank the Bishop for coming to tell him of Christ?

The Bishop returns to his boat, marveling at the Holy Man

and at his strength like a young man's. The priests, however, scoff at the people—ignorant as pigs: they cannot read; they never heard of Christ; they know nothing of religion.

Suddenly in the night a light moves over the sea. There is a man with a gray beard and a lantern, walking over the waste of waters. The priests, crossing themselves, ask God to help them. The Bishop says it cannot be a man: that would be a miracle! But it *is* a man—the Holy Man.

He is afraid that he has disturbed His Excellency, but he has forgotten part of the beautiful prayer, and has come to learn it again. . . . How did he come, the Bishop asks, over the unbridged sea?

The Holy Man replies that whatever you love in this world loves you in return. He loves the water, for it is sweet and pure and is never tired of cleansing, and the water loves him. Anyone who loves water can walk on it; but won't the Bishop teach him the beautiful prayer?

The story is told with magical grace. It suggests a mysticism that was the truth of Harris's deepest heart; if he had developed its implications, he would have reached the height of modern thought. But he could never quite walk on the water: like the Bishop, he doubted. He was never himself the Holy Man.

"The Irony of Chance" tells of a scientist whose researches led him into mysticism. He has come to know that "laws of nature and ideas in the mind are correlatives, and suppose each other as eyes suppose light"; that spiritual forces are mechanical forces raised to higher power.

Mortimer has come to know that the vegetable and even the mineral kingdoms are alive and conscious and amenable to love and hate. Stones or grasses are subject to the same laws as man: they move to the same end; a thought in the mind is a law in the star. Knowledge, which used to bring scepticism, now brings belief. Even chemical compounds move by spiritual laws: two volumes of hydrogen unite with one volume of oxygen—the

greater and meaner, even in gases, do not unite easily. Sometimes they will not unite at all until you pass an electric spark
through them: love. The atoms of even the metals are in constant
vibration, which means that they are alive. Metals, too, are repelled by hate and wakened by love.

Mortimer seeks to prove this by making a metal ball that will
respond to him. He fuses three metals; he fuses seven. For a long
time he fails; then one morning he finds the ball wobbling and
imperfect—but alive. He calls it, and it comes; he tells it to go,
and it goes. He is as God!

Yet the next morning he had lost his power: the ball is capri-
cious; he can never be sure of it. But always, after periods of despair, the power comes back.

He takes to lecturing. He tells his audiences: "The laws of
physics are the laws of thought . . . there is a positive and negative
in the electric current corresponding to the sex-division in man
and woman . . . our notion of expediency is the law of least resist-
ance . . . and the passion of love is the law of gravitation, and
moves stars and suns as easily as boys and girls." As proof, he
tells of his ball, and makes it move to and fro.

He discovers that people care little for his philosophy; the
miracle seems to them the be-all and end-all. They want to be
amused by a trick, not set free by a truth. A few are hotly spiteful:
they do not want to believe. Their scepticism weakens him. Once
the ball fails to respond: people hoot, laugh, abuse him.

He becomes frightened lest the truth of his teaching fail
with his power. Why not make the magic sure? Temptation
comes; he cuts an opening in the ball, and has a boy hide in it
and move it as he may order.

One sceptic follows him with monotonous malevolence from
place to place, always sneering. This affects Mortimer: he loses
power oftener; he uses the boy more frequently.

One evening in Birmingham, after an afternoon when the
sceptic has exhausted Mortimer, the boy asks if he can have the

evening off to see his mother who lives nearby. Mortimer is afraid
and refuses. The hour for the lecture comes. The hall is crowded,
the people enthusiastic, but the ball is only feebly obedient, as
if the boy, Walter, were sullen. Then the man with the evil face
springs up, sneering. It is all a trick!—he has followed the lecturer for weeks; there is a boy in the ball.

Mortimer answers, What if there is a boy?—the idea is true,
the ball only an illustration. But the man is resolute; the audience
is persuaded. Mortimer is tired; his soul loathes them: why struggle against this current of mud? He signs a paper, admitting that
he is a cheat; they gloat over their cleverness: Birmingham is
too wise not to see the trick in the truth!

As Mortimer sits alone, a door opens and Walter hurries in.
He is sorry. He did so want to see his mother; but the ball moved
just the same, did it not?

In this great story Harris affirms the future: a scepticism of
scepticism, a faith in faith.

The greatest story, however, is "The Magic Glasses." (Harris
wrote to Bennett: "I am so glad you like 'The Magic Glasses':
it is the story I like best too.") Rich with the colors of the spectrum, it extends also into a realm below red and beyond violet.

The hero, Matthew Penry, is sixty. He is in trouble: several
people—a laborer, a tradesman, a cleric—accuse him of having
sold them glasses under false pretenses, magic glasses to reveal
the truth of things. The judge, to test the evidence, tries the
glasses; he is delighted to see the audience and the lawyers in
bleak truth ... until a solicitor dryly asks him to look in a mirror.
Then brusquely he remands Mr. Penry for further trial, under
heavy bond.

Penry represents a part of Harris: the mystical poet and prophet.
But there was another part of Harris, less worthy, more worldly.
Therefore the story is told by an observer—a man sympathetic,
able, in a worldly sense, to help, but unable to reach the insight
that has become Mr. Penry's sight.

This chance-found friend goes bond for Mr. Penry, then sees him home. He learns Mr. Penry's story. Matthew Penry was the son of a famous maker of glasses; by work and study he has risen to be himself a master workman. By chance Rossetti happened into his shop and laughingly suggested that each painter has a peculiar vision because of which he paints the world in his own way. Why not find the secret of the eyes, then make glasses which will enable others to see as the painter has seen? Mr. Penry works out the suggestion; studying Rossetti's eyes, he finds their peculiarities and makes glasses to reproduce their vision in normal eyes. He fashions Claude glasses and Tintoretto glasses (a matter more of color than form). These—especially the rose-colored Claude glasses—have a vogue.

Bit by bit the vogue fails. Meanwhile he has become interested in more intrinsic things. There is, he notices, a certain quality common to all painters when working at highest pressure: they see things as they are; they see with the immediacy of God. He tries, therefore, to fashion glasses that will reveal the soul of things as the great masters saw it.

Gradually he left the shop to his assistant, and let his business take care of itself. By the time he had succeeded, he looked around to find his wife was dead, his daughters grown up and gone, his business a last year's bird's nest. He had found the magic glass, and lost the world.

Now no one cares for his glasses. Most people are blind to truth: how can they understand his glasses? The small minority who have a glimmer of sight complain that the view which the glasses reveal is not pleasant.

His new friend comes to love Matthew Penry. Penry has little flaws and faults of course—irritabilities, trivialities of temper, undue depression when he depreciates himself, undue elation when he overestimates himself. To most people he might seem flighty, uncertain; but his passionate devotion to his work lifts him as with wings.

But Mr. Penry's greatest work lures him on to destroy himself with victory. He realizes that there are areas of being yet inaccesible to man, and sounds on the other side of silence. Our senses are limited; they are incapable of seizing vast fields of being which, our minds can prove, exist. On the thermometer (which also, in its way, measures color-range), man's life is not even centered in the register of heat, but vibrates in a little space near the warmer extremity. And the gradations of heat above and below this are "represented by colors which no human eye can perceive, no human mind imagine." Matthew Penry determines to fashion glasses that will open man's prison into a world of freedom, and show him colors as yet unseen, forms as yet invisible. His glasses will even penetrate the future, because they will see the eternity within time.

He succeeds in making such glasses; he does not succeed in finding eyes to use them. Not even his new-found friend, for all his sympathy, can see; not even Mr. Penry himself. Somewhere he must find eyes innocent and pure enough, yet also keen and brave enough, to look into the ultimate.

The trial comes. The workman, whose testimony had been fairly favorable before, is not in court; the tradesman, Mr. Hallett, testifies adversely. The worst evidence comes from a Canon Bayton; he half praises the earlier rose-colored glasses, but speaks with burning bitterness about the new truth-glasses: they destroy the beauty of life, the sanctity. The flesh falls away; the death's head grins. They destroy the flowerlike ideal; they reveal the wormlike root. The glasses are "a blasphemy against God and an outrage on human nature."

The judge is hostile. He asks, "Who wants to see the truth?" When Mr. Penry answers, "Very few," the judge insolently asks him why, then, he should make the glasses.

Mr. Penry, angered by the hounding, puts on a pair of the glasses and peers around the court. There are few in England, he says, who can even begin to see the truth; and he has found none such in all the court. He has seen, however, a child in the next room, the judge's daughter; she, unspoiled by the world, may be able to test the glasses. Let her verdict be final!

The judge, surprised that Mr. Penry can see through walls, agrees; though the foreman of the jury declares that it is needless, as the jury is already agreed. The child is given the glasses; she exclaims at the ugliness of all save Mr. Penry: *he* is beautiful. She looks at her father—and blushes. "I don't like these glasses," she says, laying them down. "My father doesn't look like that."

Mr. Penry, seeing her innocent purity, hands her other glasses—those that see into the future. Even the solicitors and casual spectators become tense. The child, staring round, at last speaks in fright. "I see nothing. I mean there is no court and no people, only great white blocks, a sort of bluey-white powdered as with sugar. Is it ice? There are no trees, no animals; all is cold and white. There is no living creature, no grass, no flowers, nothing moves. It is all cold, all dead." In a frightened voice she adds: "Is that the future of the world?"

Mr. Penry leans toward her: he bids her follow the light—to follow the light upward.

The child, looking about her, says petulantly: "I can't see anything more: the light hurts my eyes!"

The story ends with a clipping from the *Times*: Matthew Penry has died in prison, from syncope.

"The Magic Glasses" is a symbol of man's highest search. Mr. Penry is the artist, philosopher, scientist, seer who in any field passes sight and reaches insight. In his character, his goal, and his fate, he represents the height of man. He transcends the senses, and mere matter; he reveals us as less than half-men in a whole universe. Harris is sceptic of time, space, and mortality; a brilliant seer into worlds invisible.

Biographically, the story is full of intimations. When Rossetti bids Matthew Penry travel the world and discover the eyes of the living great—Corot, Renoir, Monet—it is Carlyle telling Frank

Harris to write *Contemporary Portraits.* The development of
Matthew Penry is that of Frank Harris: first the magic glasses
(the art) of the senses, then of the intellect, and finally of the
soul. The inspiration of the story is so pure that Harris prophesies
the way of his own death—in loneliness, persecution, and obscurity, from heart failure.

The worldly part of Harris tells the story, the lesser Harris
who writes of the greater Harris; he can go only as far as his
intellect will carry him. But Matthew Penry (who is the greater
Harris) is the poet, the saint, the seer; in him is incarnated the
highest vision Frank Harris ever attained. Here he fashioned
for us the magic glasses, through which those of us whose eyes
are innocent and brave and pure may look into ultimate truth.

After *Montes the Matador, The Bomb, The Man Shakespeare,*
and *Unpath'd Waters,* Frank Harris quoted the lines from "Andrea del Sarto" that he loved so well:

> *Some good son*
> *Paint my two hundred pictures—let him try!*

These books show the true Frank Harris. He edited great magazines; he made money on the stock market; he spent vacations on
the Riviera gilded with wealth and golden with sun; he traveled
in Africa, and met Rhodes and Oom Paul; he drove fast horses
and fine automobiles; he heard Rachel in Paris and Wagner in
Germany; he lived a rich outer life. But meanwhile the true
Frank Harris lived in lands not charted on any map: azure coasts
more golden than the Riviera, a heart of darkness more profound
than Africa, the Interpreter's House of which Vanity Fair knows
nothing. Most biographers of Harris, knowing only the way of
all flesh, could not comprehend the way of all spirit. The spirit,
to Rodin, was a beautiful but hampered power surging mightily
up out of the uncouth clay, yet ever entangled and hindered by
the lag of the heavy earth. Frank Harris's life was like a statue
of Rodin's.

Chapter IX

HAMMER OR ANVIL—WHICH?

(1894-1914)

THOREAU, BLAKE, AND SHELLEY match the pure intensity of their
work with the pure intensity of their lives. They upset conventional standards, but they do so because they are *above* the world's
standards. There are other geniuses who do questionable things,
yet in an unworldly way: Vincent van Gogh, marrying a prostitute out of pity, or sending the *fille de joie* of Arles the mad gift
of his ear. And there are geniuses who attain the highest integrity
in their work, yet fall short of it in their lives. Such are Villon,
Cellini, Bacon, Swift, Voltaire, Wagner, and Gauguin. These
are the ambiguous geniuses, open to the sneers of mediocrities
who, without the genius, preserve a tepid equanimity of conventionally "moral" action. One must regret the equivocal politics
of a Bacon, the Whig-and-Tory shifts of a Swift, the sharp practices of a Voltaire, the vices of a Verlaine, the world-involvements
of a Gauguin, the shady intricacies of a Wagner. It is pleasant to
find the quarrel of genius with the world motivated from above,
not from below. But as Frank Harris wrote in *The Veils of Isis,*
"Artists all strain after peculiarities, and the quest is dangerous:
the preterhuman is not always the superhuman, oftener indeed
it is inhuman."

And Harris, though greatly sinned against by the world, also

sinned against himself. His sins were not what they were superficially supposed to be—sex, lewdness, lying. His flaws lay in a
frequent worldliness; in his love of good living; in his necessity
for luxuries; in his excessive need of too expensive foods and
wines and comforts. As Art Young wrote, "Harris always needed
money—more money. He had to have his wine—and wine of the
first vintage." [1] Harris never sold his pen; but sometimes he
wasted his pen on journalism when he should have been busy with
eternalism. What had he to do with such lesser papers as the
Candid Friend or *Vanity Fair?* With a hotel in Monte Carlo?
With various brash financial schemes? With speculation on the
Stock Exchange? He lost money as lavishly as he won it easily,
then fell into debt for the luxuries he could no longer forego;
thus he mortgaged his peace of heart, or distracted his genius.
Shaw gives the indictment blunt force: "God forsook you in
righteous indignation and delivered you into the hands of a scrib-
bler too silly to know how to steer clear of the law. You got two
weeks where Wilde got two years. You deserved hanging. What
had a man like you to do with the dregs of bucketshop finance
and journalism?" [2]

Harris had made a fortune from the sale of the *Saturday Review*. With part of his money he lived richly; with another part
he won leisure to write. But because he was a man of regal resources and imperious powers, that did not seem enough.

He had always loved the Riviera; he had always had a superlative talent for wine and food; now he thought that both these
interests might serve him, till on a human plane he might perform the miracle of changing the water into wine, the loaves and
fishes into a feast.

Often he held waiters, hotel proprietors, and master-chefs mes-
merized by his discourses on food. He was an artist in gourman-
dry, a connoisseur of the cooking of nations. French cooking, he

---

[1] Art Young, *On My Way*. Liveright, 1928.
[2] Letter from G. Bernard Shaw to Harris.

said, was too promiscuous: it destroyed individual flavors by mixing them hodgepodge, until the character of each taste was lost. A potato should be cooked in its own skin; a partridge should not be made a *chouchou* with cabbage. English cooking was better, for it sought to cook each thing by itself and so save the soul of its taste. Yet the English kept game till it was putrid, to make it tender; disliking such a ghoulish mess, he found that if you cook game the same day it is shot, it will be as tender as the most ancient corpse. Gerald Cumberland said that Harris should write a book on cookery. Could he not, then, start a hotel where entertainment was a poem, and lift living into genius?

He did start a hotel, but his carelessness with money, his lack of *routine* brains, doomed the venture. He heaped a second venture upon the first, and a third upon the second; the whole crashed. In frantic desire to escape complete loss, and in genuine confidence in his schemes, he involved Lord Alfred Douglas and finally Lord Alfred's brother in his own failure, persuading them to invest thousands of pounds. Chagrined, pricked by creditors, he thrashed about like a gamey bass on a line, trying to shake the hook out of his mouth. One cannot be greatly concerned with such self-caused troubles; neither should one be acidly censorious, as his "modern" critics self-righteously are, concerning what they choose to see as "financial rascality." Harris foolishly involved himself in business; once in debt, he tried his bold best and panicky worst to free himself; he floundered about like a fish maneuvered into a few inches of water. His fault was not incidental unscrupulousness, but a central error: he had no business in business. Apollo must serve Admetus in this world; let him tend Admetus's flocks and herds—but never speculate in buying and selling Admetus's cattle. Harris's desperate remedies (which only intensified his plight) give his biographical enemies material for gleeful strictures. The Chinese proverb says: "In shallow waters the great swordfish finds himself the butt of shrimps."

Lord Alfred Douglas said: "He [Harris] has no financial conscience, only an artistic one." In financial matters, indeed, Harris affords an excellent rebuttal of Nietzsche's idea of beyond good and evil. Dante was wiser: "Abandon hope all ye that enter here." Harris's amorality in finance led him into literal hell. He had said in his life of Wilde that there is no such mortal enemy of genius as poverty—except riches. Of the two, riches is the more dangerous: for poverty is a rough fellow with a club, whom we can all recognize; but riches is a smiler with a knife.

Frank Harris himself recognized the duality of his own nature. In "A Mad Love," and again in "A French Artist," he shows a genius who falls into aberration and destroys even his art by madness. Harris himself was Hagedorn or Piranello: great, yet half destroyed (as they were wholly destroyed) by some of the world's temptations. In him it was not jealousy of a man or lust for a woman; it was the desire to enjoy the world when he ought to have transcended the world. He knew the strait gate and the narrow way of the artist's salvation; but he was too often "Adam, who finds a larger freedom in disobedience and a wider kingdom in revolt." [3]

There is a picture of Harris in these years by Alvin Langdon Coburn. He rests his head on his clenched hand, as on a fighter's fist; his hair is black and parted in the center with rakish care, over a wide forehead that seems low. The nose is broad, prominent, sensual; below it an aggressive flowing mustache curls with a seductive fullness, hiding the straight lips. The chin, large and firm, is softened by high light. One ear, bulking large, seems to listen to the gossip of the world. The eyes are disturbing: under a black thatch of brows they look into a light that makes them half sly, half staring.

Compare the bust made in 1929 by the French-Hungarian sculptress, Perina Meszlenyi. The head rises out of the stone on a thick strong neck; it is turned toward the light. The hair, still parted in the center, is the ripple of a wave; the forehead is deli-

---

[3] Frank Harris, *Love in Youth*. George H. Doran Co., 1916. P. 199.

cate as well as strong; the ear is finely chiseled and less prominent; the cheek has a sweep that sinks to a firm base in the chin.
The mustache is smaller; beneath it the lower lip is sensitive as
well as sensuous. The nose, large but fine, rises to a cleft between
the brows; the brows are frayed granite; the eyes are candid,
seeming to look through, yet over, the world. It is an artist's face.

Whatever happened to Harris between the two likenesses was—
if tragic—good.

In a letter to Kate Stephens, July 4, 1915, Harris wrote an intimate account of his activities in these years. "I sold the *Saturday
Review* eighteen years ago and all my fourteen books with two
exceptions have been done since. Whenever I wanted money (and
I've spent it like water) I've gone back to London and made it on
the Stock Exchange or through it as a Company Promoter. I did
one Company with Pierpont Morgan for thirty millions of dollars: had he gone on and done the second as he promised, I
should have been a very rich man. As it was I made money easily
and spent it without counting. After the first success in 1886 I
never let myself be without ten or fifteen thousand dollars: as
soon as I got between these figures I returned to London to make
money and put books and plays out of my head for the time
being. . . ." One need not accept the figures. The atmosphere,
however, seems literally true. It is the worst of Harris. It would
have been better for his fame—far better for his work—if he had
had nothing, and had given himself to art.

The worst is that Harris "had to have" money—and made it at
the expense of more important things; the best is that he spent
his money, for he could not keep it. One must remember, too,
that he never made money by his books (except once or twice
later), and did not try to: art lay outside the Market Place. He
told Gerald Cumberland that his books had brought him practically nothing—for *The Bomb,* fifty, or not more than a hundred pounds at most. "If I had been compelled to live by what
my books have brought me," he said, "I should have starved. Yet

it is not long ago that Arnold Bennett assured me that I should be able to earn five thousand pounds a year if I gave my whole time to fiction. But Bennett is wrong. My books since *Elder Conklin* ... have been enthusiastically praised, but they have not had large sales. Most authors must find book-writing the most unremunerative work in the world." In a letter to Bennett, October 26, 1908, Harris wrote: "I have received nothing as yet for what I have written, not even enough to pay the cost of printing and paper, which seems to me too little." And if he made money lavishly, he spent it as regally—to live well, and to help friends. Hesketh Pearson wrote: "He [Harris] has pawned his things a hundred times in order to help friends in distress (no doubt accompanying the deed with loud and savory oaths) and he is one of those strange, occasionally awkward people who are quite incapable of attaching the smallest consequence to money, except for the immediate use it has in helping others or in spending royally. He is indeed a monster according to all conventional standards, but his monstrosity only offends the shallow people who can't see beyond it—to the soul of greatness underneath it—and they are the people who simply aren't worth propitiating." [4]

Harris's money-making did not make him snobbish, sever him from reality, harden him into conservatism, or blunt his sympathy with rebels against money. George Slocombe tells of Harris as editor of "the semi-scandalous sheet called *Modern Society*." The *Daily Herald* had been compromised by an editor who featured a royal marriage on the front pages of that republican sheet. The editor was dismissed and the paper was without a guide. Harris came to look it over; he offered to edit it—"on condition that he be given a free hand, and that if he went to prison for libel they would continue to run the paper in his absence. The committee of staid trades-unionists looked at Harris askance. The reference to prison frightened them. Lion-hearted little Ben Tillett alone was for taking a chance and giving Harris a run for his money.

[4] Hesketh Pearson, *Modern Men and Mummers.*

But the invitation was rejected." [5] (Sad that Harris did not go to prison for such a cause!) "With all his faults, which were many and obvious, his lack of scruple, his vain-glory, his truculence, I delighted in the man. There was a strain of greatness in him. A vein of pure gold ran through his tinsel shams and brittle vanities. He was, with certain remarkable exceptions, almost unfailingly sensitive to beauty and aware of genius. . . . My own experiences of him were unsullied by any action that was not generous, honorable, and courageous." [6]

Frank Harris descended into the world's depths in a diving bell. When he came up there was mud on his leaded boots, and weed and slime on the glass of his helmet; yet in spite of his immersion in the world's terrible pressures, he came up as he had gone down—Frank Harris.

In those last years in London Harris engaged in petty journalism.

After the high seriousness of the *Fortnightly* or the free brilliance of the *Saturday Review,* why did he allow himself to edit the *Candid Friend,* the *Automobile Review, Vanity Fair, Hearth and Home, Modern Society?* He did not have to, if he could make the money he says he did in other ways; he did not need to, if he could spend his genius on great books. What was the motivation of his recurrent descents? He wished to influence the intellectual life of London; he aspired to be the Angel that troubled the waters of the pool so that healing might come; he loved to feel himself a man of literary affairs. He loved to associate with writers; the smell of printer's ink intoxicated him; the sense of power that an editor has seems to have fascinated him. He would not admit to his heart what his head must have known: that the powerful of England were bitterly against him, so that they would never allow him to regain the heights.

The mere number of magazines in England edited by Harris

[5] George Slocombe, *The Tumult and the Shouting.* Macmillan, 1936. See pp. 29, 155, 223.   [6] *Ibid*).

is amazing. Einar Lyngklip, from his long and intimate association and study, complied the following list:

The London *Evening News* (1883-1887)
The *Hawk* (some time after taking over the *News*)
The *Morning Mail* (1885)
The *Fortnightly* (August 1886—November 1894)
The *Saturday Review* (December 1894—November 1898)
The *Candid Friend* (May 1, 1901—August 9, 1902)
Judy, or Pick-Me-Up (about 1906)
Vanity Fair (January 2, 1907—1911)
Hearth and Home (1912 for some six to eight months)
The *Lady* (a short time in 1912)
Modern Society (September 6, 1913—April 19, 1914)

The helter-skelter titles and dates of the papers after the *Saturday
Review* suggest his restlessness and quick loss of interest.

Frank Harris was not happy as editor of these lesser papers.
The dignity of the *Fortnightly,* the brilliance of the *Saturday Review,* held him long and enlisted his best. But he could not make
these lesser ventures great; he soon tired of them, and then they
rapidly declined. He was careless when the best in him was not
employed; after winning Austerlitz and Jena, could Napoleon
get excited about a skirmish with shotguns at a provincial cross-
roads? So Shaw could jestingly ask if these papers had not been
edited by the office boy—a question that suggests a *truth* if not
a *fact.* Harris was incapable of mediocrity—even in failure.

The *Candid Friend* declined, in its approximate year of life,
toward lesser things. After the heady liquor of the *Saturday Review* it was a mere chaser.

Vanity Fair was an enigmatic paper. Its very title suggests that
Harris, on his pilgrimage to the Celestial City, was dallying where
genius is in mortal danger: he belonged, rather, in the Interpreter's House. His fellow editor was T. H. Crosland, a literary acid-
thrower of talent, who died in poverty, years later, with a copy
of Shakespeare's sonnets in his pocket. Shaw called him "Thyr-

sites Crosland"; Harris is reported to have said, "There are two things I never hope to see: the bookkeeper drunk, and Crosland sober." Crosland helped underline the worst in Harris's editing, and then sneered at what he had helped to create, under pseudonyms, in other papers.

Hearth and Home was Tom Sawyer writing a cookery book for Aunt Polly. Gerald Cumberland (a distinguished writer, a loyal friend) tells of it wittily. "I went to live in London, and called on Harris in Chancery Lane. He was running a curious illustrated weekly, entitled *Hearth and Home,* and I remember sitting in a little back room in his office turning over the files of the magazine and wondering what on earth he hoped to do with such a publication. It was tame; it was watery; it was feeble. I looked at him quizzically.

" 'What do you think of it?' he asked.

" 'Well, don't you see—' I began hesitatingly, 'don't you see that —well, now, look at the title!'

" 'Title's good enough, don't you think?'

" 'Oh yes, good enough for Fleetway House. Why not sell it to Northcliffe? But you've got no Aunt Maggie's Column, and no Beauty Hints, and no Cupid's Corner! Oh, Harris!'

"He laughed and invited me out to lunch.

"I never discovered what strange circumstances had conspired to make him possessor of this extraordinary production. No doubt he had bought it for nothing, with the intention of rapidly improving it and selling it for something substantial later on. But I believe it died soon after—perhaps urged on to its grave by some verses of mine which were printed close to an advertisement of ladies' wear. . . ."[7]

Hearth and Home, in the tragic elements of Harris's life, was like the comic relief in *Macbeth*—the knocking at the gate, the porter's sleepy interlude, the talk of a primrose path to the everlasting bonfire.

[7] Gerald Cumberland, *Set Down in Malice.*

The final word on these ventures is Shaw's. He wrote to Harris, September 27, 1918: "I may be quite wrong in this or that detail as to your career in London journalism after the *Saturday Review*. . . . Your letter is the first intimation of the screaming joke which you mention so seriously: to wit, that you were once editor of *Hearth and Home*. I feel that I may see you editing the *Leisure Hour* and *Good Words* before I die.

"But I read the *Candid Friend* because you sent it to me from the office, and because Lady Jessica, who knew my wife, tried to get hold of me when she was editing it for you. After the first two numbers I don't believe you wrote fifty lines in it all told before it expired.

"Your *Vanity Fair* never came my way except when the Press Cutting people sent me its invariably scurrilous references to me. I did not suspect you for a moment of writing these, not on sentimental grounds, but because you could not have written so badly if you had tried for a year. At last there came a surpassingly bad article, apparently written by the office boy; but when he actually used your signature (which you seldom used yourself) I concluded that you had become utterly reckless. . . . It may very well be that the paper had passed out of your hands, and that some Freddy Hicks or Frank Hodges was airing himself in it. But there the article was, anyhow; and it was quite in the style of the things that had been coming to me during the time when you were the reputed editor. . . .

". . . It was clear that *Vanity Fair* was no more like the *Saturday Review* than the *Mystery of a Hansom Cab* was like *Hamlet,* and that you were living in Monte Carlo. The conclusion was that either you were leaving your newspapers to be edited by anybody who happened to be on the spot, and not even troubling to keep the standard up to Lady Jessica's . . . , or else you had fallen off as a literary hand to an extent that could only be accounted for by utter demoralization, and that your character had collapsed with your talent. As I came across you a few times, and saw that the latter was not the right explanation, I fell back on the former.

"But you suffered also from your personal style. Like everyone else, I took you to be much more of a man of the world than you really were. As I told you, it was Julia Frankau who first opened my eyes to the fact that the buccaneer of Monte Carlo, the impressive editor of the *Fortnightly* and the *Saturday,* the financier who gave tips to Hooley, and the scorner of the transparent and trivial West End, was a romantic boy and even a sensitive child, without the ghost of a notion of the sort of society he was living in, and the people he was up against. You were so surprised and indignant at finding that England was England, and human nature human nature, and so hurt by the knocks that seasoned adventurers in London soon cease to feel, and, what was worse for you, so absurdly unconscious of the shock and jar of your *Anschauung* against that of Eton and Oxford, and of the Saville Club's resentment of your scale of literary values, which reduced most of its members to pygmies, and piffling pygmies at that, that you never really knew where you were, or what you might say or do with impunity. You often seemed to be brutally and truculently outraging susceptibilities which no doubt would not have existed in a community of Napoleons and Maupassants, but which are the whole life of the London you had to steer through. . . . Now it is hard enough on other people to know that you think you know more than they do. It is not possible for the most vigilantly considerate man of high talent to go through the world without moving those who feel at a disadvantage with him to furious moments of hatred and envy; but when you openly scorn these victims, and wipe your boots on them publicly, you sow dragon's teeth in all directions. You certainly sowed a great many in London; but you did it naïvely and unconsciously to a much greater extent than anyone could have guessed from your style, which was that of a man who knew every corner of society and human nature, and did nothing without knowing it. Whereas

. . . half the time you had not the least idea of the pain you were causing or the fierce animosity you were rousing.

"Publishing your books at your own expense, as I have done for many years in England, is the price you had to pay for your independence.

"*Pearson's* proves my case as regards the papers you didn't edit. *Pearson's* is quite evidently edited by Frank Harris. Whenever you really edit a paper, there is no mistake about it. And when you didn't edit it there is no mistake about that either. . . ." [8]

So Shaw pours light on the troubled waters of Harris's later editing!

These later years in London were illuminated by one of Harris's major friendships, which flourished until it became, in 1914, one of the casualties of war. It began when a "Mr. Tonson," a reviewer for the *New Age,* wrote of Harris's books. Harris, grateful for genuine understanding in a world generally given to ignorance, wrote Mr. Tonson a note from the office of *Vanity Fair,* October 26, 1908. He found that Mr. Tonson was Arnold Bennett.

Bennett was a foursquare, genuine man, honest and kindly, full of a love of letters and a knowledge of life. There was less envy and more of the cream of human kindness in him than in most writers. No jealousy seems to have curdled the cream he poured for Harris. He liked Harris's work, and said so—publicly. The same honesty marked Harris's response. He wrote, September 14, 1910, "I can only tell you that your letters to me are like manna in the wilderness; they bring tears to my eyes."

The association was not an incorporated society for mutual reviewing: it was a friendship based on common interests and on stimulating differences. Harris was true to his first name: he wrote of the excellent qualities he found in Bennett, but he made vocal his differences. He expressed in his letters to Bennett, almost better than anywhere else, his own philosophy of art.

On November 27, 1908, Harris wrote one of his finest letters.

[8] Shaw's letter to Harris, quoted by Harris in his *Bernard Shaw.*

"And now, how am I to write to you? We represent the extremes of two opposing theories of art. . . . We owe each other frankness —you and I—entire sincerity—that is the measure and proof of our mutual esteem.

"I've read your three books; but of course *The Old Wives' Tale* is the one you would wish to be judged by. . . . The workmanship is astounding. . . . The style is always beyond reproach; thoughts, emotions, incidents, all perfectly clothed. The architecture, too, as Goethe called the skeleton, perfectly designed. . . . The story-teller's unique faculty everywhere apparent—then a masterpiece?

"Halfway through the book I thought so. . . . Then the disappointment. You've made a fine creature; just when we are vitally interested in her and her tragic deception and the chances of her growth, she falls to the ordinary! True to life, yes, perhaps—but not truer than the wild chance that she should pass the open portal into the future and become a symbol. . . .

"If I am wrong you must forgive me. I thought you had painted the dull conventional English life of the home-staying, conventionally correct sister at such length to give the contrast point, to make Sophie credible to us. I wanted her abandoned and seduced, and then I wanted her to take her life in her hand and go on making her body the servant of her spirit, determined to grow, to realize all that was in her, to get the knowledge she craved for, and to reach the heights! I saw, too, that such a woman would inevitably, sooner or later, come across a man big enough to appreciate her—a man who would have money, place, everything. The confession of such a woman to the man who loved her and whom she loved, seemed to me enormous. Then, the marriage, and the life in a foreign country, the great life she is born for, and then come yearnings and a visit to her stay-at-home sister and the contrast between the mangy tabby-cat and the superb wild animal.

"And you could have done it all; your description of the execution and Sophia's rise above her ignoble husband—all show the true flame, and you preferred to bring her down to dullness and make her a lodging-house drudge and quench her noble spirit in petty economies. You give her a muckrake instead of a soul. . . . It depresses me, disappoints me. The book seems to me but the pedestal of the statue. Or is this merely a proof of my thirst for ideal things, for figures greater than life, carved out of some enormous cliffside by a greater than Aeschylus? I should like to trace gigantic ebony figures out of the night itself with a flaming torch. I want the realism; but I want also to see the soul conquering its surroundings, putting the obstructions under its feet; heaping up the funeral pyre, if you will, from which the spirit may take flight.

"You must not ask me for more than I can give. I am partly in sympathy with Ruskin's criticism when he talked about 'the sweepings of a Pentonville omnibus.' If they live the usual Pentonville life and like-minded die the usual Pentonville death, then I have no use for them. But Pentonville is as free to the night-winds and stars as any other part of this visible globe. . . ."

The two men were very different. Bennett was a master of mass: he built up the background of the Five Towns, the minutiae of human character, with immense marshaling of weight and amplitude. He realized the world in complex vastitude. But sometimes the huge orb of clay outweighed the informing spirit —dulled it, dimmed it. Bennett could do the large canvas: the wide-flung sky of the novel, the scope and area of life's extensions. But he was more successful in showing earth's extensions than in showing life's intention. Harris was not so apt in painting a wide canvas, in giving area and amplitude, in creating vistas of time and space, or in realizing characters that developed slowly. Bennett's novels seem to say: "We are large: we contain multitudes." Harris was the intense swift genius, whose lightning-flashes of vision lit up life's night for a flaming instant. He gave the emotion, the mood, the meaning—and stopped; his forte was not to realize earth's amplitude of space, but the magnitude of man's spirit.

Despite all differences, they were friends. They were men of the world, rising above code and prejudice; they loved books, paintings, and France; they liked good food and wines: often they dined together, lingering over savory dishes, and losing all sense of time in the glow of eternity. Bennett relished Harris's relentless intelligence; Harris relished Bennett's intelligent generosity. Too often it was not so with others! Friends praised him to his face, and dispraised him to the world. He wrote Bennett: "I do not know whether my book is going or not. My friends have tried to massacre it: Massingham told me it was delightful and he wrote a review of it in the *Athenaeum* that was as grit in the eyes and ashes in the mouth. As Max has been praising it extravagantly and Wells, I expect they will do their best to murder it." The way of all friends! Even Christ, bidding us love our enemies, forebore to urge the harder task of forgiving one's friends! Bennett was not so. His free, unenvious mind, his generous heart, let him write publicly what he spoke privately. He even sent a telegram about *The Man Shakespeare;* in reviews he did not retreat from his easy private praise, but underlined it in public print.

Bennett was a realist. He saw life without sentiment or mysticism, yet with mystery and atmosphere. Harris was a realist in means, but a romanticist in intention. He suggested the strangeness of life that extends where only mysticism may come. "I wanted to show," he wrote, December 17, 1908, "that the scientific imagination at its height was always penetrated with a sense of mysticism." Yet a sentence or two later, denying his own words, he calls the mysticism of Wallace and Crookes "childish superstitions!" Bennett remained an artist of the three-dimensional world; Harris approached the fourth dimension.

Yet what understanding Bennett had! Harris wrote wistfully

(December 17, 1908): "Your criticism is the only helpful criticism I have ever received, except a few letters from Meredith 20 years ago, which were rather helpful through encouragement than through insight. How true it is that all the praise one gets is worthless to one because it is what the French call '*à cote*,' because it is not on the level where we are living and working. Your criticism of *The Bomb* is the only criticism the book has got."

And still further about criticism, Harris wrote revealingly: "I am afraid you do not realize what enemies I have managed to make in twenty years of frank journalism. I daresay I have been mistaken many times and have ruffled a hundred dovecotes; but what I am astounded at is the malice people show me toward whom I never felt any malice. Here is this book, now, of Noyes' on William Morris, one of the worst books I have ever read in my life: he misses the heart of Morris and his significance, and writes vilely about him. I let him down as easily as I could, but I have to say that he has done bad work. On the other hand, here is a book by a little journalist called Rutter, a book on Rossetti . . . which is not bad, always sympathetic, and often interesting. The little man does not see what 'Dante's Death' is, or how it will affect English painting for two hundred years at least. He has no idea where Rossetti is. . . . Still, he has written about him so that one can read it, whereas Noyes has written wretched piffle about a man who stood practically on his own intellectual level. I venture to say I have made two enemies in fifty lines, and the Ford Maddox Hueffers and the Garnetts are not likely to be friendly to me. Still, you have to deal with these things as seems fitting. . . ."

Bennett disliked Nice; Harris loved it. Bennett loved Switzerland; Harris detested it. "I hope to get off to the Riviera. I simply love it. I would rather live on the heights above Nice than anywhere else in the world. The sunshine and the light-heartedness and the gaiety and the mixture of frivolous French and shameless Italiante [*sic*] English are simply charming to me. When I have made money again and done with journalism, that is where I shall pitch my tent, for the winter at any rate. You hate Nice; I loathe Vevey and the lake of Geneva: there is a smell of Calvin concentrated in Geneva that spreads all over the lake, mixed with whiffs of Byron and Voltaire and Gibbon and Rousseau which are simply poisonous, not to be redeemed even by stories of Casanova. Geneva is cold, bleak, and clean, like a shaven nonconformist face. It is as bad as England."

Harris wrote of his travels. "I made excursions all through Calabria and made some wonderful 'finds' in the art way. Old columns and walls, funeral urns and medallions half life-size, things to me of infinite value. Then I had a gorgeous day or two in the Naples museum among the bronzes that would fecundate the soul of an English publican or a French grocer. . . ."[9]

Such was their friendship. The strong river, however, dwindled with the years: Bennett rose in prestige and power, Harris declined. It was hard to bear. Bennett, more kindly, less temperamental, could not understand why the "Yours ever" stiffened to the "Sincerely yours," and why the waters ran out in sand and cactus. The World War loomed like a desert; in its waste the last of the river was drunk up. Bennett wrote publicly of Harris's being bought by German gold, and spoke privately of his former hatred of an America in which he had now taken refuge. Harris wrote of Bennett as a mediocrity, subject to the conventional prejudices and pruderies of England.

Meanwhile Harris was increasingly isolated and alien in London.

He was now an established pro-Boer; a certified friend of rebels; a critic who trod the grapes of mediocrity and who saluted genius terrible upon the mountains; a creator of stories that startled with French frankness; a thinker who treated conventional religion with lucid irony, and who *also* tossed the Ark of

[9] April 7, 1910.

orthodox science on the floods of mysticism; a champion of the freedom not only of the sexes but of sex. In politics, journalism, art, society, finance, religion, pedagogy, he had made his enemy that anonymous giant, Everyman.

Shaw was faithful ("a very Abdiel he"). Here and there among the younger men he had disciples, some of whom would be faithful always; others of whom would later show him (as Robert Frost says) that for destruction "ice is also great." But he was largely alone.

Now by his descent in journalism to papers at which mediocrity could safely scoff, he seemed to be approaching his debacle. It was easier to hurt this Harris than the Harris who, even if one hated him, was editor of the *Fortnightly* or of the *Saturday Review.*

Rumor indicates the world's mood. Kenneth Hare humorously suggests the effect Harris made upon many, at least according to the wags of the day. Hare imagines a meeting between Elizabeth (the Virgin Queen) and Harris.

" 'Hoity-toity, Master Harris,' she would have observed coyly, 'You are talking to a virgin.'

" 'And that is no fault of mine, Madame,' Frankie would have made answer with his most engaging bellow." [10]

Such is the shadow, caricatured by humor, that Frank Harris cast!

The humor, however, was thin ice over hostility, and Harris soon broke through into deep water. Austin Harrison had become editor of the *English Review;* he solicited an article from Harris, called "Thoughts on Morals," which, appearing in 1911, precipitated Harris into the lake.

The article seems temperate enough today. It says that morals are not static but dynamic, and that for the health of the soul the body should lead a natural life. It praises normal freedom in sex; it says that abstinence is abnormal, even harmful, in youth.

[10] Kenneth Hare, *London's Latin Quarter.* John Lane, 1926.

As life goes on, however, chastity is a way to win back strength, and temperance is wholesome. There was no virulence, certainly nothing vicious, in the article. Yet it incited St. Loe Strachey, the editor of the *Spectator,* to cancel his advertisements in the *English Review* and to censure Harris in an editorial.

Harris wrote a letter in reply which is a classic of controversy. Freedom is desirable, he said, not only for what it says outwardly, but also for what it releases inwardly. We should bare our souls to freedom as we bare our bodies to the sun whose rays kill disease and nourish health. Without freedom, English literature could not find a vocabulary, to say nothing of a soul; without freedom, English life was a foul swamp whose miasma was hypocrisy.

More than forty authors, including Thomas Hardy and D. H. Lawrence, signed a protest against the action of the *Spectator.* St. Loe Strachey said that he did not find the list impressive: so Queen Victoria in Heaven, hearing Cervantes read *Don Quixote,* might say, "Sir, we are not amused!" Yet the protest was more professional solidarity than a defense of Harris; the attack was more representative of England.

Two years later, in 1913, Harris began what Slocombe calls "his unlucky adventures with a semi-scandalous sheet called *Modern Society."* This had little value; Harris himself, on the evidence of style and content, took little interest in it. It was a journalistic stopgap. But this editing is important in his life, for it led to his famous and from every standpoint unfortunate imprisonment.

Harris's version of the affair is that, while he himself was away, a subordinate published an article that he would not have passed. This has been denied: one biographer declares that someone told him that he saw the proof sheets marked "F.H." There is no proof of this wholly anonymous and extremely questionable statement. The truth is undoubtedly what Shaw suggests. Harris had so little heart for what he was doing that he gave little care

or time to it. Either it became the habit of some subordinate to
sign proof "F.H." or Harris did it with the automatic regal carelessness of one who cannot be diverted by trifles. He certainly felt
himself spiritually guiltless, so he pleaded "Not guilty." (As Shaw
says about Wilde, such a plea is a question not of fact "but of
morals: the prisoner who pleads 'Not guilty' is not alleging that
he did this or did not do that: he is affirming that what he did
does not involve guilt on his part.") [11] The article dealt rather
sordidly with a divorce case, one of the corespondents in which
was Lord Fitzwilliam. On January 30, 1913, Lord Fitzwilliam's
attorney asked the judge, whose unfortunate name was Horridge,
to commit for contempt the editor and manager of *Modern Society*.

If Harris was not guilty of direct complicity, he was at least
involved in editorial carelessness.

Harris was stubborn, however. He felt that he was not guilty,
since he was away; and that he had a right to publish the article
anyway, for the press should be free. Therefore he refused a
written apology. When the matter was brought to court, he
offered to apologize, according to one account; he refused to
apologize, according to his own. Judge Horridge was a symbol
of the stiff, stupid legality that had sentenced the sun-natured
Oscar to Wandsworth Gaol. Thrusting his fighter's jaw belliger-
ently forward, Harris stared at the high justice who cloaked injustice under the quaint traditional wig. The judge dryly suggested
that Harris had a certain disdain for the court. Harris replied: "Oh,
if I could only express all the disdain I feel for this court!" Whatever formal apologies his attorneys may have filed and induced
him to sign, he was too scintillant with the contempt whence
words flew like sparks to permit any doubt of his meaning. The
fierce glance, the magnificent voice, made his contempt clear.
Here was an eagle, caged, but staring from eyes that had looked
into the sun. What had the eagle, the brother of storms, to do with

[11] G. Bernard Shaw, Preface to Harris's *Oscar Wilde*. Edition of 1938, p. xxvi.

courts and commitments for contempt? The judge, feeling the hostility, grew more hostile. He had Harris committed to Brixton Prison, where he was to stay until he should satisfy the judge that he was sorry.

The finale was a draw. There was some sort of formal apology, some compromise of attorneys, to satisfy the judge; there was enough contempt to make the judge's satisfaction a pallid thing. The eagle came out of the cage fiercer than ever, his eyes more lightning-amber.

Frank Harris declared that he suffered horribly in prison. There is little evidence that he did: his wife was allowed to visit him each day and bring him food; Max Beerbohm dined with him. His sprightly pencil proves Harris to have been anything but crushed. Compared with the imprisonment of Emma Goldman in America, or of Karl Liebknecht in Germany, his jailing was a minor thing. It was not a crucifixion. In his wisest hours, Harris knew it. He wrote of Emma Goldman: "We went to gaol for our trumpery sins, and she for her deepest convictions." [12] His enemies triumphed in this—they managed to maneuver him into a minor role, an *opéra bouffe* Calvary. He was denied the consecration of tragedy: no *De Profundis* or *Reading Gaol* could come from so slight a thing. His sin was neither so evil nor so great as Wilde's; his tragedy not so symbolic. How much greater if he had gone to jail for editing the *Labor Herald,* or for helping Wilde escape from England!

Harris was not crushed. The proof is the cartoon by Max Beerbohm: "The best talker in London with one of his best listeners." The scribbled words beneath are even more intimate; they speak of the "happy fortune" that has made Frank his friend "for the past thirty years." It shows an untamed Harris; his head looms fiercely in the air, the hair aggressive and thick, the nose like a cavalry charge with lances, the eyes fiery and large, the left hand expressive in ample gesture. Across the table, protected by

[12] Frank Harris, *Bernard Shaw.*

a bottle of wine, Max sits, small, neat, thin, with a mouselike, rapt attention, his eyes more entranced with the bravura of the visible Harris than his ears with the words for which the picture provides no sound track.

There were publicity and protest. Austin Harrison called it a shame to England that such a man was pilloried by prison. Partly, perhaps to avoid a *cas célèbre,* partly because they had so minor a basis for what might become a major matter, the authorities released Harris after a month.

The case, seemingly casual, was actually causal. Harris seemed to have fallen into trouble over legal technicalities; his real trouble, however, was his truth-telling, his mordant boldness, his quarrel with the world's values, his genius. Harris, Shaw thinks, did not realize the effect all this had on London; and he undoubtedly did not. Yet he had always a sense of the tragic destiny of genius; he wrote in *The Man Shakespeare*: "Some will say that Shakespeare was perhaps condemned for dissolute living, and did not come to honor because of his shortcomings in character. Such a judgment misapprehends life altogether. Had Shakespeare's character been as high as his intellect he would not have been left contemptuously on one side; he would have been hated and persecuted, pilloried or thrown into prison as Bunyan was." So in his own imprisonment, if the reason seemed a petty trick of circumstances, the cause had a profound basis in character.

Harris felt a deep shock and a blazing anger. At last he realized the truth: his life in England was ended; there must be an exodus if he would find a new genesis. The trial convinced him that success, or even life on terms acceptable to his pride and need, was impossible in England. With this realization there went, unfortunately, anger like a fan stirring a fire into fury. It disturbed the flame and distorted the light. England, actually, had been less unkind to him than Holland to van Gogh, or Florence to Dante, or America to Whitman. He should have used his minor

Calvary as Christ used His major Calvary. But let him that is without anger cast the first stone!

Like Dante, Harris must now go into exile and find how salt the bread of others, how hard the going up and down another's stairs; perhaps like Dante he would write his *Divine Comedy*.

In *The Life and Confessions of Oscar Wilde* Frank Harris asks about the fallen Oscar: "Hammer or anvil—which?" The question was now his own—and the answer: would he prove an anvil to be beaten by the blows of the world; or a hammer to strike sparks from the world and forge it into new forms?

Meanwhile he fled from the storms of his own life to Paris, and found himself in the path of a world-storm.

Chapter X

REED SHAKEN IN THE WIND
(1914-1920)

FROM PARIS shaken by the Germans (whose power he had long realized) Frank Harris wrote: "I'm just back from the frontier. . . . This war of nations is going to test every man with fire before it's over. It will be long in spite of Mr. Kipps and Bernard Shaw. The Russian masses will hardly come decisively into action (they have scarcely any railways and no good roads) till next May or June, and long before then, or rather in a couple of months from now, the French will be pressed back to within twenty miles of besieged Paris, when I hope the English forces on the flank will stop the German advance. Then will begin the slow process of driving the Germans home, which will be quickened by the Russian might behind Cossack pricks. Fancy one man having the power to set 400 millions of men fighting for their lives. . . ."[1] This prophetic letter proves that Harris knew Europe like a great general or a great statesman.

In the same letter he wrote: "When you have done great work you feel it is not yours, but given to you: you are only a reed shaken in the wind; you can judge it as if it had nothing to do with you. Moreover you see that this failure to recognize greatness

---

[1] Letter to Gerald Cumberland, August 29, 1914. Published in Gerald Cumberland, *Set Down in Malice*.

is the capital sin of all time, the sin against the Holy Ghost which He said could never be forgiven. Modesty is the fig leaf of mediocrity—don't let us talk of it. . . .

"I am the Reconciler; though my cocked nose and keen eyes may make you think me a combatant. Twenty years hence, Cumberland, if your eyes keep their promise, you'll think differently of me. I remember as a young man getting Wagner to praise himself and saying to myself that no man was ever so conceited as the little hawk-faced fellow with the plowshare chin. Did he not say that the step from Bach to Beethoven was not so great as from Beethoven to Wagner! And yet for these fifteen years past I have agreed with him and find nothing conceited in the declaration. Only weak men are hurt by another man's conceit; are we not gods also to be spoken of with reverence? . . . Now at nearly sixty I am about to rebuild my life; my own people have stoned and imprisoned and exiled me. Well—the world's wide. In October I shall be in New York, ready for another round with fate. . . ."

In Paris he waited and watched, talking with Frenchmen in high position, while the German masses rolled southward with the apparently irresistible impetus of an Alexander crushing the Sacred Band. The danger did not daunt him, the might of the Germans did not deceive him: "The French will be pressed back to within twenty miles of besieged Paris, when . . . ." But it was hard to make a living as artist in war-torn Paris. In America he might find a nook of quiet wherein to do his work. He was no silver birch, its life limited to decades, relatively fragile like Dowson or Keats; rather, like Tolstoi or Whitman, he was an oak— late to branch and leaf, long to gnarl into final strength. Now fifty-nine, he was beginning a new life. He entered his exile, even at that age, with high courage, ready to "rebuild his life," ready for "another round with fate."

He reached New York in October, 1914. He had landed once, a mature boy of fourteen; he landed now, a young man of fifty-nine. Once he had come too early for fame; now he came too late.

Shaw said that doubtless as soon as Harris landed he would claim to have been the first to discover the continent. This side that exuberant jest, Harris was content to describe New York like a philosopher-poet. "This New York is hard and shallow and greedy as an old whore: the most terrible city in the world for the weakling or artist or scientist, or, indeed, any man of genius or distinction. This people loves education and endows it with an incomparable magnificence, but it cares nothing for the flower and fruit and object of education—men and women of talent." [2]

Of Washington Square where he lived, he wrote: "This square is as large as Trafalgar Square. Fifth Avenue runs into the middle of it and at the juncture there's a meaningless arch, which, however useless and in itself foolish, has in winter, when festooned with snow or gleaming with icicles, a certain aesthetic value. To-night I saw it in hard frost, the sky purple with rain of diamonds, and above the arch a cross in golden fire on the spire of some Catholic church. . . ." [3] In such painting he was the Whistler of Manhattan—but stronger than that butterfly brushing mist-tones and star dust from his wings.

He lived first on Washington Square; then at 40 Seventh Avenue—a house of Chelsea style, now torn down, opposite St. Vincent's Hospital. One who lived next door wonders that so sensitive a man could have endured the noise of that traffic-thronged avenue.

Those who saw Harris supposed him to be a man of thirty-five, or forty-five at most. Joseph Wood Krutch, who saw him even later, speaks of his "ferocious vigor." William van Wyck, meeting him in 1917, wrote: "Power was the first thing that impressed me about Frank Harris. I have never before or since seen such dynamic qualities as he contains." His face in its bitter yet victorious strength, had a "granite look." Michael Monahan described him

[2] Letter to Hesketh Pearson, February 3, 1915. Published in Hesketh Pearson, *Modern Men and Mummers.*   [3] *Ibid.*

as "a short clipper-built man" who "never looked his age." George H. Doran, his American publisher, wrote in his *Chronicles of Barabbas*: "Having nothing to fear, I was more fearful of Frank Harris than of any other human being I have ever met." Guido Bruno tells of one who doubted Harris's knowledge of all the great men concerning whom he had written: "'Because' he supported his argument, 'look at Harris, he appears to be forty or forty-five, but though he is fifty, how could he have met Carlyle, or Flaubert, or Spencer, and all the others?'" Harris was then sixty-four.

The best likeness of Harris at the time is by Marcus. The hair, black and abundant, curls with a vibrant ripple at either side of the straight, long, low forehead. The eyebrows are divided by cleft lines of concentration. The nose thrusts forward with a bold strength over the black mustache; the full, half-hidden lips are sensuous but sensitive. The chin is a thrusting yet fine termination and foundation of the cheek; the cheek, a wide sweep of light, gives distinction. The ear is finely proportioned, delicately chiseled. It is the face of a sage who seems ageless: in it one sees the maturity of sixty, yet the vigor of thirty.

A greater revelation is the earlier bust by Jo Davidson. The hair, a silken sheen to reflect light, is crown or halo over the low, long forehead; the center of the forehead is cloven by a scar of shadow, like the gravure of pain. The eyes are deep-set and dark; they seem to half close and yet to stare from hollows like craters on the moon. The nose is a bold rudder of light. The mustache, not accented, hides the full lips and mitigates the crag of the chin. It is the face of God's Spy.

But though he was a reed shaken by the wind of God, men seemed to have little use for him. He tried to find work with newspapers or magazines; he hawked his great *Portraits* about, but the editors thought them too much this or too little that; too romantic and imaginative, or too factual and bitter. He wrote Hesketh Pearson, "But Alas! here no one seems to want my work especially. I've hawked about my *Portraits*, and no one will take 'em. . . . [They] will not take my stories either. . . . Bit by bit I'm getting poorer, though I'm once more after a fortune. Well, it's on the knees of the gods, and I don't whimper, for their judgment must be a vindication in time."

The explanation is easy. America had little knowledge of the great in Europe, in spite of a Huneker crying in the wilderness. It was concerned with its own revival of the "New Poetry"— *Spoon River Anthology,* "The Congo," "Chicago," *North of Boston.* Amy Lowell was gaily tossing her colored balls about, and dazzling the yokels with her snip-snap about red slippers. She was influential in a fashionable, superficial way; and of Harris she said to a young poet: "He is not a *nice* man." In criticism, the sweetness and rushlight of a Howells had not been shattered by the literary Fourth-of-July of Mencken. Henry Sydnor Harrison's *Queed* was a best seller; Poole's *The Harbor* was to make a stir. A parlor socialism, soon to yield to Mencken's boob-baiting, was the literary fashion. Harris was too savage for the writers of the Right; too civilized, world-experienced, and romantic for the writers of the Left. Timeless, he did not appeal to any time.

There were, as always, editors whose minds had never traveled; they did not know who Frank Harris was. One of them, talking with him, wondered if he had not written "a book."

His misadventures with the New York *Sun* are characteristic. First trumpeted in its pages as "The Famous Writer, Frank Harris," he was paid five hundred dollars for each of a series of weekly articles. The first three were the gist of his book: *England or Germany?* The first was a cloud across the *Sun;* the others were *Sun*-spots. So the second article was captioned: "By the Well-known Writer, Frank Harris." But his incorrigible incorruptibility continued; so the third was headed: "The English Writer, Frank Harris." He himself called it: "A Prophet's progress from fame to infamy in his own country in a month." Still, he had a contract with the *Sun;* the editors, thereupon, proposed that he should avoid politics and write on literature. But—*ex pede Herculem!* If Frank Harris had said the word "parallelogram" he would have made it quite his own. His first article, "American False Estimates of Greatness," disturbed the editors by its transvaluation of values. What a red banderilla of a picador to flaunt before thunder-swollen throats!—that Longfellow was a sweet singer of nothing, that Mark Twain was a wife-frightened provincial who wrote for adolescents! (Harris detested the intellectual immaturity and moral timidity of Mark Twain. He was once reading aloud "Mark Twain's rhapsodical praise of the Jungfrau mountain. Suddenly he closed the book, raised his head, and said scornfully: 'Jungfrau the Virgin! Why Virgin? Why not Old Prostitute? Everybody's been there!' ") [4] He acclaimed David Graham Phillips as the leading novelist of America. Such judgment not only upset the applecart, but also called the vender's favorite apples rotten, and cried up the peaches on a nearby counter. Harris was a rebel in literature no less than in politics. Everything he wrote was as surely himself as every canvas van Gogh's brush touched was his before he signed it.

The editors of the *Sun* wished to pay Harris five hundred dollars for a weekly silence, rather than continue the contract; Frank Harris, the supposedly unscrupulous, simply tore up the contract.

Frank Harris's greatest handicap was his reputedly pro-German attitude, brought to a focus by *England or Germany?* published by the Wilmarth Press in 1915.

In the foreword, Harris said that Germany was universally hated; but do not men often hate their superiors? So the Athenians hated Socrates: "We mortals crown our greatest with thorns." Germany had done great things in industry, philosophy, music, literature, science; her population had grown; she had abolished poverty. Was this not enough to make her hated by nations that had not had the wit to emulate or the wisdom to

[4] Raymond Thomson.

surpass her? We must make allowance for this prejudice against superior virtue: "Those who would stand upright must lean against the prevalent wind in proportion to its strength."

On the other hand, as Heine saw long ago, there were hateful things in England: oligarchy, snobbishness, hypocrisy. Yet Heine had been unable to see the full virtues of England: the humor, the loving-kindness, the sunny goodness. The English working people were the salt of the earth; and in their humor the pepper, too.

There were good things on both sides; the war was equal tragedy for all. It was a blunder and a shame; it might have been avoided if England had had Germany's virtue in scientific planning, and if Germany had had England's humor and loving-kindness. Now it should not end through savage butchery, but in a peace of reason. France, though involved by a natural defense of *La Patrie,* was above the battle. Her real destiny was complementary to Germany's, and was not to attempt to cancel out a nation that she had neither the strength nor the need to crush. As for Russia, who was sure to profit most in a material sense either in victory or in defeat, "It is the Tsar and his counselors who are fighting and not Russia; Russia is as yet without national policy or purpose; the brain and heart of her are not geared properly to direct the huge body. Thirty years ago I wrote that sooner or later Russia would express herself in a new birth in religion or a new form in society. It is perhaps the mission of Russia, Holy Russia as her children call her, to found the United States of Europe."

In the body of the book, Harris wrote: "The truth is, all the peoples engaged in this war are almost equally to blame. Behind all the moral pretensions there was hard national selfishness." There might have been legitimate criticism of William the Witless; but the conservatives of the world had praised him for his weak and evil things, and had wished to destroy the good that Bismarck had begun. There was, on the plane of the world's

huggermugger, rivalry on both sides—a resolve to crush the growing trade of Germany, or a resolve to seize the dwindling trade of
England. If Germany had been wiser, she would have avoided
war and grown quietly up to stature that none could challenge;
if England had been wiser, she would have realized that one
could not confine a nation with the potency of Germany in a
small country no larger than France.

Shaw, defending Harris in a letter to the *New Statesman,* saw
the true motivation of *England or Germany?* Its dynamic was
disappointment with England, its cause a wounded concern:
Harris was an idealist whose vision had proved vain. England,
Harris wrote, was an aristocracy corrupted by oligarchy: it had
no use for genius; it distrusted intellect, and persecuted when
it did not ignore; its upper-class life was the pleasantest in the
world, but it was founded on the degradation of the poor. England's treatment of artists, scientists, and philosophers mingled
amused contempt with spasms of hatred; her law was venal and
fair only to the privilege that was the shadow of the Golden Calf.
In waging the war, England would muddle through; Carlyle's indictment stood: there was no place in England for the Great
Captains of industry or battle.

Germany had greater virtue. Her aristocracy was not taught
to sponge and idle, or to despise intellect and art as dilettante
follies—all this "seeping down like water in sand, to infect those
below." There was provision for artists, musicians, scientists;
agriculture and forestry were subsidized. There was social planning: slums were cleared, men were employed, poverty was
abolished, utilities commonly used were run by and for the
commonwealth. Thus industry expanded; life for the masses was
fuller and richer; population grew. Even freedom was greater,
where it counted: in art, literature, science and philosophy. English art went in blinkers; German art was for men who dared
look into the eyes of life.

Germany should be generous to France and heal the wounds

of that foe who should be a friend. She should make peace with Russia too. Then, if she fought by striking at that commerce which was necessary for England's life and which England's misgovernors had not had the imagination to protect by the right sort of navy and air force, she could starve England into revolt. The greatest catastrophe for England would be to win the war without fundamental social change. "The one hope of progress in England is sharp defeat in war. . . . Everyone who loves England should pray for the bitter lesson. More than a hundred years ago Tom Paine declared that nothing would civilize England till the blood of her children had been shed on their own hearthstones. It needs a defeat in war to wrest the land of England from the lords who stole it and give it back to the people." On the other hand, if Germany is defeated, it will mean her eventual strengthening: "She will spring to power quicker than before." There was sad truth in Harris's prophecy that England would not profit by victory: her artists fell into weary passivism and the illusion called disillusion; she became the land of Hollow Men and their futilitarian poets who gloried in their shame, their rats' feet making whispers over glass. In her treatment of workers, in her attitude toward international morality, the England of Baldwin, Macdonald, and Chamberlain was nihilistic. Only the defeat of Dunkirk and the dive of doom from the air awakened her. Harris's prophecy of the rise of Germany is unfortunately underlined in red on the ledger of history.

What are the limitations of this prophetic book? If Harris had lived his London years in Berlin, he would have seen Germany's regimentation and arrogance and looked toward London as a city of light. He would have idealized the free speech and fair play of England. Were the militarists who dictated the treaty of Brest-Litovsk, or the Junkers who murdered Liebknecht and Luxemburg, superior? Was a nation that so soon burned the books of his favorite Heine a nation kind to art? If history has shown Harris right in seeing the power of Germany, its social kindness to the many, its use of intellect to attain its will, it has also shown that he did not feel deeply enough her malevolence. The lack of humor and light that leaves the German mind heavy with robot-seriousness he overlooked. Later, when he visited post-war Germany, he etched the pedantry of the German spirit in the ferocious acid of "Gargoyles." [5]

But Harris gave no secret aid to Germany. In everything he was open and headlong. What he thought, he said. He who ran might read; if he refused, Harris would pursue him and blare his words truculently into his ears.

Frank Harris did visit the submarine *Vaterland* when it reached New York, and wrote two articles for the German magazine, the *Fatherland*. One, February 10, 1915, entitled "Snobbery in Excelsis," was an exposé of the aristocratic prejudice shown in British relief; the other, October 27, 1915, "Truth at Last," was a review of a book by a Professor Clapp on England and the slavery of the seas. Harris received no bonus for his views; his pen was not a commodity. His attitude, on the other hand, hurt his material interests in America and tarnished his welcome.

Later, Harris saw the light and changed his views. He condemned the infamy of Germany's course toward Russia, and Germany's brutalities that grew with her defeat; he modified his position so completely as to desire the defeat of Germany as a measure of world salvation. This required courage and integrity. To Hesketh Pearson (April 30, 1918) he wrote: "The moral aspect of the war has changed. The shameful aggressions of the Germans in Russia, the disgraceful stealing of Batoum and Kars, and the handing over of the whole of that fertile province of Georgia to the unspeakable Turk, is one of those crimes that can never be forgiven, and for a year now I have seen that the Germans must be beaten. We go perpetually the wrong way about it, but still it will be done; so for the first time I am at one with

[5] Frank Harris, *Contemporary Portraits, Fourth Series.* Brentano's, 1923. P. 252 ff.

my kind, and though not so savage as the majority of men have managed to make themselves, perhaps not less determined." [6] Thus Frank Harris joined the war.

He wrote brilliantly about Allied soldiers, Joffre and Haig, or about Clemenceau. He wrote about grand strategy; he believed that the stalemate in the West, the wurrawurra in the trenches (trading yards for lives) was stupid: the English fleet should force the Baltic at any cost and invade Germany from the rear, where she was least ready and would suffer the pangs of battle on her own soil. Meanwhile the slow decision by discovery of who would first bleed to death seemed lethal. He championed a peace of reason and justice; not a compromise, but a synthesis of conflicting worldly interests for the good of the world.

Beyond all controversy concerning politics, Harris had done some of his greatest work in art. He brought with him to America a volume of stories, *The Veils of Isis*; it was published in 1915 by George Doran. (The English edition, under the name *The Yellow Ticket,* had been published by Grant Richards in 1914.)

The stories were preceded and followed by novels: *Great Days* in 1913, *Love in Youth* in 1916. *Great Days* is the better novel; full of incidental wisdom it also contains some autobiography. Yet one remembers something vivid here and there—the description of revolutionary France, the estimate of Napoleon, the episode of the two love stories—rather than a coherent architecture making for a single impression. *Love in Youth* is less purely a novel, yet it glows with beautiful things. Jenny, describing her love, says: "There's all the difference between being in love and loving. I fell into love as if I stood against a parapet and leaned and leaned, and it suddenly gave way, and I fell and was lost. I went about like someone hurt to death, and I couldn't bear to speak or be spoken to, and yet I could not endure to be alone, and all the while words of yours would come to me and make me burn and throb. . . ." Still finer is Harris's summation of life: "This

[6] Hesketh Pearson, *op. cit.*

incomprehensible world in which realities are dreams and dreams realities—this world in itself so mysterious with the surprise everywhere of beauty, in spite of the simplicity of things, and the miracle everywhere of happiness in spite of the eternal sameness of things as they are." The book is great in its flowers of wisdom that we may cull along the road. It does not have a single destination. Several roads diverge—one leads to the beauties of France through which the lovers travel; one to their love; one to the nature of England and the English; one to the character and story of Jenny's father, the American millionaire, Mr. Foxwell. The story is partly autobiographical: Jenny is a finer Laura; her worldly petulant mother is Laura's. In spite of the incidental grace of passages in the novel, the wind of God was blowing more strongly over that lovely shaken reed, *The Veils of Isis*.

The Veils of Isis is one of Harris's great volumes. (In England, under the inferior name, *The Yellow Ticket,* it included the sad, noble "In the Vale of Tears" instead of the poignant "Within the Shadow" and "The Kiss.") It was not so well received as *Unpath'd Waters,* because of extrinsic imponderables, not its intrinsic qualities.

The title story is a masterpiece. Amanthes, a young Egyptian, has been devoted by his parents and his own heart to the priesthood. He will not worship Osiris, for he was defeated by the dark; he will devote himself to Isis, "the woman-Goddess, the giver of life, for her creed of joy and hope must last as long as the earth lasts and the sun gives light." He tells his father and mother to look upon him as dead, "for he had given himself to the servitude of the Goddess with heart and life and for him there was no looking back." He learns all forms and ceremonials easily because of his love, and seeks ever the most intimate services. The priest long refuses him permission to perform them, holding before him a ten-year apprenticeship of study; but Amanthes proves that love is the best interpreter and amazes all by his reading of the oracles of Isis. One day—even while the priest counsels longer waiting—the door of the inner shrine mysteriously opens, and Amanthes strides in, defying the death which the priest forebodes.

From that time on he dwells within the shrine. Night by night he speaks with the Goddess as with a woman; he touches her as if the marble limbs were flesh. Love is his guide; the Veils of Isis begin to fall, and he becomes a reed under the wind of the Goddess's will. The usual scribes and commentators sneer and object and hint foul calumnies. But the priest who watches in secret only hears him entreat the Goddess to drop still another of her veils, since now only the last remains; hears the Goddess answer that it is for his sake—his whom she loves—that she refuses; and sees her lay her hand upon Amanthes' head. Amanthes replies, "To refuse one thing is to refuse all: love knows no denials; I would see you as you are, as the Gods see you, face to face."

Isis answers: "No woman's soul can resist love: tomorrow it shall be as you desire."

The priest warns Amanthes, asking him if he is not afraid. "Afraid?" he answers. "Tonight is the night for which I was born."

Opening the doors next morning, they find Amanthes dead before Isis. She is veiled as usual; her hands, that had touched his head, are now at her side.

The priests are glib in explanation. The mortal, seeing the Immortal, must die. Beyond the Gods stands the death's head of Fate: when the last veil fell, Amanthes died of the sight of Death. "No," says another, "the last veil fell to show him the Goddess only a woman—disillusion killed him."

But the people know better. For outside the temple, a woman cries: "The truth is plain! Having at last found a perfect lover, the Goddess took him with her to Amenti, the Land beyond the Darkness!"

"The Yellow Ticket" is the story of a Jewess who, denied a

passport in the old Russia of the Czar, and desirous of the education that she cannot get without it, attempts to win the "yellow ticket" of a prostitute, so that she may find a place in placeless Russia. She meets a man who, instead of demanding that she pleasure him, buys her a better passport as a Russian.

"The Ugly Duckling" is a great story: a parable—shining, subtly simple like those of Hans Christian Andersen—of Harris's own life. To understand him, one must read it: the beginning among his watery brothers and sisters who are pure ducks; his flight to the Anglo-Dorkings across the pond, who are hens (with snobbery of worship for one scrawny old rooster called a "Lord," and with prudery that denies the flesh); his experiences with Cochins and the Geese across the pond. At last he finds a swan, and out of the duck pond he springs up on strong wing exulting and follows the sun around the world.

"A Daughter of Eve" is a study of the eternal feminine. A girl, who by her presence among lonely men upon a ship can disrupt their fellowship with lust and anger, unthinkingly destroys her sister and her sister's husband. And finally, taught by tragedy, she rises to the height of goodness.

"A French Artist" is one of the most beautiful of Harris's stories, greater indeed than the better-known "A Mad Love." It has the same general theme, but in terms of painting. Piranello is a genius—as wise as he is masterly; he has an insight into mysticism, too, and feels that the world rises to meet our desires and to give us the fulfilment of any wish we are great enough to fashion clearly in our hearts. But he fails—as Hagedorn in "A Mad Love" fails—through some flaw in his character, some lust in his love. He is killed symbolically by the crucifix that he himself has fashioned; it falls, as he stumbles in lust and violence, and crushes him—"the cross of his own making."

"A Fool's Paradise" is a slighter interlude. It suggests that power to see life strangely is not something to shrink from, not something easily to be given up for the dull conformity of usual sight. To cure an idiosyncrasy may ruin a life. Yet one may regain the individuality upon higher ground. "All you have to do is to set yourself to learn and to grow so as to become wiser and gentler and more loving than your fellows, and you will see the faces of men and women once again in a hundred different facets, and they will move you to laughter or tears. . . . But men and women will hate you for your superiority and punish you for it; you will be thrust out of the paradise of ordinary life, and be made an outcast and a pariah. . . . The Vision Splendid has to be paid for, and the price is heavy."

"Within the Shadow" stands with Conrad's "Lagoon." It reveals Harris's knowledge of China; his insight into the passion and cruelty, the wisdom and devotion, of the Chinese soul. The lovely "Flower of the Waters," child wife of the shrewd elderly mandarin, Phang, falls in love with Wilson, a ship's officer. She gives herself to him in dear and desperate love, willing to pay with death. Discovered, she is taken before the magistrate; she lays her head quietly upon the block of stone, so that the elephant's foot may crush out her life. "He shifted his weight from one foot to another uneasily, but after a tap or two he lifted his right foot and put it down quietly on the girl's head, which squelched like a ripe mango."

Veils of Isis has beauty of style and depth of insight. It reveals Frank Harris—autobiographically in "The Ugly Duckling," symbolically in "The Veils of Isis." Much of his life is implicit in the tragedy of Piranello: the cleft in his nature, the motivation of his fall into worldliness. *Veils of Isis* is, next to *Unpath'd Waters,* his best volume of stories—a book of poignant beauty and heroic meaning. Harris is one who, like Amanthes, looked—beyond all veils—on beauty bare.

As the final music of the reed shaken by the wind of God, Harris published work which, already largely written in England, came into being during his life in America. The first series of *Contemporary Portraits* appeared, soon to be followed by other series of the same and his *Life and Confessions of Oscar Wilde*.

Contemporary Portraits had been begun long before. Harris's conversations with Carlyle had precipitated them: when the Scotch seer had told him to preserve the great whom he met "in their habit as they lived." Even before, the love of great men and the design of seeing and chronicling them had been implicit. It was his destiny to be the Boswell of the great of his day—a greater Boswell of greater men—a Boswell with a philosophic mind and a poetic style. To Hesketh Pearson he wrote, April 5, 1916, "I always felt that St. Paul and Ben Jonson missed the chance of their lives by writing their own life stories instead of the histories of the greater men whom they met. . . . No one will ever write of Carlyle or Renan or Davidson or Maupassant or Verlaine or France, in the future, without bottoming himself on my work. Every new 'Portrait' I do of the Shining Ones I have known is sure to increase my readers in all time to come." Harris was like his own Mr. Penry, he used the magic glasses of his own genius to show us that of the great masters of the world.

The *Portraits* are not biographies. Biographies are the novels of human lives; *Contemporary Portraits* are the short stories of biography. Or they are intense swift intimations of body and soul such as El Greco created.

The sitters for the first series of *Portraits* were among the greatest that he was ever to meet; the memories of these men, too, had gathered longest in his soul. They begin with the grave, noble realization of Carlyle, a verbal counterpart to Whistler's painting. This contains controversy: Carlyle's alleged sexual impotence and abstinence. But the interpretation of Carlyle's nature, of his destiny as a statesman of the deed, of his stature as man and artist, is a work of integrity and grandeur. There are portraits, too, of very different men: Renan, that lucid Gallic candle with a sprinkle of salt in the flame, with his clear, limited intelligence, his sentimentality like the music of Gounod, his candor up to the limits of his character; or Matthew Arnold, the English Renan, with his austere scholarly poetry and his fine thin mind, chilled by English prudery till it could call Keats' letters "underbred." There are the suave salacious Anatole France; the lesser Maeterlinck; the tragic realist, de Maupassant, whose heart was too sensitive to the hurt of pity and the lure of lust. There are Oscar Wilde; and the stinging brilliant butterfly, Whistler, with his fighting clarity of wit, his mist-tones and arrangements, his austere puritan portraits of motherhood and Carlyle. There are the artists who, breaking out of decorum, wrote and lived with headlong ferocity—Verlaine, Burton, Middleton. Slighter essays deal with Swinburne and Browning. Harris never "saw Browning plain": the English reticence baffled him; the romantic purity (not Puritan!) escaped him; the interpretation of life in terms of adventure not terminated by death was beyond him. But there were great portraits of Burton and Davidson, both frustrated by an England that scorned poets; the stallion spirit of Burton, greater Raleigh whose Elizabeth was Victoria. Meredith is also well portrayed, and Rodin. Reading such portraits, Shaw in sheer admiration was constrained to call Harris a greater Plutarch. Only Harris, Shaw thought, could play the part of Ulysses among the suitors: he alone could bend the bow!

Many have objected—often friends or relatives of those pictured. "Lies" is a frequent stone; "libels" a peculiarly jagged brick. Mediocrities forget that Harris's essays on Carlyle or on all the great make them immortal: he had malice only toward the base, and charity even for Herbert Spencer. Moreover he made it a rule at first to write only of those he could love. He felt that the real was enough—if only it was crowned with stars. He thought love was the way—for love alone saw into the soul; love alone, also, could see that even shadows (the faults, the vices) were merely the dark relief that made the noble qualities more intensely real.

Did the good burghers like the way Rembrandt painted them in "The Night Watch"? Yet his shadows, like his lights, came from love: he bestowed immortality on their protesting hearts. To notice shadows is a part of love; to leave them out is to write truly with hate. Are we not familiar with the "family biography" where the blemishes are removed and the man made inhuman? What sort of man never casts a shadow? Mediocrity also labels that "exaggeration" which is actually only a greater ability to experience life. When the lady objected to Turner's sunsets, "But Mr. Turner, I never saw a sunset like that!" he answered, "Madame, don't you wish you could?"

The sober fact is that overwhelming evidence shows how well Frank Harris knew, and how well he was known by, the great of the earth during his time. There is a published list of letters from one hundred and forty-five different people—autographed— that were selected for sale from the thousands that Harris had received. They included seven letters from Arnold Bennett, two from Lord Arthur Balfour, five from Coventry Patmore, *eighteen* from the Rt. Honorable Winston Churchill, two from Mrs. Patrick Campbell, two from Joseph Caillaux, four from Sir Charles Dilke, four from John Davidson, three from Eugene Debs, one from Ernest Dowson, seven from Lord Dunsany, one from Froude, three from King Edward, three from Thomas Huxley, two from Pierre Loti, one from Henri Matisse, two from Maeterlinck, one from Guy de Maupassant, twenty from Ouida, one from Walter Pater, one from Rodin, one from Cecil Rhodes, three from Olive Schreiner, two from Theodore Roosevelt, seven from George Russell (Æ), one from Christina Rossetti, three from John Tyndall, four from Beerbohm Tree, one each from Verlaine, Alfred Russell Wallace, and Whistler, four from Yeats, and one from Zola. The correspondents cited are only chance selections from a wealth of names. And these letters were only a few—probably the least of all in essential value—that were selected, out of thousands, for sale! Among the letters received from Winston Churchill there was a *wedding invitation*. And Winston Churchill was so very anxious to have Frank Harris attend his wedding in London that *he not only sent him an engraved invitation with a card to attend the church services, but he also pleaded with Harris by cable, urging him to attend the ceremony*. Surely after such evidence of Harris's knowledge and friendships, the most sceptical should be assured. Even doubting Thomas believed when his fingers touched the nail prints in the hands!

The reception of *Contemporary Portraits* was comparable to that of *Leaves of Grass*. The *Nation* patronized him: "Mr. Frank Harris has patronized a number of the great men of the earth." It called him "condescending"; it said it was a pity he could not "eliminate himself." (Would one ask Whistler to "eliminate himself" from his portrait of Carlyle, or El Greco to "eliminate himself" from his Toledo?) The *Springfield Republican* noticed, with the usual pathological bias of Harris critics, the sex angle: it was a "scandal book" which, even as scandal, failed. Only Mencken did Harris justice and redeemed America. "I know of no more brilliant evocations of personality in any literature. . . . Here is an American, who, when all values are reckoned up, will be found to have been a sound artist and an extremely intelligent, courageous, and original man—and infinitely the superior of the poor dolts who tried so childishly to dispose of him." [7]

Harris wrote Kate Stephens, July 18, 1915, "Have you seen the contemptuous brainless notice of *Contemporary Portraits* in the New York *Sun*—'journalism . . . bright . . . the earliest are the best.' And the joke is no one knows which are the earliest! A poor foolish blind guide who doesn't see that the whole book is the first defense of the artist and seer and prophet which has appeared in literature. I kept the book by me in print for years; correcting this, rewriting that! and this is my reward—like Don Quixote to be trampled under the hooves of the swine!

"The incurable malignity of the mediocritie! Joubert says 'moderation in praise is the best sign of mediocrity.' I would say of the

---

[7] H. L. Mencken, *Prejudices: Third Series.* Alfred A. Knopf, Inc.

second-rate, for surely *hatred* of the new and good work is the symbol of mediocrity!

"Still what *does* it matter! . . . The most awful text in the Bible is: *Neither did His brethren believe in Him.* And as His pretensions grew—the sign and proof of His sincerity—the disbelief grew acrid; He declared: *I am the bread of life . . . and from that time many of His disciples went back and walked no more with Him.* How their withdrawals must have bruised His heart and tinged with sad despair His resolve to go up to Jerusalem for the supreme ordeal!"

Harris wrote to Michael Monahan (August 24, 1916): "I explain such extravagances of praise and blame by the fact that there are no masters in America. You get accustomed to treat every one as second or third rate, and generally you are right. But now and then you are wrong. And while extravagant praise can't do much real harm, extravagant condemnation can do a great deal. You said once of something of mine that it was very clever and interesting and all the rest of it, but I am not a 'Titan.' I have used the phrase somewhere. You are quite right, I am not a Titan, but one of the Immortals. Nothing Titanic about me, but Olympian. I write all this to you because instead of commencing by self-praise, as Shaw and Schopenhauer did, I am ending with it, like Meredith—driven to it by that dreadful moderation in praise which is the mark of the mediocre." [8]

Contemporary Portraits, Second Series, appeared in 1919. It is the greatest of the volumes in at least two portraits: those of Ernest Dowson and James Thomson. It contains a sprightly appraisal of Shaw (with Shaw's witty rebuttal) and the etching-in-acid of the fortunate George Moore. The portraits of Dowson and Thomson are studies in love and sorrow, lyric dramas of deepest understanding and highest style. Harris gives us Dowson essen-

---

[8] Published in "Recollections and Impressions of One Who Knew Him." *The Catholic World,* December, 1932.

tially—the poet of grief's monotone, the singer of Cynara; and also overtones of the doom of every poet betrayed by some *Belle Dame Sans Merci.* The portrait of Thomson is like a stormy sea lit by blood-red gleams of Turner's sunsets. It is a clamor of mighty waters lifted against the pull of the dead moon. One cannot forget its cadences: "The weary weight of this unintelligible world lay heavy on me and the builded desolation and passionate despair of Thomson's poem took complete possession of my spirit. Verse after verse, once read, printed itself on my brain; ever since they come back to me in dark hours, and I find myself using them as a bitter tonic. . . . Such words sink deep into the heart as meteors into the earth dropped from some higher sphere." It is music comparable to a death-march by Chopin; it looms like some statue in black marble by Michelangelo.

Contemporary Portraits, Third Series, is good—but not better. That it contains fewer men of major stature was not Harris's fault. Wells was lightly sketched, deftly appraised; Upton Sinclair was fairly, even fondly, done in water colors. Winston Churchill, John Galsworthy, and several younger men, were sketched in black and white. There was one failure. Harris was unable to do justice to Chesterton, that Don John of Austria fighting his Lepanto against modern nihilism, that poet of the great *Ballad of the White Horse,* that fighter in Cobbett's style for the People. The best portrait is of Cunninghame Graham: he rides through the pages as the Jeb Stuart of literature. Arthur Symons is there too: delicate poet, critic in pastels, brave under the ravaging of the years. And Harris gives us Alfred Russell Wallace: greatest scientist of evolution, broad and sane like the earth of the prairies. Strange that mysticism could come out of materialism, like honey out of Samson's slain lion! Harris could not hear the celestial harmonies that "piped to the spirit ditties of no tone"; but he respected the man who did hear. Harris paints Huxley, too, a man more limited—a John Bull of the mind. Finally there is Walt Whitman, in whom America became a man.

Contemporary Portraits, Fourth Series, deals with a larger number of living contemporaries, whom Harris had known for a shorter time. The portraits are limited by lesser knowledge and the restraint of existing relationships. But of one contemporary he painted a great portrait—that of the noblest woman he ever knew, Emma Goldman. The greatest portraits were those of Wagner and Turgenief. Harris called Turgenief's a snapshot; he felt that he had seen the great Russian only in passing by, and had been tangent to his genius; but the picture endures and glows for all its brevity and its regret for things unsaid. The portrait of Wagner is memorable. It has been challenged; but if Harris never met him (as the sceptics claim), the marvel is all the more: and is it not possible for a Daumier to paint a Don Quixote whom he has never seen? Wagner comes alive: the little hawk-nosed fellow with the plowshare chin, the genius who suffered too deeply from the envy of the mediocre, and who knew his own worth with all the plangency of one of his own operas.

In *Latest Contemporary Portraits* Harris rescales Himalaya. There is a study of saint and seer in Ireland, the great "Æ." There is an essay on the ignored immortal, Louis Sullivan, the architect in the windy sprawl of Chicago. There are portraits of the heroes of the human cause: the good exile, Peter Kropotkin; the woman not glamorous in body but heroic in mind, Annie Besant. There is the essay on Housman, who never grew up though he lived eighty years. There is the memorable meeting, when Harris recited:

> *Oh, God will save her, fear you not:*
> *Be you the men you've been,*
> *Get you the sons your fathers got*
> *And* God *will save the Queen!*

He recited them beautifully, but made the last verse sarcasm—as he supposed it was. Housman replied sharply that it was not so, not so at all! He had meant exactly what he had said. How could anyone misread it? He added fiercely, "I can only reject and resent your—your truculent praise." (What a word for some of Harris's criticism: "truculent praise"!) What more was there to say or do? Only to pay the bill and leave. They had met without meeting. Harris had done his best; he had meant no offense and was puzzled that the poet should take any. But what a poet Housman was!—of monotone, to be sure, but in his highest formulations of his single mood, how poignant!

> *Here hang I, and right and left,*
> *Two poor fellows hang for theft:*
> *All the same the luck we prove*
> *Though the midmost hangs for love.*

In the portrait, as elsewhere, Harris quotes what he thinks are the greatest lines:

> *Be still, my soul, be still: it is but for a season:*
> *Let us endure an hour and see injustice done.*

When Harris died there were on his desk manuscripts of other portraits. Many have been lost in the shuffle of war, but years before his death Harris gave one to Einar Lyngklip, who brought it to America and tried again and again—vainly—to interest some American editor. A quotation will show its quality.

"GABRIEL D'ANNUNZIO"

"Popularity is the varnish of talent, as fame is the patina conferred by time on genius. The varnish brightens the colors, holds them together, tends to preserve the picture: but it is not otherwise important. We know all about fame: it comes from a man's peers, and it is slowly built up by generation after generation; but popularity is a sort of wind-blow, and falls at haphazard. For many years now d'Annunzio, the Italian poet and novelist, has been living in a perfect blare of applause. Whatever he says is noted by the papers and trumpeted abroad; his every movement is a triumphal progress; he is throned as a monarch and holds a sort of Court with a vast retinue of admirers.

"Naturally one hears now and then what one might call a caesura in the hymn of adulation.

"At a reception one evening d'Annunzio dropped his handkerchief by chance; a young lady picked it up and handed it to him with a pretty smile. . . .

"D'Annunzio bowed and, seeing she was pretty, replied with royal amiability: 'Keep it, Madamoiselle; you may keep it in memory of me. . . .'

"The American girl's smile vanished; holding the handkerchief carefully between finger and thumb, she walked to the fire and dropped it on the embers. A smile spread on every face but the Italian's. Such incidents, however, hardly supply discord enough to spoil the universal harmony. On all hands d'Annunzio is hailed as a genius, a great writer, a lord of words, a master of deathless music.

"Snobbishness is responsible for half the fuss, and jingoism for nearly the other half. The pyramid of praise stands on its apex. . . .

"In person he is insignificant: a little fat man of five-feet-four, or thereabouts, with podgy figure, tightly cased in ultra-fashionable clothes (open war between vanity and gluttony). He looks like a typical Southerner of sixty or sixty-five; his head is quite bald, his mustache preternaturally black; his nose well-formed, his eyes remarkable—large, almond-brown, vivacious, bright.

"His works every Italian knows: half a dozen novels, all stories of passion, or jealousy, or hate engendered by desire. Himself the hero always, half panther, half poet, human-cruel; an irresolute sensual artist who is utterly unable to see himself from the outside and is without any faintest gleam of humor. Now and then a woman is recognizable as the Duse by cicatrices of age and the malady of an unhappy love. The figures seem to move before us as in a furnace; the half-naked bodies glow like baking clay in the vibrating heat-mist. The prose is like a soft carpet under one's feet, and silken curtains, half-hiding, half-revealing.

"His poems show d'Annunzio's literary gift better than his prose: they are full of pictures, full of sonorous, beautiful cadences, with now and then hints of life, suggestions of desire, but he has never yet written a poem that can live with the best of Leopardi or Carducci. His plays, on the other hand, discover the essential weakness of thought, his want of originality, of what Goethe and Carlyle called genius. D'Annunzio is certainly not a *seer;* but lives with unconscious complacency within all the modern conventions. An almost perfect type of the man of talent, he has a superb gift of rhythmic, sonorous speech: it is as if an ordinary and very sensuous nature had been endowed with an astonishingly melodious and beautiful voice. . . ."

At the end Harris ironically notes the reward of the worldly talent: "His allegiance to Mussolini has been superbly acknowledged: he has been made a Prince and given a great villa-palace by the Italian government. All the approaches to his mansion are guarded by black-coated Fascisti soldiers and the interior is graced not only by Aubusson carpets and splendid tapestries and pictures, but also by marble presentments of his coat of arms. It is the bare truth to say that no poet, no writer, no heaven-sent genius, has ever been so rewarded in all recorded time."

Harris told Einar Lyngklip that he intended to use this in the Sixth, or possibly in the Seventh Series of his *Contemporary Portraits.*

In all the volumes one finds no gossipy chitchat by a sly, knowing journalist, lost amid superficial facets, surface facts, social adjustments; here is a master jewelsmith, studying diamonds to determine the water, and then perfectly describing the luster of each gem—and the flaws and strains. A usual question is: "But are they *true?*" Does one ask of El Greco's portraits of priest or grandee in that lost Spain: "But are they *true?*" Does one ask of van Gogh's painting of the woman of Arles: "But is it *true?*"

Do we mean true to the wits of Main Street—or true to the vision of God? Could the very man portrayed, or the most intimate of his friends, tell us if the pictures are "true"? For the function of the painter is to see more than the man himself sees, more than his friends see.

The climax of *Contemporary Portraits* was *The Life and Confessions of Oscar Wilde*. This was Harris's most successful book: even during his life some 40,000 were sold.

Shaw called it the great life, by which Wilde's reputation must stand or fall. In 1939—twenty-two years later—he wrote a preface to a new edition. There he reiterates his former verdict: "Now that I am better informed, am I going to stick to my old estimate? I am afraid the reply must be, 'More than ever.'" Mrs. Harris tells how the last preface by Shaw came to be written. The fiery Robert Sherard—to whom Wilde once wrote, "Don't fight more than six duels a week"—had written a book which Shaw calls "frantic," entitled *Bernard Shaw, Frank Harris, and Oscar Wilde;* its purpose was to prove that Harris's life of Wilde was an imposture. Mrs. Harris had long wished a new edition of the book, and had repeatedly asked Shaw to write a preface. Shaw had refused, pleading his age, his preoccupation with his own work, the needlessness of prefacing such a book, the general hatred of Harris and the impossibility of yet defending him. . . . But when Sherard's book appeared, Shaw cabled Mrs. Harris that he would write the preface.

Mencken called the *Life of Wilde* "the best biography ever written by an American—an astonishingly frank, searching, and vivid reconstruction of character—a piece of criticism that makes all ordinary criticism seem professorial and lifeless." [9] Twenty-five years later, Arthur Leonard Ross wrote to Mencken, asking him if he still rated the book so highly. Mencken answered: "On reflection, I can't think of a better."

Harris himself knew its greatness. Upton Sinclair wrote him

[9] Mencken, *op. cit.*

that it was among the four or five great biographies of the world. Harris replied: "Name the others."

The greatest quality of the *Life of Wilde* is not patient accuracy of detail, but glowing realization. The book is not a mere chronicle of movement through time; it is a poetic and philosophic interpretation. Harris integrates Wilde with life; he shows him as a symbol; he makes his life the drama of the fate of genius. The book continues to sell steadily through the years, and is already that rare thing called "a publisher's classic." Beyond all count of sales, it lives among the great biographies of the world—a grave splendor.

Chapter XI

THE SIDEWALKS OF NEW YORK

(1914-1920)

FRANK HARRIS published between 1914 and 1920 much of his greatest work; behind him lay fame as editor and man, and a record of great books; yet American editors did not know him or want his work. What was he to do, since the power and the glory would not bring him the daily bread? Like Carlyle, he turned to lecturing. If few read his work, more might listen to his voice: the imperious personality, the magnificent speech, might (as the Americans said) "put him across."

He lectured in New York City, at a hotel in the Catskills, and in the Middle West. The program of his lectures at the Bear and Fox Inn in the Catskills is a collectors' item, and is practically unprocurable.

As a lecturer, he had an imperious, even arrogant, presence; intense magnetism; a voice like ocean tides. Beyond these there were the play of a great mind, a distinction of style, wit, allusion, anecdote, philosophy, epigram, image, pity for the world's victims, anger for the world's ways with them. He lived his lectures—as artist who fashioned, as actor who gave.

Often he did not keep to the topic: scheduled to lecture on Shaw, he might at the door—or halfway to the platform—decide to speak on Shakespeare.

Once he learned that two ladies were present who had come to hear him because he had been in Brixton Gaol. Toward the close of his lecture, he asked both to stand; when neither obeyed, he castigated English injustice, declaring that for his beliefs he would gladly go to jail and stay till he rotted—till he *rotted*.

Gerald Cumberland gives a vivid acccount of an earlier lecture in Manchester, England, which may paint his American manner too. Cumberland describes the assembly of "pale men and spectacled women," the fiery provocative Harris, scattering ideas like sparks, girding at respectability; upholding "a wonderful ideal of chivalry and nobility and condemning, en bloc, the whole human race and particularly that portion of it seated before him." Rustles from "ladies of both sexes" testified to the wind of his eloquence among the aspens. One lady, when he paused, applauded; a few weakly joined her; a brave soul ejaculated "Bravo!" Harris, thrusting out his chin, went on to attack the idol of Manchester, Professor C. H. Harford. Harford had just called Harris's *The Man Shakespeare* "a disgrace to British scholarship." Harris proceeded to flay Harford alive, as Hercules flayed the satyr: he used "scalding invective and the most terrible irony. Each sentence he spoke appeared to be the last word in bitterness; but each leaped above and beyond its predecessor, until at length the speaker had lashed himself into a state of feeling to express which words were useless. He stopped magnificently and this time the room rang with applause. . . . They applauded him with enthusiasm, and they did so because they had been deeply stirred by eloquence that can only be described as superb and by anger that was lava-hot in its sincerity. Briefly, the lecture was an overwhelming success." [1]

Of Harris's American lectures, Raymond Thomson writes: "I opened the door at 57 and had my first sight of Frank, who was at the moment telling some seventy-five persons in a mixed company about Clemenceau out of his personal impressions. Frank's face was a formidable first impact: a face that seemed more com-

[1] Gerald Cumberland: *Set Down in Malice*.

bative than John L. Sullivan's, with a challenge in the combed-flat hair, long narrowed eyes, and black Kaiser-like mustachios. . . . The impression of combative challenge was deepened by a rich, resonant, bass-baritone voice which Frank used with subtle intonations, and always with athletic vigor.

"He was saying: 'There was good wine in Clemenceau. Like Burgundy, one of the great wines of the world. But if you take a barrel of Burgundy and put an onion in it, within a month you will have the sourest vinegar you ever tasted. Well, life supplied Clemenceau with the onion! Do you remember his story of the blind Chinese who regained his sight and after looking about him asked to have his sight put out again?' (The written transcription of his talk is like words without music.)

"From the first fighting impression on through a series of first-hand memories of some of the greatest (including, of course, Wilde 'the greatest companion') Frank, like a great explorer, took us deeply into his revelation of Shakespeare; and even more wonderful remains his insight of Jesus ('Subject reverently treated' we were assured by a card in the window of 57). A subject that Frank himself said should be approached on one's knees, though he added critically: 'No man can be an ideal to us. But Jesus will remain an influence.'

"Frank's voice . . . with its dramatic or wistful undertones and overtones sounded the depths and heights of feeling, the Hell and Heaven of human being, though he could not even imitate the high notes of the upper registers. Still, in the thoughts that wander through eternity and in the soaring glance staring at the sky, he used his voice like a skilled musician on a cello that thrilled and won the hearts of many women and the admiration and sometimes the envy of many men. But it is like trying to describe a cello solo with orchestral accompaniment, this merely verbal attempt to describe Frank's voice.

"However, one remembers a night at the Rand School auditorium when Frank, during a talk about Shakespeare ('just as if he had gone out of the room') turned to telling us about Cleopatra. Without any make-up, but in his own very masculine appearance, he clasped his hands over his chest and slowly came forward on the platform while repeating the death-speech in which the woman 'cunning past thought' rises to the majestical height of a queen-soul in her everlasting farewell to the earth. In spite of his appearance, with the magic of his voice alone, Frank wrought the wonder of re-creation before our eyes. As acting alone, it was miraculous.

"Six years later, when Einar Lyngklip returned after several months in Nice, he told of being at a table in a restaurant with Frank, who was telling of Sarah Bernhardt's power to move her hearers to tears by the recitation of the multiplication table. Then Frank remarked, 'I can do it too.' Einar was not easily moved to tears, but he confessed with enthusiasm that Frank *had* so moved him by reciting the multiplication table—something he would not have believed possible."

(The reception was not always favorable, of course. Mary Austin, in *Earth Horizon,* says that Harris overpraised David Graham Phillips; kicked a chair; acted like a spoiled boy.)

Harris's mind was too swift for mediocrities: he would not return and explain. A champion on a toboggan, he took the curves at sixty and did not stop to pick up the passengers who were shaken off. When some dunce interrupted him with questions to which the answer was obvious in his books, he would fume and explode. Yet in a few moments he would calm his irritability, and, smiling, would soothe his listener with grace and charm. As lecturer, Harris was like Macready—who, as Othello, terrified his Desdemonas because in his heat of passion he was liable literally to strangle them. Frank Harris lived his lectures with the same heady passion.

In the course of his lectures he came to Lawrence, Kansas. He asked the address of Kate Stephens, the "slim girl with the heavy-lidded eyes" as he beautifully called her, his fellow-student and

Smith's fiancée. He corresponded with her from May 8, 1915, to October 19, 1916. His letters to her in their brief span embrace a comedy of character and a tragedy of friendship.

His first letter was written May 8, 1915.

"Dear Miss Kate Stephens,

"It is more than forty years since I last had the pleasure of seeing you. The other day I lectured at Lawrence, Kansas, and saw the excellent portrait of Professor Smith which called back to me all the scenes of that bygone time with a magic of representment.

"I asked about you and got your address and heard of your book on Professor Smith, which I should like to read:

"I want to have a talk with you. Will you let me come and see you some day and renew our friendship? I should like to very much." [2]

Many letters follow—generous, brilliant, touched with the desire to be the friend of the girl who had been so true to Byron Smith. He wrote her some of his most intimate, life-confiding letters; he trusted her utterly. He addressed her variously as "Dear, dear Miss Kate," "Dear Constancy," "Dear Diotima," and spoke with reticent kindness of her books; he dealt gently with her Kansas morality when sending her his *Wilde:* "I think it will flutter the dovecotes of Puritan sensibilities in your breast." She regarded him as a bad boy who had at last decided to be good. "Every erring child" (she wrote, July 12, 1915) "should have a bit of mother's apron-string tied to him. When you need the apron-string, come." Harris wrote: "So you expected to meet a hard cynical man-of-the-world and had to put up with the 'kid.'" Evidently she thought she found a child in him, for he writes: "You persist in calling me a child, and young, and I suppose anyone who can look forward to producing four books in one year may

[2] This and the ensuing quotations dealing with the Kate Stephens episode are taken from *Lies and Libels of Frank Harris.* Edited by Gerritt and Mary Caldwell Smith. Copyright, 1929, by Kate Stephens.

pass as possessing some of the productivity of youth. . . . Still,
that's how we halfmen live!" He treated her as an intellectual
equal, a woman of the world; she scolded him like a naughty boy
and called him "laddie."

He wrote graciously in another letter, "Your *Redbud* poem
delights me. I have found the lovely tree all along the slopes of
the Western prairies where the sky is higher than it is in other
lands."

Proof of his trust is his letter of July 4, 1915, telling of his love
for Laura, his first marriage, his financial adventures in England.

But meanwhile rifts were forming in the lute of this strange
impossible friendship. They began with her. She persisted in re-
garding him as a naughty child, at last sorry and willing to be
good; she lectured and scolded him (the comrade of Carlyle, Ruskin, Meredith, de Maupassant, Renoir, Taine, and Oscar Wilde!)
as if she were his spinster aunt. She waxed angry at his ideas: he
saw little idealism—none of her "magnificent idealism"—in
America; rather, he saw "savage individual greed run mad," "a
thin superficial culture without morals or even manners," and
idealism only "here and there in some starving heart." He was
also against the war, which to her was a crusade of pure white
against pure black. Worst, she thought him lax in morals: a
friend had seen him "with a blonde in a picture hat." The two
were so incompatible that the marvel is that their friendship lasted
so long; it lasted because Frank Harris was the tolerant, patient,
understanding friend, while she was the harsh, petulant censor.
The final break came because of Byron Smith's letters. She let
Harris read them; he marked certain passages; she thought them
too brief and few. She grew angry. He told the story of Smith's
supposed sexual weakness, and she was furious: it was "a lie and
a libel!" She became berserk, and ran amok in *Lies and Libels of
Frank Harris.*

His reaction was a quiet irony that infuriated her the more.
One of his last letters to her reads:

"Dear Kate Stephens,

"It is no use. We speak different languages, and are aeons apart.

"Your friend who saw me one evening with 'a blonde in a picture hat' probably saw me with my wife. He or she certainly did not see me with any other man's wife.

"I am glad you are feeling 'good.' Your optimism must be an excellent protective."

Apparently they never met again; and indeed they never *had* met.

Kate Stephens had been younger than Byron Smith; his student, she had fallen under his intellectual spell and had said yes to his quietly delayed proposal. She told Einar Lyngklip about it: "We had no regular courtship days. . . . I never saw Byron Smith regularly. I saw him daily in class. He came to the house whenever he could. He was very busy in those days teaching. . . . I never saw him alone. He came to the house generally on Sundays when he came in effect to see the whole family. I never went out with him except when we went for occasional buggy-rides. These were always during the day; I was never alone with him in the evening." Of her memories (on which she based her refutation of Harris) she said: "I did not keep a diary, and I found afterward I could not be sure of the exact order of many of the events." She added, "The letter dates and certain other records helped me to set it straight. I didn't have any private talks with Byron Smith. Our conversations were generally in the classroom before other students, or on the campus, or at my home while members of the family were present."

None can question Kate Stephens' integrity; all must question her capacity. She wanted to tell the truth about Harris, but she was not one who could, any more than Aunt Polly could tell the truth about Vincent van Gogh. She wrote that she wanted him married—he was already married!—to "a deep-bosomed woman" who would cook him "puddings" and "in the absence of a valet, would see that his stockings and necktie had no violent vendetta."

Her *Lies and Libels* is written with an acid that, as she wrote, she spilled over her own angry, shaking fingers. Its "facts" are based (as she told Lyngklip) on memories and guesses that were at least as fallible as any of Harris's. Many of the "lies" are quite unimportant; others are debatable; all ignore the reality that truth is an atmosphere and spirit, not the figures computed by an adding machine. The "libel" is Harris's belief that Smith suffered from a sexual wasting. Harris was almost certainly wrong; but, to him, it was nothing vicious: it gave pathos and reality to Byron Smith. Harris loved Smith, and praised him as the star-kindler of his whole life. Harris, far more than Kate Stephens—more even than Byron Smith himself—has lifted Smith into eternal note. One cannot read her book without feeling a pettiness gathering about the memory of Smith. One cannot read anything Harris wrote of Smith without feeling the splendor of the man, the valor and value of his life. The "lies and libels," as she calls them, are no crown of thorns, but a halo.

Meanwhile Frank Harris walked the sidewalks of New York. In outward presence he was fiery and original. Einar Lyngklip paints him to the life. "We were walking south on the west side of Fifth Avenue. At the corner of 42nd Street, we turned to cross. We had been talking about Jerusalem and Troy and archeology and cathedrals, Spain and the Alhambra, of Louis Sullivan and Wright and architecture; and Frank was telling me about his experiences in Chicago and what Sullivan said about the Grand Central Station in New York, when he suddenly decided to cross. Traffic was against us. He was impatient to show me something about the Grand Central Station and an inscription on it. He looked up and down the street, fuming, tapping his black walking stick on the pavement.

" 'Is there to be no end of this?' He leaned forward like a sailor looking into the wind and glowered into the line of traffic. 'Where is the policeman? Why doesn't he stop these mad drivers? Where do they think they're going? If they have pilots' licenses, they should be taken away for flying too low!'

"I was on the verge of daring to suggest that we wait until the lights change, when suddenly he raised both arms high in the air and stepped off the curb into the street. Alarmed at the mad look in his eyes, I jumped in front of him. He shut both eyes tight. A powerful push with his left arm shoved me aside. He lifted his right arm, and, with eyes still shut and cane held out in front of him and pointing directly ahead, he walked straight into the line of traffic.

"I stood breathless.

"Much later I realized that I had heard brakes screech. Tires on locked wheels screamed against asphalt. Men groaned. I saw cars leap to a stop in a locked line a block long in each direction. I smelled burning rubber. Drivers shouted and cursed. A woman fainted. Then I heard a whistle blow—it seemed far off.

"I was frozen with fright. I got a glimpse of him . . . in the center of a mass of steel and smoke and noise. Here was the end of him for sure!

"But when I looked again he seemed all by himself in the center of a clear path, walking resolutely through the almost perfect lane that had shaped itself for him as if by magic. His head was high, his cane still held rigidly out in front, his eyes still closed. When he stepped up to the opposite curb, he turned, happy and smiling, to wave to me, 'Come on!'

"When I had run over to him, I got there just in time to hear a man who was holding both hands to his chest gasp as if coming out of a trance. 'God-damned fool!' he shouted, 'Are you crazy?'

"Just then a traffic officer appeared, who drove his excited horse up onto the sidewalk straight at Harris, calling the author of all this everything he could lay his tongue to. But Frank choked him off in the middle of one colorful sentence, causing him to swallow half of it.

"Drawing himself up to his full five-and-a-half-foot height

(which seemed still more) he thundered: 'Well! Where have you been? Where were you when I wanted you? And here is something I want you to know. . . .' (I have no slightest notion of what it was he said, for I was as dumbfounded as the cop.)

"The policeman, indeed, sat open-mouthed on his horse as we walked away, and the crowd thickened from all sides and continued to mull about, asking how many had been killed.

"I was not the same again that day (nor ever again, since, in my feelings about Frank), but he went on with his discussion upon exactly the same note and from precisely the same point at which he left off on the other side of the street, and as collectedly as if in the interim nothing at all had happened."

When Frank Harris went walking in Central Park, he was so entranced by conversation that he did not notice any impediment until he was almost upon it. Then with a swift leap he cleared the park bench or child's tricycle like a bounding tiger. Once on Fifth Avenue, when he was about sixty-five (and looked forty), he encountered a young man. Harris was on the right side, but the young man would not give way. Frank stopped him by his imperious presence in the path, stood and stared, and then remarked in a deep angry voice: "For two pins, I'd knock you into the middle of the street!" The young man stared back in consternation; decided that his strange adversary would do what he said; and, stepping aside, let him pass.

Frank Harris once sought in Camden the house where Whitman had lived. Stopping the first policeman he met he asked the way. The policeman answered that he did not know any "Walt" Whitman: did he have a job in the mayor's office? Harris could hardly be restrained from lodging a complaint against a policeman who did not even know that America's greatest poet was dead.

Frank Harris's inner life in Manhattan was of a different sort. Raymond Thomson remembers how Harris would quote from the world's greatest poets, often unconsciously bettering the originals. In one of his sonnets Shakespeare writes:

> *They that level*
> *At my abuses, reckon up their own:*
> *I may be straight, though they themselves be bevel.*

Frank Harris, quoting, unconsciously changed it:

> *They that level*
> *At my abuses, reckon up their own:*
> *I may be straight,* though all the world *be bevel.*

The greater intensity of combativeness, hate, and defiance in Harris's fighting nature had reached a depth of feeling beyond that even of the goaded Shakespeare, who confessed himself only an enraged sheep in anger, who, "being much enforced showeth a hasty spark or two and straight is cold again." Frank was only rarely cool. His temperament blazed like an oil-soaked cloth.

Again, Keats, in one of his greatest sonnets, wrote:

> *I must die*
> *Like a sick eagle looking at the sky.*

Frank Harris, quoting, unconsciously changed it for the better; his passionate sense of defeat reached an inner intensity by saying:

> *I must die*
> *Like a sick eagle* staring *at the sky.*

In prose, too, Harris bettered even the greatest English. The thirty-eighth verse of the twentieth chapter of The Acts, the King James version, reads: *"Sorrowing most of all for the words which he spake, that they should see his face no more."* Frank Harris slightly but subtly changed it to perfection—*"Sorrowing most of all for the words he spake, that they should see his face no more forever."*

Thus Frank Harris, despite his lack of the native gift of song, was a poet. His soul, deeply brooding, concentrated in passion, found the great word; he who can by a single word better Keats or Shakespeare or the King James Bible is indeed a poet!

Through Manhattan Frank Harris walked largely unknown, as he had through London. Who saw Nietzsche in Zurich, or van Gogh in Arles, or Cézanne in Paris? Even in this world, the flesh has to fall away before the spirit can live. Frank Harris was, to most who met him, a man of wild opinions and spectacular dynamism. Yet he was all the while straight though all the world was bevel; and, if a sick eagle, one who, through the bars of his cage, stared at the *sky*.

Chapter XII

PEARSON'S MAGAZINE

(1916-1922)

"I HOPE TIME may be given me to do all my work," Harris wrote to Hesketh Pearson (September 19, 1916). "I have a sort of belief that no one dies in this world until his soul dies, and I am afraid my time may be near at hand because I do not seem to have grown in America. There is a sort of arrest in my development through the transplantation. It is a harsh unfriendly climate for the soul—this one of New York—and I have no roots here. I put out one little tendril now and then, but they all get nipped." [1] It was a natural but passing sadness. His soul was far from dead; it was growing toward some of its finest manifestations. One of them was *Pearson's Magazine.*

But first he was advertising manager for the Chesapeake and Ohio Railway.

This is not surprising. He had always loved railroads; he had written beautifully of them in *Confessional.* "The railroad and ocean liner have made change easy and travel a delight and wonder. Turner was the first, I suppose, to depict the poetry and mystery of the railroad; and to me, a wanderer from boyhood, the shining straight way has always been at once a magic symbol and an aspiration. 'Aladdin's Carpet,' I call it to myself with a shud-

[1] Hesketh Pearson, *Modern Men and Mummers.*

251

dering sense of ecstasy and delight; at any moment I can close my eyes and hear the *chunk-chunk, chunkety-chunk* of the blood beating in the great heart of the monster who will carry me to the home of Heart's Desire.

"The great railways of the world are to me beneficent Titans who have beauty and health and wonder as gifts and are always prodigal of bounty. Think of the Canadian Pacific, whose imperious purpose holds arrow-straight from Quebec to Vancouver, through untrodden pine-forests, over unchristened lakes and uncharted prairies and heaped up mountain-ranges to the great ocean where West and East are one. Think of the New York Central which follows the Hudson quietly for miles and then flings itself coil on coil over the Adirondacks to dart, straight as a serpent striking, to Chicago, a thousand miles away. Or recall for a moment the Cape Railway, like a homing pigeon circling around Table Mountain before it finds its line due north to Victoria Falls, the first breathing-place on its breathless flight of seven thousand miles to the Mediterranean Sea. . . ."[2]

Harris was employed as advertising manager for the Chesapeake and Ohio Railway Company on November 9, 1915, for a period ending May 1, 1916, at a salary of $400 a month plus traveling expenses. On the same date a contract was made with him by White Sulphur Springs, Incorporated, for his employment for the same period as advertising manager at a salary of $100 a month plus traveling expenses. He wrote a book on White Sulphur Springs which he intended to publish, but after submitting the manuscript he was told that a number of statements in it seemed unsatisfactory to the management, and that they could not agree to the publication. Harris declined to make any change in his manuscript, and as a result the work was never published. He did not prepare any advertising matter for the Chesapeake and Ohio Railway, but was "employed for the specific purpose of writing a book about White Sulphur Springs and . . . his duties

---

[2] "Travel in France." In *Confessional*, pp. 117-19.

were not supposed to cover any other activities." [3] The Chesapeake and Ohio Railway is most courteous in its references to
Harris, and was most courteous in its relations with him.

Mrs. Harris says that Frank was discouraged about the book
on White Sulphur Springs, and let the manuscript drift around
until it was lost. The matter illustrates his originality, which was
too intense ever to be used in the usual channels of "advertising";
and his integrity, which would not yield on artistic questions,
even in a book devoted to advertising.

But Frank Harris could not stay away from literature. If magazines would not publish him, he would find a magazine in which
he could publish himself.

In *Pearson's Magazine,* July, 1916, appeared a letter of policy
over his signature. "There are not many magazines in the United
States which I would consent to edit. *Pearson's* is the only magazine that suggests itself to me. It is frankly opposed to the mad
individualism we Americans misname Liberty; it advocates the
nationalization of the railroads, the telegraphs and telephones,
and the municipalization of public utilities; besides, its columns
are free, not bound by advertising or money interests of any kind
—a forum for sincere opinion, for the Truth and nothing but the
Truth.

"Consequently I welcomed the invitation to edit *Pearson's
Magazine.*"

He went on to outline his program. He wished to do what
Shaw said he had done for the *Saturday Review:* to gather
young writers of talent now lonely, unappreciated, without voice;
he wished to oppose a war which he regarded as worldly in the
evil sense and to advocate peace for the world; he wanted to set
up standards of international criticism, as meteor-exposer and
star-finder. "In fine, I am going to make a great many enemies

[3] This quotation and the preceding material come from a full and courteous
letter from Mr. Walter S. Jackson, Advertising Manager of the Chesapeake and
Ohio Railway, dated September 6, 1942.

for myself and few friends, but with that I shall have nothing to do. I shall sow with both hands." He concluded by asking his readers' indulgence, for "it takes some little time to learn how to steer a ship or a magazine."

So Harris became editor of *Pearson's*. The circulation grew amazingly. After four months of his editing, Arthur Little, the former full owner and manager, set down the following table. The sale of *Pearson's* in the New York Subway stands alone had been:

August, 1916 - - -	96
September, 1916 - -	191
October, 1916 - - -	330
November, 1916 - -	633 [4]

Pearson's had been passing through "muckraking." Like other popular magazines of the time, it had advocated a populism that, on its negative side, attacked "privilege," "money," and "pillage." Its official orientation was "radical," though, as usual then, it had no political connections and no formal economics. It had the tone of a radical D.D. who had gone into the Labor Movement. It was heavy, serious, righteous. It would not have sympathized with Wilde's wish to be a snake charmer and lure "the cobra to stir from the painted cloth or the reed basket that holds it," and "to sway to and fro in the air as a plant sways restfully in a stream." It would have been more apt to call a capitalist a cobra and to kill him with the first convenient club.

In introducing Harris, Little admitted this. Writing farewell to James Thompson (its editor for three years), and hail to Harris, Little said: "No reader can picture the unceasing war that has been waged against *Pearson's* for almost five years by the representatives and advocates of the power of pillage. . . . A couple of months ago I read two comments upon the magazine which caused me a lot of reflection. . . . One comment read: 'The only interesting thing about *Pearson's* is its policy. . . .' My own common sense told me that the comment was just. Carried away by enthusiasm of public-spiritedness *Pearson's* was being permitted to drift into an overbalanced state of seriousness." He had sought, therefore, a man who, continuing the policy of *Pearson's,* would at the same time make it brilliant. He had found Frank Harris.

If one can imagine William Jennings Bryan suddenly superseded by Oscar Wilde "feasting with panthers," he will realize the change that startled readers into attention. Yet Harris, unlike Wilde, wished to "wrestle with Caliban" as well as to "sport with Ariel." He continued the radical ideas of *Pearson's,* but he gave them style. It was as if *Uncle Tom's Cabin* had turned overnight into the grave might of a more brilliant Tolstoi. Shaw declared that he read every word of *Pearson's*—which was proof ultimate that Harris was really editing it.

The magazine *was* Frank Harris. Before him, it had been a painting by a member of the Royal Academy; now it was as personalized as a Rossetti or a Turner. Harris wrote most of it under his own name; much of the rest of it under pen names. When he did not write it, he discovered writers of talent: one of the foremost was Konrad Bercovici. Harris published his articles that no one else dared to—articles mordantly written on the ways of organized charity with the poor. Eugene Debs contributed papers on men whom he had known—Ingersoll, Riley, Wendell Phillips —in a strong homely style like winter apples.

There were at the time in America two magazines that had recognizable souls: The *Masses* and *Pearson's*. Others were well edited, well written, impeccable; but they were distinguished rather by occasional contributions of authors already established, for which they were able to pay munificently. *Pearson's* could hardly pay at all. Other magazines could afford Wells, Conrad, Kipling, Shaw; Harris (who had discovered most of them) could not. Having little money, he had to compensate for its lack by genius. And, with nothing to speak of in the way of money, he was able to outdo the magazines that had money, prestige, advertising, subscribers, and famous contributors. To reread *Pearson's* is to discover ageless youth. One must set the magazine with the brittle but brilliant *Dial* of Margaret Fuller, with the early *Atlantic* that published Emerson and Thoreau, and with the *Masses,* as one of the history-making magazines of America. And *Pearson's* was the greatest of them all.

Frank Harris was a star-finder. He was eager to discover new talent, generous in his appreciation, never one to use the "tepid praise which is the hall-mark of mediocrity." To one young poet, at the time otherwise unknown, he wrote: "Fancy the genuine thing sung in America! I take shame to myself that I do not know your work." Such words were as if Roland on his way to the wars paused to give accolade to a little lad by the roadside.

In poetry Harris's taste was both daring and conservative. He had no need to prate about a "New Poetry," for poetry had never grown old. Poetry, he knew, is neither new nor old: it is beyond the mere criterion of time. What is newer than Homer, what is older than today's sweet singer of nonentity? There is only high poetry—and verse. He was too good a lover of Shakespeare and Blake to succumb to the easy acclaim of Masters, Sandburg, Amy Lowell; or even to the uncritical acclaim of Edna Millay and Robert Frost. He discovered some fine and lovely things here and there by poets ignored by the ballyhoo of the dominant cliques. Two poems, without allocation to any definite authors, are especially lovely: "Little Roads" and "Last Year's Love." Harris himself contributed one poem that shows his own best singing strength.

FRANK HARRIS'S CONFESSION

This Friday is my birthday.
If you want to know my age,
You can work the following problem
On the margin of the page.

I'm nineteen when I'm happy,
  And ninety when I'm sad;
I'm forty when I'm sensible,
  And nothing when I'm mad.

I'm seven in the country
  And a thousand in the towns,
And as old and young as all the earth
  When I am on the Downs.[5]

I'm green in love and grey in thought—
  That's all you need to know.
Never you mind how old I am
  As Februaries go.[6]

Harris published the fine "Pagan Chant" of Joseph Freeman (June, 1921); the lovely shining "Mood" of Arthur Symons (February, 1919); the excellent "Summer Passes" by George William Browning (January, 1918); the poignant "Winter" by Frederick Manning. He adopted, too, the wise custom of publishing lesser known great poems by less popular great poets of the past, like James Thomson and William Blake.

In his leading articles—far too personal to be the usual "editorials"—he spoke his own mind on great themes. He was against the war, for both sides; he was against American participation. He criticized the way it was waged, the lack of audacity and imagination, the stupid catch-as-catch-can in the mud and blood of the trenches. But he did not confine himself to such issues. There were articles by Bercovici on charity and Rumania; by Charles Edward Russell on "The Inside of the Pork Barrel"; by O. M. Simons on Labor; by Guido Bruno on Greenwich Village. The most living things were Harris's portraits of the great he had known; his brilliant comments on life and literature; his re-

[5] Near Tannersville in the Catskills.
[6] *Pearson's*, April, 1920.

views of books; his own great stories. He republished "The Magic Glasses," "The Irony of Chance," "The Ugly Duckling," and others. Thus in the coarse pulpwood pages of *Pearson's* appeared masterpieces of world-criticism, masterpieces of world-fiction.

In the book reviews he relentlessly exposed the comets that the populace took for stars; and he boldly affirmed the splendor of stars and even constellations that the usual critics ignored. He was merciless to the puffed mediocrity of Wells' *Outline of History*. He was penetratingly appreciative of *The Way of Martha and the Way of Mary*, by Stephen Graham; of the first novels of Frank Swinnerton; of the strange black flame of D. H. Lawrence; of W. H. Hudson's *Far Away and Long Ago;* and of so fine a poet as Gladys Cromwell.

He discovered several who later made their place as brilliant shatterers of shams or as candid commentators: among them, J. L. Spivak [7] and Elmer Davis. [8]

He himself was a prophet. In June, 1919, he wrote on "The Coming World War": "Already one sees shaping itself in the womb of time this triple alliance of Germany, Russia, and Japan. . . . Great Britian and France will not fight for Poland [did they, at first, beyond a pitiful gesture?] nor for the Czecho-Slav Republic, nor for Rumania, nor for Jugo-Slavia, nor for anything but their own existence. God help Poland!" He went on: "Now the Allies forbid her [Germany] to have more than 100,000 men: she will have 1,000,000 of the best surely, and her chemists will supply them with more terrible weapons than cannon or submarines or Zeppelins. . . . America is going to use her brains to get rich; Great Britain is on the same tack; France and Italy too, in a milder way. Germany is forced to use her brains to get strong in a military sense. In ten years God pity Poland!" He wrote this in 1919; the tragedy of Poland came in 1939—two decades later, instead of the one he allowed.

[7] March, 1919.
[8] August, 1917.

In "Napoleon's Tactics" he told how a truly modern war would be fought by genius—anticipating much of the lightning-war of Hitler; this (he pleaded in vain) should be inaugurated by the generals of the Allies.[9]

The result of all this was a growing subscription list and a genuine love for *Pearson's*. The letters to the editor focused an even wider delight in a magazine at once so true to the principles of social advance and in itself so brilliant. Upton Sinclair wrote: "Congratulations on the magazine you are making. Assuredly you are the most interesting writer we have in this country!"

A letter to Hesketh Pearson (April 30, 1918) describes Frank Harris's daily life as editor. "You ask for details of my daily life. I wake at about eight in the morning, get a grapefruit and a couple of cups of tea, and write or dictate till twelve-thirty; then I get up and dress. I try to go out for five or ten minutes' walk or run before my lunch at one-thirty; from two-thirty to three-thirty I snoozle; at three-thirty I go to the office to see people, deal with correspondence, calls, etc.; from six to seven-thirty I take a walk if I can; then I come in and have a cup of soup, no bread; afterwards I either read or correct manuscript till one o'clock. Then I am supposed to go to bed; but if I have taken any coffee during the day, and it is a perpetual temptation to me, I probably do not sleep till three or four and pay for it by feeling tired and worn out next morning." [10]

His methods of editing are illuminated by Elsa Gidlow. An unknown Canadian girl with a talent for writing, she came to New York; Frank Harris employed her on *Pearson's*. To give her a lesson in editing, he set a problem: *Pearson's* was printing and selling little masterpieces as booklets, among them "The Inheritors" by de Maupassant. This was a couple of paragraphs too long for a certain specified number of pages. Harris sent her the proof, telling her to cut it without omitting anything essential.

[9] *Pearson's*, May, 1918.
[10] Hesketh Pearson, *op. cit.*

It was like asking a journeyman to chip a Kimberley diamond. After the better part of a day, she surprised him by returning the proofs with the requisite omissions. He had supposed it impossible. He was so pleased that he raised her salary from $25 to $30 a week. Two weeks later, displeased by something, he reduced her salary from $30 to $25 again. Miss Gidlow comments: "I think Harris got the best out of those around him because he made a direct appeal to what little (or much) greatness there might be in each individual, and assumed they would give of that greatness in dealing with him."

His action came from his conviction of the divinity of the individual: he wished to help men to find themselves; otherwise it was futile for man to gain the world. "No teacher so far," he said, "has even thought of helping men and women to find out the particular power which constitutes their essence and in-being and justifies their existence. And so nine men and women out of ten go through life without realizing their own special natures: they cannot lose their souls for they have never found them." [11]

As editor of *Pearson's* Harris was often asked to lecture. It helped the magazine, for it advertised the editor; it helped him, for he needed the money. (He made only a precarious living from *Pearson's*.) In his lecturing he traveled into the Middle West again, sometimes to Chicago, which, he felt, would become the true capital of the United States. It had always been a city of space and winds, grandiose and savage like a fierce Sioux chief with broad shoulders, and skyscrapers of eagle-plumes, and bangles of lights. The river, now changed from the very direction he had known as a boy, was no longer a slow open sewer, but beautiful —especially at night. The lights beside it, mirrored in it as golden arcs, gleamed like those beside the harbor waters of the Antwerp that Rembrandt had seen. But the houses were mean, especially millionaire's row along the lake: did the sky there owe its height to its aversion from such atrocities of man? It seemed to him, sometimes, that Americans had signed a private declaration of

[11] *My Life and Loves,* Vol. I, "Foreword," p. xviii.

independence from beauty, so that each might be free to follow his own ugliness.

But one day, passing the Auditorium, he stopped to stare. "Unmistakable—great height, long lines unbroken, leading the eye up and then horizontal mass cutting the sky without a break, one of the great buildings of the world, fit to compare with the Cathedral of Chartres or San Sophia, and modern at that, wholly modern." [12] How, in God's name, did it get there?

He found that it was the work of Louis Sullivan, an ignored immortal. He discovered two of Sullivan's buildings: the Schiller Theater with its "unmistakable great air"; and the department store of Carson, Pirie, Scott & Co., "which made all other stores and office buildings in the world look tawdry and foolish, or merely pretentious." The greatest architect since Christopher Wren, perhaps, working ignored and unknown!

And there was the Chicago Art Gallery. In that shelter of grace he could shut out the welter of commerce, the driven hurrying thousands. He sought a Japanese *kakemono* and a fight between two animals by Sosen, and stumbled suddenly into another room. It was glowing with the magic of Monet—Claude Monet at his best. "By the door water lilies in a pond; nothing but the white blossoms against green leaves in the *glauque* water . . . here in front some rosy buds half open; the whole thing a miracle of truth and beauty interfused." And nearby was another Monet, "an herbaceous border of flowers leading in the distance to a little arch in his own garden. On both sides of the walk common flowers of every sort are growing higgledy-piggledy as in nature; they are all represented miraculously; but withal there is vista and a beyond, atmosphere of the rarest, the whole scene transmuted into the ineffable, lifted so to speak, by sheer genius, till a bit of this earth of ours became a part of Paradise." No one had ever painted better, he said; no one ever could paint better. A world's masterpiece! And there, on the other wall, a Whistler!— Waterloo Bridge "pictured with all Whistler's magic, and then

[12] "Louis Sullivan." In *Latest Contemporary Portraits*, pp. 169-70.

the towers of Westminster seen through the mist, and finally the mean hard outlines of Charing Cross Railway Bridge, made wonderful because seen through a haze of transfiguring beauty." [13] An interlude of art, here in the city that was hog-butcher to the nation, dusty with the toil of piling job on job!

In Chicago he debated with the witty Percy Ward: *Is Life Worth Living?* In cataract of oratory, headlong, scornful, gravely vibrant with hope for the Kingdom of Man and with joy in the tragic adventure of man's pilgrimage, he urged that we should say *Yes!* to life. The true Harris was here; the fighter, the adventurer, the creator who rejoiced even in the night because it was the blackboard on which the sun could write the day.

But meanwhile bad luck shadowed his editorship.

At the very beginning, a number of employees, led by Ricker, the business manager, had used the mailing list for promotion of oil stock. Thus Harris took over a magazine already tainted by trickery of which he was entirely innocent.

He had hardly got the magazine stabilized when America entered the war. The Postmaster General consistently threatened to revoke his mailing privileges. In order to avoid the expected demand that a certain issue should be held up until it could be examined, Harris brought the magazine out early each month. Friends at the Post Office Department warned him when the magazine was to be held up. He offered to submit the copy regularly in advance and let the authorities pass on it: they refused. Postmaster General Burleson never found anything that was seditious; he never suppressed any issue. Yet he continued to keep the magazine from the mails as long as he could each month, sometimes making an issue two weeks late. His purpose was to destroy the paper financially rather than provoke the odium that would result from suppressing it outright. He succeeded in starving it by blockade; but thanks to Frank Harris, he could not kill it. Harried by such tactics, Harris came to feel that the United States were becoming "the Benighted States."

[13] *Ibid.*

Also he fell into disfavor with the authorities by attacking the New York Night Court. He introduced his investigations thus: "I intend to go about New York with a lantern, . . . and turn the light in many obscure corners. The underworld of poverty and suffering, in this the capital city of Christendom, is appalling and should be known. . . . I hope to be able to illumine some of the dark places. But I am particularly anxious not to put in heavier shadows than really exist, for they are black enough." He thought that the aim and purpose of the Night Court were wrong, its methods often excellent. The aim was to *punish,* not to *prevent* vagrancy, drunkenness, lechery. That, to the Christian, was wrong. Hospitals should supersede prisons. But, given the bad aim, the execution was well conducted. The cases, however, Harris discussed candidly: he was a Dante of the poor, revealing their woes in the cycles of the damned. As his investigations proceeded, he grew more critical: he found that police, detectives, even judges, had professional interest in convicting. He met, of course, great opposition. Sumner and his Society for the Suppression of Vice did not like Harris's freedom in exposing Night Courts and white-slave traffic, and (as Harris said) "made a flank attack." But they could not silence his artillery of facts, his brilliant marksmanship of wit. When one District Attorney tried to demolish him with a letter, he routed his opponent by a counterattack which ended: "The best I can say . . . is that if he were a fish, I would throw him back."

Because of his bold integrity, all the powers of conservatism— the great papers, magazines, advertisers, business and money— were against him. The "liberal" government of Woodrow Wilson, which on the basis of the New Freedom should have been his ally, was his enemy. He had few champions among professors, editors, critics, reviewers; he had no support from the great stores and companies that spend most for advertising. Again and again he had to send out personal appeals to the subscribers— most of them poor—begging for money. Thus again and again he saved *Pearson's* for the people.

Meanwhile he was writing the little gemlike *Parables,* the noble *Beatitudes.* He planned a book to rival *The Man Shakespeare,* about Jesus: for him the thorn-crowned was the star-crowned. Too sceptical by nature for the mysticism of a John, he knew that among the disciples he was doubting Thomas. He planned to write a *Gospel of Thomas.* It would have been perhaps his greatest book.

Meanwhile the situation of *Pearson's* was growing desperate: the task of both editing it and supporting it was too great for a single man, even a superman. To write the whole magazine and fill it with one's spirit would have been an exhausting task for a young Greek god: Harris, by 1921, was sixty-six; and he had been fighting the hard fight since 1916, not to speak of his lecturing, his new stories and books, his day-by-day living. He was weary. In 1921 he was ill; overwork, exasperation, and the weight of the years were afflicting him. He suffered from headaches that made work almost impossible: "a torture cap."

At last he left the magazine to Alexander Marky, who had been editing it well during an interlude while its editor had visited Savannah. Harris went to the Riviera; visiting the Genoa Conference, he sent brilliant articles back to *Pearson's.* Gossips, however, mingled intoxication with his wit.

Once more in America, he prepared to leave *Pearson's* forever. He had made it unique but already under Marky it was becoming a different magazine; after his leave-taking it became irrecognizable. Marky wrote about Dr. Abrams' electronic diagnosis and cure, perhaps a sound thing in spite of the hostility of organized medicine, but certainly a sensational thing. The difference is characteristic: Harris made *Pearson's* a sensation by power intrinsic in himself; Marky sought to keep it going by exploiting sensations extrinsic to himself. Harris sold the magazine to Marky, who continued it for some time, but was unable to bring it to success.

In the issue of *Pearson's* for September, 1922, Frank Harris wrote his last editorial.

"For six years I have edited *Pearson's Magazine* and written most of it. . . . Time and again during the war . . . persecution took the place of prosecution. . . .

"I won every case; but could get no compensation for the injuries done the magazine by the richest government in the world in direct violation of my rights under the Constitution.

"I make no complaints; I merely state facts to make it clear to my readers that certain promises of mine were made impossible of fulfillment by the government.

"Now I have my own work to do, my autobiography to publish. . . . I cannot publish it in America. . . . I must hand *Pearson's* over to younger, stronger hands. . . .

"It now only remains for me to say 'Farewell' to the readers of *Pearson's* who have sustained me through all these years of the war with unflagging kindness and support. I am more than grateful to them. They have become my friends and it is very painful to me to say 'Goodbye!' But I am sixty-eight [14] and can no longer work as I did. The unmitigable years force me to rest. . . . Now to all I say 'Goodbye, my friends, goodbye, and my best thanks to all of you!' "

One of his *Parables* is fitting final commentary on his experiences with *Pearson's*.

"Once upon a time a mole was walking in a garden when a snail that had climbed high into a lilac-bush lost his hold and fell heavily to the ground. He lay there groaning with pain.

" 'Why do you moan like that?' said the mole. 'It was your own fault; you should have taken care. I never fall.'

" 'You never climb,' replied the snail."

Frank Harris left the offices of *Pearson's*—the famous 57 Fifth Avenue—forever. Then it was vibrant with his personality, resonant with his voice; now it is a salesroom for pianos: where his voice thundered, the ivory keys twinkle and the silver strings sound.

He worked at Tannersville, in the Catskills, on his autobiogra-

---

[14] Actually, sixty-seven.

phy; a few months later he left America for Nice. One of his favorite poems—the greatest, he thought, of Whitman and of America—was "The Prayer of Columbus." As he left the shores of America, he turned it in his mind and fashioned it with his lips. For he knew that he was a Columbus, too—the Second Columbus, who does not discover a mere outer continent, but who strives to *create* a New World of the Spirit. Like the first Columbus, he was now old, outcast, unappreciated, yet great.

> *O I am sure they really come from Thee,*
> *The urge, the ardor, the unconquerable will,*
> *The potent, felt, interior command, stronger than words,*
> *A message from the Heavens whispering to me even in sleep,*
> *These sped me on. . . .*

> *The end I know not, it is all in Thee,*
> *Or small or great I know not—haply what broad fields, what*
>   *lands,*
> *Haply the brutish measureless human undergrowth I know,*
> *Transplanted there may rise to stature, knowledge, worthy*
>   *Thee,*
> *Haply the swords I know may there indeed be turn'd to*
>   *reaping-tools,*
> *Haply the lifeless cross I know, Europe's dead cross, may bud*
>   *and blossom there.*

> *One effort more, my altar this bleak sand;*
> *That Thou, O God, my life hast lighted,*
> *With ray of light steady, ineffable, vouchsafed of Thee,*
> *Light rare, untellable, lighting the very light,*
> *Beyond all signs, descriptions, languages;*
> *For that, O God, be it my latest word, here on my knees,*
> *Old, poor, and paralyzed, I thank Thee.*

Chapter XIII

THE MENACE OF THE YEARS

(1922-1931)

"NICE, NICE, NICE! The clanging ceases. . . . The *Promenade des Anglais* and the marvelous *Baie des Anges,* the blue sea laughing in the sunshine; the sky like a blue bubble above, luminous toward the horizon, resting lightly on the waters; the clean, clear air; the mountains in the distance; about us palms and umbrella pines—the livery of the South. . . ." [1] Such was Nice—where, if Frank Harris could not be born, he was to die.

He settled on that azure coast. He lived first in a white villa in the hills looking over the blue sea—*Boulevard Edouard VII, Cimiez*—with windows that flashed in the westering sun, behind stone walls and iron gates. Around him were the things he loved: the first editions, the statues, the busts, the pictures, the letters from the great of the earth. . . . He might have sold these treasures many times when he seemed falling into poverty, but he would not, for he "could not live without them." All his life he loved beauty as the *Koran* bids—"If you have two loaves, sell one quickly and buy a flower, for the soul, too, must be fed."

The poet, Allan Dowling, one of the truest of his friends, describes Harris in these years. "Harris always impressed me as a man of medium height, rather than short. I should guess about

[1] "Travel in France." In *Confessional,* p. 194.

five feet six. I was in his bedroom one day when he was getting on the heavy underwear that he always wore in later years when the natural heat of the blood was leaving him, and, having been an athlete myself, I can testify that he was muscularly well developed—far above the average. Any feats of strength that he boasted of having performed as a boy are quite credible. His hair and mustache at that time were half gray and half dark, going a little grayer as time went on. I never saw the slightest evidence of his having dyed his hair, as some people claimed he did.

"You ask me about his eyes. I recall—and my wife confirms me in this—that they were a grayish green, light in color, and rather small. Quite a hard glint could come into them at times; and his lips were thin. The 'famous voice' . . . was really a magnificent instrument, deep, powerful, and beautifully controlled—one of those splendid bass voices that are often found among Welshmen; and Harris, wherever he may have been born, was, to me, typically Welsh.

"To complete the physical aspect of the man, a word must be said about his clothes. On the whole, he dressed well. His clothes were always of the first quality. The winged collar and stock were conservative. The spats and checked waistcoat with the gold watch-chain strung across it were just a little on the loud side—a pleasant reminder of his days as editor of a London racing sheet.

"Whether in his first apartment on the hill of *Cimiez,* or in the later one down in the center of Nice, the general atmosphere was the same. The furniture was very well chosen, but the walls were overcrowded with pictures—signed etchings, prints, and paintings; also photographs of celebrated friends. Whistler, Wilde, Fantin-Latour, Rops, and a score of others were represented, and the period from 1890-1910 seemed to be very much alive around one.

"I lunched and dined there often. The food was always excellent, with a pleasant local white wine to go with it, and good coffee and a glass of cognac to follow. Tine, the pleasant-faced

Italian cook, was a good one; and Harris was an expert in fine living. Sometimes there were interesting guests, though I never found them so interesting as the host; and at other times I was there with no one but the family—which consisted of Frank and Nellie and her sister Aggie. Aggie was an odd sort of person, very plain, although she had the same beautiful red hair as her sister—and very quiet, but with a good sense of humor. Harris would do most of the talking, while I responded like a good audience, put in a remark or a question now and then, and frequently laughed till the tears ran down my face. After lunch, he always retired to the livingroom for a nap, and left me to read a book or manuscript until he awoke.

"The years have passed since he died, and I have had plenty of time to think about him. I still think he was one of the most interesting men that ever appeared on this earth. His combination of wide knowledge and worldly experience, sensuality, unhesitant rebellion, and at the same time a deep sensitiveness to the finest shades of truth and beauty, made him a fascinating person. He was extremely easy to approach, open-handed to a fault if he liked you, and frankly contemptuous if he didn't."

Frank Harris had many a day of sunshine in Nice. Those who have seen many lands declare that few places are as beautiful as the country behind Nice in the Maritime Alps. Harris had a tremendous enthusiasm for it, and he loved to take short automobile trips through the lovely land. Sometimes he stopped at small hotels for lunch; at other times he had picnics on the grass by the road. He had no car; but he had a favorite driver named Scotto, whom he often hired for the day. The exchange was favorable, and everything in Nice (apart from a few big hotels) was inexpensive.

There were interesting people in Nice. A ruling Rajah, when Harris took the first taxi that drove up to the hotel, and the Rajah had to go back and wait for a second, stuck out his tongue at Harris—a gesture natural but not regal.

Matisse had his home in Nice. Harris would rather hear Matisse criticize a gallery of paintings than any one else. For he thought that Matisse saw not only the color and the basic drawing, but the spirit behind the space of canvas—the very passion of the artist's purpose.

In Nice there was Bréal, too, with his paintings of "the hard, cold, side-glancing eyes of the Gitana"; and Fortuny, with his paintings of Spanish beauty—the passion and the teasing, the flower, the little curl, the dancing eyes. There were landscapes of the Marne, "drenched in rain and sadness"; there were seascapes of the Riviera, with the red rocks and flaming mountains of "the sun-blessed land."

He met Blasco Ibáñez in Nice. The Spaniard had quarreled with the King of Spain from some hidden motivation of patriotic love; he was barred from his own land because he had loved her too much! Kipling also came to Nice; Max Eastman, too, and Richard Le Gallienne.

Thus in Nice he had not only the red rocks and flaming mountains of the sun-blessed land, but also creators of visible beauty and writers of the word. Most of them visited him; the best of them he visited.

Once, as he was walking in Nice, he passed an Englishwoman. She was beautiful; almost without consciousness of what he did, Harris put out his hand and touched her, as if to assure himself of the reality of her graceful flesh. She turned on him with words of hot resentment. Reflectively he studied her till her tirade faltered under his glance; then he said, "Madame, you are not as kind as you are beautiful."

Another time, as he and Nellie were strolling in Nice, an Englishman jostled him; and Harris nudged him fiercely with his elbow. The Englishman confronted Harris immediately with the challenge: "Are you a gentleman?" Frank peered at his inquisitor in surprised wonder; but Mrs. Harris quickly answered,

"No, he is not a gentleman: he is an Englishman." Her repartee left the fellow at a loss; he stared, while they walked away. Harris, quite unconscious of his own gesture of pugnacity which had incited the incident, asked her (in the Irish pronunciation he always used for the word), "What ailed the eejit?"

Morris White, a young American, visited Harris in Nice. They went to a cinema. During the show, two men began to argue: at once Harris—ignoring the less graphic shadow-shapes on the screen—leaned forward to study the moving passions flickering over their faces.

Frank Harris was one of the world's great letter writers. In these last years he wrote letters that show how finely he loved and how wisely he criticized literature.

He wrote to Allan Dowling, May 21, 1926, "I thank you for an excellent letter, the greater part of which I agree with, but when you talk of Swinburne as you do, you make me smile. I don't think of him as one of the greatest technical masters ever known, but he has brought new music into English poetry, and now and then all the powerful rhythm of syllabification of the best Greek work. There are choruses in the *Atalanta in Calydon* that have never been equaled in English, and his 'Hertha' is one of the poems that live with me, like his 'In the Orchard' and 'The Leper.' You go on to say that 'it is the easiest thing in the world for one with a feeling for rhythm to acquire the knowledge and facility in verse of Swinburne.' Go to it, my dear man, I shall believe it when you send me something as good as

> *The seed and the sower,*
> *The deed and the doer,*
> *The dust which is God.*

But I am not a poet so I can put no limits to what you may do in that art, but your short story I shall be glad to read; that, I think, I can measure better than anyone now living.

"It has been a great pleasure to meet and know you. You are the first American whom I have met who is on the topmost level in knowledge of English poetry; the majority of so-called poets there made me gasp. Miss Amy Lowell told me that I definitely over-rated Blake, 'And if you were a poet you would know it.' Poor old school-mistress!"

Again he wrote (December 16, 1926): "I had already noticed in my *The Man Shakespeare* that it would be possible to guess a poet's voice by his writing. I am certain that I said it about Shelley, the shrillness of his treble startled me; but Shakespeare's voice was high too, I feel certain, and believe I could prove it to you if you were here for five minutes."

He wrote, December 22, 1926: "You say I was pleased at being compared to Swift. Swift was an admirable writer and his Lilliput and Brobdingnag are real creations and have their place in English literature. But he wasn't a great man. He had no reverence in him and very little love, and these shortcomings dwarfed him. It is curious to be told that I am the best writer of English prose and at the same time to find myself after three years of the hardest work I have ever done poorer than I was before writing the masterpiece.

"I only write to wish you all good things for the New Year. We shall be glad to see you with or without bride."

February 15, 1930, he wrote: "I wanted a fifth volume of 'My Life' and put in it the gist of my sex experiences in India, China, and Japan, compared with those in London and Paris, but my wife doesn't want me to write it and I don't know whether I will ever get it done."

In a letter to Abraham Frankel he wrote a gem of Olympian humor: "I always pray to God that He may let me live up to my vain opinion of myself!"

And in the beautiful autobiographical letter to Roy Butera, he said: "Always meet the great man with reverence and avoid the little one without too signal a disdain."

Such flashing arrows from the Bow of Ulysses prove that in these years at Nice Frank Harris was vividly alive!

From some letters, and from the fact that he did not leave enough money to buy him a grave, he seems to have been poor. This is true—in a relative sense. Again and again he besought friends in America to send him money, and often complained because they could not. Isar Levine, his friend and agent, was constantly under appeal; and constantly, he says, sent Harris money —"large sums of money." Harris's American attorney, Arthur Leonard Ross, got *My Reminiscences as a Cowboy* taken by Charles Boni, and even secured the unprecedented advance of $7000 for the *Life of Shaw*. How, then, can Harris have been poor? The answer is that he had no conception of money except its value in buying life. He never hoarded, seldom made a *long-range* investment, would not take thought for the morrow. Money was something to be spent for abundance of life—it was the servant of one's desires, never itself a desire to be served. He had made money easily, he spent it as easily; he was accustomed to abundance as inexhaustible as air and sunlight: does one hoard the air, or put sunlight in the bank?

No persons of note, whether friends or enemies (in secret), came to Nice without visiting him. He entertained them with the choicest wines and foods. It was his pride not only to keep the House Beautiful but also the House Bountiful. When he went out, no matter how many dined with him, or how low his funds, he must pay the bill. Ross tells how once in New York, when Harris had little money, a large group gathered to dine with him. All knew his lack of funds and wanted to pay, but each hesitated —knowing Harris's pride. At the end of the dinner, Harris turned to one of his guests and "borrowed" a bill of large denomination to pay for the entire meal.

One of his secretaries in Nice, a girl, feeling his greatness and his need, wrote long letters privately to some of his friends. She was worried by Frank's worry: it was not so much his lack of money as his fear of lack, and especially his fear that he could not do all that he wished for Nellie. Creditors hounded him, too, and when money came it was already spent.

Yet nothing kept him from his work, neither worry nor age. (He never flew the white flag, he said, even in his hair!) He did what he had not been able to induce Wilde to do: poor, in exile, in ill-health and aging, he held himself to the task and joy of art. One of his favorite quotations was:

> *Death closes all, but something ere the end*
> *Some work of noble note may yet be done.*

He had commended Shakespeare for gathering his failing forces and shaping them into *The Tempest*. Now he himself would do the same. The Indians of the plains had sought death in the glory of battle: old, they would arm a prisoner and give him his freedom if, in fair fight, he could kill them. He, too, like the Sioux of the plains, would go down fighting, in lifelong unsurrendering battle with fate.

A magnificent example of the pith and clarity of his mind in these last years is a letter to Arthur Leonard Ross, written from Nice, November 17, 1924.

"My dear Mr. Ross,

"I read the article you sent me from the *Jewish Tribune,* 'Frank Harris, Anti-Semite,' and I think it one of the cheapest and vilest pieces of work I have ever seen, and certainly don't regard it as worth answering. Take one of the first things. He says I have spoken of a Jew's view of Heaven with golden streets and pearly gates. Mr. Herzberg complains that I don't tell him 'just where in Jewish literature this view of Heaven is presented.' If he reads the Bible he will find out, but his criticism is a fair sample of his work. He admits that when I am talking of the way the world treats its sacred guides and leaders two of the three names I mention are those of Jews. He might have added that when I spoke of the greatest women I have ever met I say all three were Jews—another proof in Mr. Herzberg's opinion that I am an anti-Semite.

"Frankly the man's an Ass, and does not see what has been patent to everyone—that I admire Jews more than any other people, and love them better than any other people except my poor Irish compatriots. In the last book of my *Portraits,* which he seems chiefly to be talking about, five out of the twenty are Jews and every one of them praised. I declare that Miss Goldman is the greatest woman I have ever met. Nobody else has ever said it, no Jew of them all, which I again suppose is a proof of my anti-Semitism. I have praised Trotsky, too, and compared him with Otto Kahn, praising both of them—another proof of my anti-Jewish prejudices, but the whole thing is an object lesson in the fact that Whistler put better than anyone—'mediocrity hates ability of any sort.'

"What always puzzles me is why the common fellows always write about the men of genius. Why don't they write about their own kind? Why don't the Herzbergs write about the Herzbergs? —and leave us who inhabit the heights to our own devices.

"I was very glad to hear from you, because you made so kindly and sympathetic an impression on me in Paris. . . .

"Weinberger has just written me that if my differences with Brentano lead to a suit, he will not be able to represent me, although in Paris he told me that he would do it gladly. I wish people would only say what they mean—it would make things easier.

"I have just sent the second volume of my autobiography to the printer. If anyone can write as true a picture of the time, and of great men as I have done, without using my freedom of speech, I want to see it done. I don't know of any such book. If you care to write to answer Herzberg you will find munition enough in this letter. I thank you and return herewith his article so that you may be able to reply to it.

Sincerely ever, and affectionately,

Frank Harris."

As Frank Harris indicates in this letter, and as he had said in his farewell to *Pearson's,* he had been working on his autobiography for some years; after leaving the magazine, he finished the first volume during several months in the Catskills. He had carried the manuscript with him to Nice. Now he published it on the continent, for he knew it could not be published unexpurgated in America.

My Life and Loves was not, as the usual reviewer who runs and cannot read supposes, an excursion into pornography. It was not, as pedants try to demand that it should be, a factual chronicle; on the other hand it was not, as some have declared, a congeries of tall tales. To Harris, it was a philosophic commentary on life, a gospel as authentic as John's. Harris was not concerned—as little people insist that he should have been—with factual events: he was concerned with the spirit and meaning of his life. If every fact in the book were false, the book still would be true. As Einar Lyngklip asked Kate Stephens, was Harris "a date-recorder or a soul-discoverer?" There is truth that the fact-mongers never know, "a great deep stream of it that flows through all Frank Harris has written. . . . In the whole story of Jesus there is hardly a known 'fact' as to dates or places or even names, yet it is the truest as well as the greatest story in all literature."

My Life and Loves is commonly compared with such autobiographies as Rousseau's, Cellini's, and Casanova's; but such comparisons are aesthetically illicit. Rousseau's was a great Sentimental Journey through his own emotions and theories, all interpreted in relation to the Return to Nature. Harris's is freer of theory, stronger in virility, wider in experience. Cellini and Casanova were buccaneers of personal prowess, supremely individual, concerned with their own conquests and sensations, lacking in social interests or high philosophy. Harris was more philosophic: he was concerned with the individual—and with society; with passion—and with self-mastery; with questions of the soul's destiny and the fate of the seer and poet in the world; with the nature of man and of great men. His width was greater, his insights deeper, his vision higher, his style far greater.

His own judgment on the comparison with Casanova rings through a letter (July 5, 1924) to a Mr. Semple. Harris writes, "Don't please compare me to Casanova; he never wrote anything but his 'memoirs' and they are anything but well written. . . . My Second Volume will strike you, I think, as the most remarkable 'memoirs' ever written and I'm pitting myself not against poor Casanova, but against St. Simon and the dialogues of Plato on Socrates.

"Casanova, my dear man, Casanova is not worthy to tie my bootstrings!—though I like the fellow. . . ."

There is Olympian scorn, like Shakespeare's high praise of his own "powerful rhyme," in these words.

It is generally supposed that *My Life and Loves* is preeminently busy with sex, in terms of pornography. A foolish reviewer even charged that Harris must have written it "in a brothel"—though Harris was proud to state that never in his life did he go with a prostitute. To be sure, as a witty woman says, "Frank Harris seems capable of sex experience in any language." Yet sex occupies probably one third of the first volume; perhaps less than a fourth of the second; approximately one fifth of the third. What man of normal virility—even *normal* virility—would give less place to sex in his own life? To Harris these "loves" were natural and pure; he regarded them as holy experiences. He made mistakes; he did not economize in the grand manner; he often whipped the senses to lust more than he roused the soul to love; he was inartistic and passion-blunting in some of his words; his girls too invariably address him as "Sir." But his purpose was to make love a natural, joyous thing; to set the body free for ecstasy, because the mind is free from prudery; to show that the flesh, no less than the spirit, is holy. His belief was akin to Whitman's, and his art (*in the aspect of sex*) superior; his reception, too, was similar. It was Whitman's attitude toward sex that, overempha-

sized for decades, caused his greatest persecutions and made
people confuse his art with infamy. (A father in those days threatened to horsewhip an anonymous young man—if he could discover him—who had sent his daughter *Leaves of Grass*.) How
does this differ from the reaction of most "moderns" to the work
of Harris? "Moderns" have, as D. H. Lawrence said, "sex in
their heads." Harris had sex where it belongs.

Some critics said that Harris was "senile"—writing with wistful memory of his past, and trying to blow into flame the coals
of spent passion. If his artistic realizations of love are senile, what
must the young Harris have been? If Jove burned Semele to
ashes, Harris would literally have burned the women he loved
to ashes too, if he had had any more glowing power.

But why prattle of sex? Harris's greatest pages and wisest interests lay elsewhere. He gave up lusts and loves, money and
place, not once but many times, for the call of an intellectual or
spiritual ideal. The greatest loves of his life were not for the girls
he possessed, but for the idealists of the spirit who possessed him
—Byron, Smith, Carlyle, Shakespeare, Jesus. His greatest loves
were not for the feminine body but for the masculine mind. All
his greatest portraits are of men; all his most enduring and dramatic friendships (save that for Emma Goldman, and here love
was not involved) were for men.

The greatest pages in *My Life and Loves* are the poetry and
philosophy of men, of books, of life. Such words as these are characteristic of his wisdom summed in the perfect image: "Gautama
Buddha always impressed me as one of the noblest of men, and
where a single tree grows to the sky, the soil and climate too must
be worth studying." Harris was concerned with the relations of
the individual to society, wherein equal justice should be done
both to equality and to freedom; with the relation of the genius
to the mediocre; with peace in place of insensate wars; with the
farthest reach of science, and the implications of mysticism that
tease men out of thought; with life in its colors and its light.

Sex was only a part of life—a part so normal that he wanted it taken in stride, with thanks and joy. Only those who notice sex exclusively make this part of his interest supreme. Harris wished simply to restore it to its true proportion in the integral whole.

There were, to be sure, flaws in *My Life and Loves*. The printing (done in Germany) was full of errors and of punctuations (notably quotation marks) that are not English. The illustrations of naked girls in the first volume are not art; they merely cheapened the book. The physical charms he describes at such length are not balanced by real differentiation of character (except in the cases of Lorna Mayhew, Sophie, and Eirene—particularly Sophie). Harris shows no sense of humor—about himself. Einar Lyngklip writes: "A group of newspaper men nearly split their sides laughing when Frank told them of the things that had happened in the printing of the first volume of *My Life and Loves*. Frank couldn't see anything funny about it, it seemed, and was merely reciting some of his mistreatments and misunderstandings, and telling about some of the phlegmatic Germans who had a hand in the printing. He was quite serious, but nevertheless these fellows roared with laughter till they had to quit eating. And one of them got up to walk around, holding his sides, saying, 'Did you really put that in *that* book? Lord help us!' Frank had been telling us that he had put at the end of the book (or was it at the end of the Preface?) these words in large caps in Latin: AD MAJOREM DEI GLORIAM."

In spite of the life not naked but nude, which cannot be published in the Anglo-Saxon world, and in spite of incidental blunders of taste, the book is great. It is grave, wise, sane; a commentary on men and affairs, on life and literature, on passion and chastity; a monumental history of the intellectual and spiritual life of the decades from 1885 to the 1920's. There is nothing like it elsewhere in the world; nothing, of its type, to equal it in modern literature.

It broke paths toward new freedom. Much of our health in

facing sex as normal and joyous, our freedom in dresses and bathing suits, our tolerance toward such books as are openly discussed today (such as the incandescent core of Mann's *Joseph in Egypt*) stem from Harris. He was a casualty of the battle; but over the dead body of his reputation, the battle was won.

The reception of the book was *hysteria in excelsis*. It was the opportunity his enemies had long desired: the lion had delivered himself into their hands! They sent beaters out to chivy him with assagais; they loaded their express rifles and prepared for the kill. The explosive bullets crashed all around him. "It reads as if it had been written in a brothel." [2] "A senile and lip-wetting giggle of an old man about his far-distant filthiness. It is a gruesome, postmortem job to read Mr. Harris." [3] "Having put himself in the class of streetwalkers he is entitled to no sympathy. The Frank Harris of years ago died long ago, and it is his cadaver that has been writing recently. The odor proves it." [4] His friend Upton Sinclair gave tongue with the pack: "It is the vilest book I ever laid eyes on."

But simply set beside these hysterical verdicts a few quotations from the book they are supposed to describe. "One incident in this life may be worth recording: Lotze, the famous philosopher who preached a God immanent in every form of life, remarked once in a Seminar that the *via media* of Aristotle was the first and greatest discovery in morals. I disagreed with him, and when he asked my reasons I said that the *via media* belonged to statics whereas morals were a part of dynamics. A bottle of wine might do me good and make another man drunk: the moral path was never a straight line between extremes, as Aristotle had imagined, but the resultant of two forces, a curve therefore, always making toward one side or the other. As one's years increase after thirty or so, the curve should be toward abstinence." "When shall we

[2] A. I. Tobin and Elmer Gertz, *Frank Harris: A Study in Black and White,* p. 313. (The words of a "prominent American.")

[3] *Ibid.,* p. 314. Attributed to Sinclair Lewis.

[4] *Ibid.* Quoted from the New York *Evening World,* August 23, 1926.

artists and lovers learn that the most highly powered engines require the strongest brakes?" "I have always fought for the Holy Spirit of Truth and have been, as Heine said he was, a brave soldier in the Liberation War of Humanity: now one fight more, the best and the last." Or he wrote that we have been "assisting at the overthrow of morality itself and returning to the ethics of the wolf and the polity of the Thieves' Kitchen." "Nine men and women out of ten go through life without realizing their own special nature: they cannot lose their souls for they have never found them. For every son of Adam, for every daughter of Eve, this is the supreme defeat, the final disaster." "Is it not written in the Book of Fate that he who gives most receives most and do we not all, if we would tell the truth, win more love than we give: Are we not all debtors to the overflowing bounty of God?"

The too hysterical clamor from too many critics makes us question their morality. It is as though they had in their souls, driven rabid into underground caves, timber wolves long starved but still alive, that slaver and yelp when they smell meat. To Harris, passion was no wolf to be starved and forced into caves, there to gnaw at the foundations of life. It was nature's gathered lightning that must break from the electricity-charged clouds in joyous tracery of splendor, ending the sullen heat and clearing the stifling air.

One American critic—and the best of the sorry time—appreciated the book. Mencken wrote: "I know no other American who shows so civilized a mind, so tolerant and charming a cosmopolitanism, so complete a freedom from the childish prejudices of his country. Compare him to the average native literatus of his generation: it is like ranging Metternich's Pauline beside a country schoolmarm. He is infinitely more learned than any of these old women in pantaloons. . . ." [5]

The book, thanks to adverse critics, was well advertised among the wrong people. Salacious individuals whose purpose was por-

[5] H. L. Mencken, *Prejudices: Third Series*. Alfred A. Knopf, Inc.

nography sought a copy even at $20 or more, whereas the book demanded an audience of poets and philosophers. The oddest fish fitted on magic glasses and peered into the mystery of things as if *they* were God's Spies. One can only hope that some of them were capable of being born again; of learning wisdom, statesmanship, and the lore of great men. The government refused mailing privileges; all copies discovered were seized and destroyed. (One wonders how many were read first!)

Distribution was by an Underground Railway, with persecution and prosecution just around the corner. Frank Harris made little: fly-by-night publishers pirated the book and reaped clandestine profits; he lost most of his capital, the sale of his other books, his public, many of his friends, and the residue of his reputation.

The first volume of the autobiography appeared in 1922; the second in 1925; the third in 1927.

Harris's own ideas of selling it are revealed in a letter (September 22, 1924) to Abraham Frankel. "Now how to sell it. I must have $5000 for the American rights. Now for the publisher. We should take a place in Windsor, Canada, where a secretary or friend would take orders and receive moneys. He should then give copies to Mencken and Viereck, on condition of long reviews all mentioning the Canadian address and stating that on receipt of $15 a copy will be sent. He can easily get $10,000—then let him send out all copies ordered and paid for in a single week from his place in the U.S., or places near it, and all by express. The book should be bound only in paper, no pictures except photos of men, and when the big money is taken, I'd offer a cheaper edition at $5 to stall off pirates and your publisher can make a lot."

Various things—the seizure of the books, the pirating immediately—made such a scheme fallible.

Harris's experiences with the book in England are revealed in a letter to Einar Lyngklip (August 22, 1925). "First of all, I believed that books privately printed were allowed to be sent anywhere in

Great Britain without let or hindrance. I had helped to distribute my friend Sir Richard Burton's *Arabian Nights*, though I disliked intensely certain pages of it that seemed to me merely bestial. He was a great man, a law therefore to himself: it was for me to help, not to hinder, him. But this noble English freedom has been abandoned: in the war fervor Parliament passed a law copied on the law of the United States, whereby it was made an offense to send what the authorities called obscene literature through the mails, and Bodkin, the public prosecutor, was eager to stretch his powers to the uttermost. Consequently when I sent copies of my first volume to my friends, he not only stopped the books in transit, but sent inspectors to my friends to threaten all manner of dire penalties if in the future such books were sent to them. Of course, in this he overstepped all measure: but that's the nature of the Bodkins. . . . I wrote to him asking why he allowed *Hamlet* to go through the post. . . . Bodkin did not answer.

"The confiscation of my book in Great Britain and the United States prevented my getting any profit from the first volume, and, worse still, the fact that I had written and published such a book injured my reputation as a writer and as a human being. Till then, I could always earn £1500 yearly by my pen. . . . Now in one month everything I wrote was at once returned (from editors) with foolish phrases: even manuscripts that had been accepted were sent back to me without a word of explanation or excuse. Men I had known well cut me in public."

The second volume was challenged in *France*. Harris describes the attack in a letter to Allan Dowling (July 25, 1926). "Since you left France, I have had a great misfortune: I have been called up before the *Juge d'Instruction* for *'outrage aux bonnes moeurs'!* He told me he had nothing to do with the first volume because it was not printed in France, but the second volume was printed and sold in France and he had been instructed to get it translated and proceed against me because of it. He gave me a list of passages objected to; and the whole story of guzzling and the gluttony of the English middle-classes, and the behavior of the Lord Mayor at the dinner with Lady Marriott, were especially marked, as was the fact that the Prince of Wales likes naughty stories.

"It seems to me that the whole attack comes from England, but I am told that it doesn't come from the Embassy. . . . In any case I am informed that the prosecution is most serious and in October or November I may expect to be brought before the *court d'assise.* My sin is evidently that I had the books printed in France and thus gave the work to French printers—but just because the charge is stupid I am frightened of it.

"If I had the money I would leave the country and certainly I would give my third volume to be printed in Italy or Germany instead of in France, but poverty aggravates every disability."

But Frank Harris found defenders. A petition was drawn up and was signed by leading French writers, as well as by many English and American writers.

"We, the undersigned artists and men of letters, earnestly desire to enter upon the records of your court our protest and our appeal.

"With unbelieving astonishment we have learned that for the first time in French history a foreign author writing in a foreign tongue is charged with corrupting public morals. It is not clear how the French-speaking public can be corrupted by English words. It is not clear why the author's far more outspoken book, namely *My Life and Loves,* Vol. I, was not included in the charge of immorality. With these considerations the charge appears obscure and disingenuous. We can only conclude that the organized prudes among our English-speaking peoples are attempting to use a French court to punish a kinsman artist whose work they fear and hate. This attempt is much more than an attack on the freedom of a single author. It is a blow aimed to strike at the very right of free artistic expression by all men of letters in the world. Therefore we protest, severally and collectively, we protest against this contemptible outrage.

"For several generations, student artists from all parts of the world have gone to France as to the hearth and home of all liberal arts. In France they have found the freedom of speech and action which are necessary to the growth of art, the supreme freedom of the mind, as sunlight and air to the growth of a flower. Is France now going to surrender the proud distinction of being the intellectual center of the world? For it is the intellectual integrity, the artistic freedom, and the illustrious leadership of France that are here on trial. Very respectfully and very sincerely we appeal to you, in our own names and in the name of all mankind, for the protection and defense of this integrity, this freedom, and this leadership, against all enemies at home and abroad."

A copy of this was sent to Shaw, among other authors. Instead of signing it, he wrote: "This is calculated to damage Harris to the utmost possible. To address it to the judge is not only an impropriety which may for all I know be a punishable offense in French law, but it must in any case give him offense as a shameless attempt to tamper with the court. It draws attention quite unnecessarily to *My Life and Loves,* as if that were likely to improve Harris's chances instead of providing additional evidence against him. All the stuff about France and art and freedom is enough to make any lawyer sick.

"I have not seen the volume in question; but Mr. Harris is in possession of my view as to how the first can be defended: that is, not as a work of art but as a document. As an invention, or as a display of art for the sake of art, it is clearly a contravention of the laws against indecency. As a record of fact and an authentic clinical study it can claim the toleration allowed to all legal and scientific documents. On no other ground can the author possibly succeed; and any attempt to claim that art, as such, is above the law, will only redouble the determination of the court to explode that heresy by making an example of him.

"I fear that it is too late to do this now, though I have heard nothing of the trial of the case. The delay has been caused by the temporary misplacement of this paper. However, I send it for what it may be worth.

G. Bernard Shaw
21/1/27"

Such was Shaw's verdict on *My Life and Loves*. As an antidote, one should read Harris's defense of freedom in the Introduction to Volume I. One should also ask Shaw why, if *science* is above the law, *art* is not. Neither Shaw nor Harris ever thought of art as an "invention" or something that exists merely as "art for the sake of art." Art, to both of them, was a creative impact of Life upon lives. What of the attempt to stifle *A Doll's House* and *Ghosts* as "indecent"? Did not Shaw defend Ibsen against his ignorant critics; would he not have defended him against an ignorant court? Or, if it had been against the law to publish "indecent" economics (i.e. those that so seemed to the Puritans of Capitalism) would Shaw have refrained from writing plays "indecent" with the truth?

Perhaps because of the protest—probably because of the civilized tolerance of France—Harris was not prosecuted. If he had been, almost his last refuge would have been destroyed.

Meanwhile there had been other work, not so monumental, yet finer in chiseled art. In *Undream'd of Shores* (1924) Harris returned to the short story. The volume contains nothing to equal "The Veils of Isis," or "The Ugly Duckling," or the supreme "Magic Glasses." But it is a gravely beautiful book of the tragic hinterlands of passion.

"A Mad Love" is almost a masterpiece. The hero, Hagedorn, is a musician of genius. He has studied the strange unkown

music of China and Japan. He knows how crudely music imitates
the rich scope of sound in the world, and he has learned to equal
the sounds of nightingale or seatide. He has absolute pitch. He
can hear the twelve vibrations by which C sharp is faster than D
flat. He is a virtuoso of sound, a philosopher of sound too—a
genius both in technical ability and in understanding. In relation
to art, he is a master; but life, unfortunately, masters him. He has
fallen in love with, and married, a dancer of genius; he is deliri-
ously happy with her. Returning suddenly one day, he sees a
journalist, whom he dislikes, kissing her; without waiting for
explanation or revenge, he leaves her and wanders all over the
world—wasting his genius in a pique of despair. It is hard to
believe that a man of the world would so quickly fall into the
illusion called disillusion, without waiting for the innocent explanation that would have been so easy and so exonerating; it is
harder to believe that so great a genius would nurse the infection
of a psychic wound to the destruction of the art he loved. (It is
Shakespeare's story, as Harris saw it, on a lower level—the mad
jealousy, the sick passion of a genius for a woman who deceives
or seems to deceive.)

A nobler love, with overtures of Chinese character and philosophy, and a central theme of cruelty like a saw cutting slowly
through a body in its path, are found in "A Chinese Story."
Harris is finely just to the genius of China; and the story itself
is intense and tragic.

The other stories, too, deal with the ways of love—whether
in men who love worldly wantons and destroy not only themselves but even their talents, or in a man who goes mad for some
months, and by his singleness of love makes his wife temporarily
the happiest woman in France. One of the stories is "The Temple
of the Forgotten Dead," the germ of his novel, *Pantopia;* it is an
attempted synthesis of paganism and Christianity. There is a
temple to the great unknown benefactors: those who discovered
fire; those who discovered the wheel; all those who went into the

darkness, leaving anonymous gifts. The volume sparkles with facets of brilliance; as a whole, however, it is—like the individual stories—not of Harris's first quality in fundamental conception. Harris in spite of what he himself thought, was at his greatest when he wrote of philosophical truths, untroubled by love. He told others—Upton Sinclair, Galsworthy, Shaw—to fall in love that they might write masterpieces. He himself, however, wrote his greatest work when love was a flower along his road to a greater goal. His best symbol was not Aspasia, but Plato.

Amid the menace of the years came an interlude of partial recognition.

In 1927 he was invited to give lectures on Shakespeare in Germany, for the *Lessing-Hochschule*. The liberty of thought which he had missed in England seemed possible under the Weimar Republic; Germans seemed not afraid to face sex in its boldest disclosures, its most intimate revelations. *My Life and Loves* was not, to them, a bogey to set children screaming. The lectures, begun in German and continued in English, were a victory and an event. Harris had a popular success, acclaim from critics, justice even from the press. He was (the papers said) a brilliant talker, a man who was active in life itself, a philosopher who was genuine: "Sentences spurt forth"; yet he was a person "of the greatest restraint and responsibility toward himself." "Frank Harris dances Shakespeare," one paper said. Berlin turned out to a dinner in his honor; among the diners was Albert Einstein. Harris returned to Nice warmed out of torpor by this generous response; fortified, also, by generous remuneration.

But Germany disappointed him. In his *Contemporary Portraits: Fourth Series,* he etches in acid the pedantic arrogance of the Prussian official. His publisher, too, tried to edit out of the third volume of his autobiography the chapters on Jesus and Heine.

In 1928 Harris revisited America. He might have been prosecuted: one friend, knowing that he was old and ailing and could not survive prison, wrote that the venture "meant death." Fortu-

nately there was no prosecution; unfortunately there was no acclaim. He returned to Nice, saying in Shakespeare's words, *" 'Tis
honor with most lands to be at odds,"* which he characterisically
changed to: *" 'Tis honor with* all *lands to be at odds."*

Yet he won some success with his books, largely because of
Arthur Leonard Ross. As a young law student, Ross had attended
some of Harris's lectures at 57 Fifth Avenue; and (as he says)
"ate them up." Harris wakened him to an interest in and an
insight into American literature. In 1924, after Ross had become
a leading attorney, the American Bar Association sent him to Europe; there he met Harry Weinberger, Harris's American attorney at the time, and Emma Goldman and Frank Harris. He spent
two weeks in Paris and was with Harris much of the time. On
his return to New York he received a letter from Emma Goldman, who had become his client. She asked Ross to become Harris's lawyer, because (she said) Harris was incapable of buffeting
the rude billows of the world's tides. Ross did become Harris's
lawyer, and served him with untiring devotion and eminent
success.

My Reminiscences as a Cowboy (the publication of which was
negotiated by Ross) appeared in 1930 as one of the paper-covered
books in Charles Boni's series. Rockwell Kent and William
Gropper made pictorial their conceptions of Harris's characters
and atmosphere; the account of his years on the plains—clear like
Texas air, spacious like Texas itself—at last found incarnation.
The book was well received; it won greater praise than Harris's
masterpieces.

In 1930 *Confessional* was published by the Panurge Press. It is
a volume of essays on men, cities, literature, life. The essays on
Columbus and Joan of Arc are among the greatest ever written
on these two transcendent spirits. Of Joan, Harris spoke with a
mastery that took him to the heart of her mystery. "The tragedy
of Joan's life is just as simple as the secret of her success. The
virtue she had amassed in those hours of solitary communion . . .

in Domremy carried her irresistibly to her achievement; but no one lives in the world without being affected by common views and common desires. Gradually Joan's stock of primitive virtue wore away. After Rheims she ought to have returned to Domremy, and in solitary communion with the highest again filled her soul with the perfume of the Ineffable. Had she done so, she would have been the greatest of the Christian Saints, dowered with the gentleness of Francis and with more than the courage of Dominic; as simply human as St. Elizabeth, as devoted as St. Theresa, she would have enlarged our conception of womanhood. "That was not to be. Joan was to make mistakes like other mortals, and like others she was to fall short of the highest, and to be punished, finally, not for her shortcomings, but for her glorious achievement. So in the public square at Rouen, where all the fiends of the Pit seemed loosed against her in hootings and hellish laughter, the brave woman-soul went again to God, and the mortal put on immortality." [6]

Great, too, are Harris's essays on places; especially the marvelous essay on great cities. No one has ever painted the soul of cities better—the atmosphere, the spirit, the destiny of these creations of man in multitude. Harris was a city man (though he loved the wild places and wide spaces), and he does beautiful justice to the cities he loved.

There are essays on the art of writing: on the short story, on biography. There is also the essay on morals which, in the *English Review*, had roused the hornets of St. Loe Strachey.

No one can know Frank Harris until he has read *Confessional*. The Panurge Press also published *Pantopia*—a philosophic novel which Harris ranked with his best. Mr. Saavedra—who is Harris as he saw himself—is statesman and prophet of an island in the Southwest Pacific, inhabited by Latin supermen. The island is protected by a cloud of electricity that brings death to invaders; if a stranger should penetrate the cloud, he is put to death to

    [6] *Confessional*, pp. 46-47.

preserve the insulation of the island. The hero somehow passes the lethal lightnings: he finds Saavedra to delight his mind and Aura (Saavedra's daughter) to charm his senses. He studies the life of this insulated people, and their nature-mysticism, which knows that plants live and feel, that climate is affected by the human spirit, that disease and crime can be cured by science if it rises to imaginative vision. There is no poverty in Pantopia, for all work in a wise way; there is no war or crime; and love is free from prudery. Religion is scientific, yet mystical; in morality the great commandment is love. There is ritual and a Temple of the Forgotten Dead, and Orders that worship different virtues (Courage, Vision, etc.) The priests and preachers of all virtues must first prove themselves adepts in practice. The island of Pantopia seems another of the great dreams of man, like Plato's or More's.

Yet *Pantopia,* though an excellent anthology of ideas, fails as a novel. It falters between a gospel and a love story. Saavedra lacks convincing centrality: at one time he seems a superman ruling his people with perfect benign power; again, like a prophet of the outer world, he seems opposed by his people; finally he dies too suddenly of pneumonia, which he should (it seems) have been able to control because of his superior wisdom and power. Aura, too, is a hybrid—a woman of the future, with advanced ideas; yet also a naïve human girl, misled about love and life, who is wakened to passion only by the visitor from the inferior world. *Pantopia* is like a fragmentary crown: gems glow here and there, out of an imperfect or broken round of gold.

Frank Harris also wrote a play, *Joan la Romée.* The subject should have ensured success: he had written of Joan beautifully in *Confessional;* he knew her more deeply and truly than Shaw did. But he wrote the play, like all his plays, with his conscious mind; some invisible censor, shutting out the subconscious, insulated him from inspiration. Dialogue short-circuited his genius. (In a letter to Arnold Bennett he wrote: "The Play is not a form of art that pleases me like the novel. I don't want the actors deforming and altering my characters as they do. If I write a play, and I have got one in mind, it shall be symbolic, and the characters only sketched in vaguely, so that they can be filled out with the actors' own obtrusive personality. They often give the flesh and blood to a sketch while destroying a picture." [7]

Harris sent the play to Shaw, who advised him to "drop the thing into the wastepaper basket with a good-humored laugh, and apologize for the surviving copies." The trouble (he said) was that Harris wished to make a short story out of everything; he always saw life by a lightning flash; you can't make drama that way. Condensation in a play can be condescension; life will not be patronized. The play was neither a play nor a story: tear it up —and write the story. Harris replied with a right and left to the jaw, minus boxing gloves and plus brass knuckles. Shaw's own *Joan* had been insufferable—long-winded history-mongering, with space given to the Caiaphases and Pilates of the world, and Joan and Jesus reduced to excuses for a treatise on sociology. Joan herself was an anachronism, bounding and bouncing like a tomboy or acrobat, and calling the King "Charlie." Anybody could present the Cauchons of the world, the ordinary politicians, the worldly churchmen; why not realize the genius of Joan? He closed with a somber insult: "I remember reading once how Cervantes praised Lope de Vega and sent him *Don Quixote* and de Vega replied he couldn't help in any way, because there was no talent in the book *Don Quixote.*"

Frank Harris's final book was *Bernard Shaw*. Allan Dowling, who was present at the birth of the book, writes interestingly: "After the completion of Harris's autobiography his interest seemed to flag. Scully kept pushing him to write a life of Shaw, and Harris made a beginning but soon tired of it. [Harris, at this time, was ill unto death.] He complained to me that he had already said all he had to say about Shaw, that Shaw had not

[7] Letter to Arnold Bennett, September 14, 1910.

led an interesting life, and so on. However, Scully kept after him, and I am sure he meant to help Harris. He persisted in getting Harris to talk about Shaw, and to write on Shaw, and when he had collected enough material he put it all together and filled it in as best he could. I had contributed a little material—not much —but when Scully had finished his part of the work he brought the manuscript to me and said, 'You know Harris's style better than I do. Please go over this, and cut out anything that you think doesn't sound like him.' I read it carefully. There seemed to me a lot that didn't sound like Harris, but I only cut out a few American slang phrases and returned it. Then Harris died, and Shaw edited the whole book himself. . . .

"The life of Shaw is inferior to the life of Wilde. . . . The latter is a work of art, and has a dramatic drive and continuity entirely lacking in the book about Shaw. The Shaw book is a medley of stuff, with some very interesting chapters; but I can tell you one thing that probably no one else could or would. I read Shaw's letters to Harris, which were many and long, and I know that some of the best passages in the book were written by Shaw himself, even when not attributed to him. The pronoun 'I' was simply changed to 'he' and the rest of it allowed to stand. I think this ought to be told as a tribute to the generosity of a man who was one of the few to stand by Harris to the end."

In the New Zealand *Radio-Record,* June 18, 1937, there is a letter of Shaw's: "The truth is that Frank Harris was very badly qualified to write a life of me. He did not want to do it; what he did want was to write a new life of Jesus as a companion to his Shakespeare, but the publishers would have none of this, and demanded a book on Shaw.

"He, being at the end of his resources, had to comply; but as he had read nothing of mine since he edited the *Saturday Review* in the nineties, and never to the end of his life understood why such a fuss was made about me, and was, besides, so ignorant of the circumstances of my life that he had to invent them all with wildest unsuccess, he made such a hopeless mess of the job that publication was impossible until I took it in hand myself. He never read the result; for he died before I got to work on it.

"I cannot tell how much of the work is mine and how much Harris's, because I destroyed the evidence so completely, and I amused myself so often by imitating Frank's style and being more Harrisian than Harris, that I could not tell with any exactness which was which."

Harris was a Plutarch or an abbreviated Boswell, not the beaver-patient chronicler of a whole life. His *Contemporary Portraits* are the short stories of biography; his Wilde—the exception that proves the rule—is a *jeu d'esprit* of knowledge and love, or of opportunity and insight. He was no research scholar; he had not the talent or patience for professional biography. Why should he have written a studious life of Shaw: had Chesterton done that? —yet Chesterton's book (Shaw said) was the best written about him. Harris's book on Shakespeare had been of that sort, too; and it had raised Shakespeare from the grave.

Harris sought to interpret and appraise Shaw. He saw him as a man of intellectual quality, unsupported by virility: he was "shy Shaw," the virgin till he was twenty-seven, the vegetarian who did not know war or women except as ideas, the Don Quixote of the pure intellect (who had, nevertheless, a worldly flair for buttering his parsnips and for making windmills, which he never really charged, means of advertisement). He was a pamphleteer, an *entrepreneur* of ideas, a dramatist of debate and brilliant talk, who had never created a real woman (save perhaps Candida) or a hero equal to Bazarov or Don Quixote. His plays lacked anti-septic against time, and central passion: they were verbal chitchat, not fundamentally philosophic; they were eclectic rather than in-evitable. As he had risen to place, he had more and more used his paradoxes as red herrings across the trail; he had been basically on the side of the smug angels at ease in Zion. He had supported England against the Boers (as always, with clever liberal rea-

sons); in spite of all boast of commonsense, he had bolstered
England in the World War. Where had he ever run counter to
the will of the Powers That Be? (Had Harris lived longer he
might have heard Shaw excuse Lady Astor and the Cliveden Set,
and apologize for the Munichmen.) Shaw was the best of modern England; but he had never pulled his weight—he was Mephistopheles, but never Faust.

Some impute such verdicts to vanity, especially since Shaw in
his golden way generously allowed himself to be persuaded into
collaboration and into abetting his own bath in acid. Was not
Harris motivated by pique? He, once fully in the sun, had lifted
the unknown Shaw into the light. Now, fallen himself into
shadows, he was obscure or hated; Shaw, on the other hand, was
the darling of two continents. Yet there is sober truth in Harris's
appraisal: Harris had known the honor of being "with all lands
at odds"; he had written of the same evils as Shaw had, and had
won his crown of thorns while Shaw had won the purple; he had
endured bankruptcy, legal conflicts, exile, poverty, for his incorrigible spirit. Compare Shaw's position in England with Harris's
persecution in America during the same days and in relation to
the same war. Could Shaw have risen to affluence and influence
in England; could he have been the approved apologist for
England during the war—if he had been one of God's Spies?
Was he a socialist?—why, then, was his fate so different from
Lenin's or Liebknecht's? Was his work truly a transvaluation
of values?—why, then, was his fate so different from Blake's
or Whitman's or Nietzsche's? Was there not something wrong
with a Christ who ended cheek by jowl with Caiaphas, as the
licensed jester of Pilate? Shaw, in his fine Postscript, feels all
this subconsciously. He tries to justify himself—and under-
mine Harris—by saying that Harris was not only "disappointed
in people who did nothing splendid, but savagely contemptuous of people who did not want to have anything splendid
done." The trouble was, Shaw goes on to say, that Harris's "always

seething susceptibility to scornful indignation" would not let him stop to ask the calm question: "What else could I have done had it been my own case?" But was not Harris right in demanding great actions from great men? Shaw himself criticizes Shakespeare for dallying in the Mermaid Tavern when he should have been shaking England with the thunder of his spirit. Is it any better to dally among the Cliveden Set? Shaw praises Shelley as no "ineffectual angel"; and Shelley, like Harris, called for drastic and splendid deeds, and died driven far from the shore and the trembling throng. Is it a sign of realism to end rich, official—and innocuous? Calvary is a better pulpit than a throne. *Heartbreak House* was an indictment of England; but what if one still lived in Heartbreak House and broke sportive bread with its architects and inmates? A prophet's path should lead to noble doom and not to ignoble dominance; to Calvary and not to the Cliveden Set.

Stark Young wrote one of the few adequate reviews. He notes Shaw's trick "of coming out all right himself as history goes forward and other champions to their ruin or martyrdom, his facility along with a conscious and unconscious slipperiness in argument, his goodness, brilliance, bad taste and overwhelming exhibitionism. . . ." Stark Young speaks of Harris, whom he saw on a long visit "from which I carry a recollection of a strong and rich nature, great cordiality, and entertaining talk in a beautiful, persuasive voice. Everyone knows something of his books, his impetuosities, the scandals, difficulties, unreliabilities, disciples, and powers of mind and body that go with his reputation. . . ." He continues: "In this little defense Mr. Shaw comes off nicely. As Frank Harris says of him, he is wonderfully cool in the face of criticism and calm in tone. As a matter of fact what happens is that he contrives to dispose, it would seem, of the whole book, and pretty much of its author. In his customary way he is unanswerable, unerringly persuasive, or is at least if you let him rush you along and never stop to see what premises you let him smother you with. . . . I have read none of the reviews of this book on Shaw by Frank Harris, but I have been told that for the most part Harris gets little credit at best, and that frequently the cudgels are for him and for Shaw the plums. . . . This note is only to point out that Harris is very likely much oftener right on Shaw than you might conclude. . . . By a certain intuition, by his long observation of Shaw and by the force of his own powers, he hits the nail on the head, I believe, more often than we might be led to think, certainly than Mr. Shaw himself in his smooth-sailing postscript portrait would lead us to think." This caution from a notable and impartial critic should give the Shavians pause.

Shaw seemed to have all the luck, as usual. Harris died before the book was completed: Shaw could write his own account of his own sex life; could add his interpretation of Harris; and in general (as Stark Young says) could "put the skids under Harris." It was the same cosmic irony that seemed to make Shaw fortune's darling and Harris fortune's fool, all their later lives. But the whirligig of time brings in strange revenges!

As Frank Harris neared the end of his *Life of Shaw,* he approached the end of his own life. Doubtless as he looked back, he sought to appraise and evaluate his own work—in his old age that was to be "a prophetic vision." What did he see; and what should the world see?

Chapter XIV

RIPENESS IS ALL

In "A Mad Love" Hagedorn says that there are two kinds of artists: the one who is the fine artist first, and the great man second; and the one who is a great man first and an artist second. Swinburne, for example, had a specialized talent for lyric verse which lifted an otherwise limited man to a precarious eminence; Whitman, on the other hand, was a great man, whose amplitude of life spilled over into the one channel of writing just a bit more notably than it expressed itself in other ways. Frank Harris, though he had an aptitude for prose equal to Swinburne's lyric gift, had also Whitman's amplitude of life. "Gifts don't matter," he wrote, "it is by the soul alone we count."

Frank Harris was a great man first, and a fine artist second. That is why his life is important. But to understand his life, the world must also understand his work.

What is the harvest of his work?—the "ripeness which is all"?

The basis of Frank Harris's style is its concreteness. Some styles are bookish—scholarly and derivative echoes of past literary grace; but Harris's style, for all its foundation in the King James Bible and its rich allusiveness, came from *life*. His expression came from his experience. He found the single symbol: the basic, sometimes homely image that incarnated abstract truth in concrete

instance. Every truth of the spiritual life had its correspondence
in the natural world. Thus, writing casually in *Pearson's*, he said
that experience is like the light at the stern of a moving ship—
it illumines the sea over which the ship has already gone, but
throws no light ahead toward the surf or rocks or open water to
come. Or he wrote, "Nations, like fish, go rotten first at the head."
Or, making abstract economics concrete, he wrote: "The other day
a rich man was complaining bitterly because he had to pay 15¢ to
get a pair of boots cleaned. I asked him what he would rather
give than clean them himself. 'I don't know,' he said, 'I would
probably give $5; I am so clumsy with my hands.' 'Then,' I said,
'unless you are asked to pay more than $5, you ought not to
complain; that's what you ought to pay.'" In *England or Germany?* he wrote that to tell the truth, as to stand upright, one
must "lean against the prevailing wind in proportion to its
strength."

How beautiful this aesthetic physics of his style! "Her eyes had
grown dark like violets in water." [1] "There was something catlike
and cruel in the hard naked eyes, something of the snake in the
flat pointed face." [2]

Harris, though a bold innovator in thought, was conservative
and even classical in style. He cared nothing for tricks of novelty,
or flashy cerebration; style, to him, was "the way great men talk."
The function of speech is to communicate. None of the Cult of
Unintelligibility for him! He did not seek to suggest profundity
by concealing his thought, but to prove his profundity by revealing his thought. He wished to make the subtlest thought
clear to the simplest mind. The profundity of fog!—what an idea!
Fog might well veil a great city or a majestic sea; or it might
just as easily be magnificent over a waste of ash heaps and rat
holes. He desired not the art of fog, but the art of the sun.

Harris does not write the poetic prose of a Ruskin, or the storm-

[1] *Love in Youth*, p. 197.
[2] *Veils of Isis*. George H. Doran Co., 1915. P. 201.

chants of a Carlyle amid eagled crags: his prose was sober and firm; it seemed sometimes almost mathematical in its logic. It was partly akin to the earth-based, brute-level prose of Swift; but there was much more—rhythm, glow, image, music. Imagination gave him images, emotion gave him music: the movement of the words, the soaring rise and dying fall of sentences, the progression of paragraphs, the natural emphasis of accent, expressed not only the outer thought, but the inner emotion.

He listed as his models in prose Donne's *Sermons*, Dryden's *Prefaces*, Froude's *Short Studies in Great Subjects*, Ruskin's *Praeterita*, Swift's *Gulliver*, Bacon's *Essays*, the King James Bible, Shakespeare's prose, and Huxley's *Essays*. He did not mention Schopenhauer, though elsewhere he often praised him.

But his prose is more like Schopenhauer's than that of any other world master. Schopenhauer among modern writers is one of the most concrete and personal: his style is so tangible that his words seem as solid as Rodin's granite or Cézanne's apples. In concrete imagery, in mordant grave power of thought, in ideas that follow the grain of life's wood, in passionate life, in ability to be allusive originally and to quote with selective artistry, Harris's style is akin to Schopenhauer's. The great German's magnificent image characterizes both his own style and Harris's: the rainbow that stands in beauty above the thunder of life's cataract.

Yet style is only the best way of communicating the best meaning. What was Frank Harris's meaning?

He called himself the Reconciler. He meant that life which in others had come to be fissured or fractured, was reunited in him in a higher synthesis.

In society there had been a fracture. There was too great poverty among the Have-Nots; there was too great wealth among the Haves. There was not a commonwealth. This came from a deeper cleavage: Liberty (a noble ideal) had become in practice *laissez faire*—the license to exploit, individuality run mad. The result was chaos and anarchy. On the other hand, Marx and the socialists would destroy the natural inequality of destinies and functions, and would level liberty into the monotonous steppes of equality. The Reconciler must show that liberty can never be the license to grab and get; yet that equality must never become the monotony of the ant heap. Thus Harris saw the necessity of change that would introduce a controlled economy and a true commonwealth; but also the necessity of a true conservatism that would preserve the soul of the individual.

He wrote, "I was a Socialist when I was seventeen; but even then I knew that equality was the worst injustice, knew that individualism was just as important to the state as collectivism: well-being could come only from a sane equipoise of both these forces. . . . Goethe and Carlyle have both drawn the dividing line correctly. Every department of industry which the individual can control should be left to him; but whenever he has had to surrender his initiative and unite with other men in order to manage the business, such industry should be owned and managed by the state. . . . But leave full freedom to the individual, for it is from the individual that all progress comes in industry, as in art, or, indeed, in life.

"I wanted to see both principles realized in life, individualism and socialism, the centrifugal as well as the centripetal force, and was convinced that the problem was how to bring these opposites to a balance which would ensure an approximation of justice and make for the happiness of all." [3]

In art, too, there had been a fracture. On the one hand, genius moved toward insulation, partly because of its disillusionment with men, partly because of its own weakened, rootless life. On the other hand, society had lost contact with art; ignored art, or persecuted it. Genius should be integral with life: the artist was not a decorator, a fashioner of petty prettiness, a playboy of beauty. Life should be integral with art: the bulk of men had bought

[3] *My Life and Loves,* Vol. I, p. 260.

a ticket to Hell when they ignored or destroyed genius; nations could live only as they had vision, and there could be no vision where the artist perished. Art must be vital; life must be artistic. "As force and matter are indestructible, I saw that spirit was everlasting and the spirit of man one and universal. A new vision and a new reward came to me from this understanding. In measure as you grow, I said to myself, so your ideas and feelings will become a forecast of the future of the race and just as you embody in yourself today the chief experiences of the long-forgotten past, so will you be able from your own growth to divine what is to come thousands of years after your death. . . . I felt that it lay before me and in my power to become a sort of beacon to generations of men yet to be born; if I chasten myself to feel the joy and suffering of others as deeply as my own, I too may yet become one of the scared guides and in spite of all insufficiency help to steer humanity across unpath'd waters to undream'd of shores."

And again: "To say of a man that he's a great artist ought to imply that you regard him as one of the choice and master spirits of the age, one of those whose judgment is subtly fair because he stands in true relation with the visible world, as well as with the viewless mysteries."[4]

There had been a fracture, also, between life and love. Puritanism and brute animalism had, between them, destroyed love. Men, and especially women, had been taught to despise the body or fear it; to feel that physical love was "dirty" or "evil." The revolt of women and their overpitched emphasis on the vote came because they had been frustrated in love. Either false ideals had rendered women incapable of enjoyment, or men had been so blinkered and blinded that they knew nothing of the fine art of love by which alone women (and men) could be happy. The garden of love had been turned into a prison or a marketplace; love, seen as lust, had lost its joy. The thwarted impulses of men

[4] *My Life and Loves.*

and women had either been inhibited into neuroses, or had broken out into animal lewdness of desire: prostitution, Bohemianism, fierce excess, orgies of joyless lust ... the Wild Oats of Poetry. The Reconciler must reveal love as a natural function—necessary, joyous, holy—life's dynamic. "Blessed are the sensuous," he wrote, "for their roots are strong and their continuance sure." The Reconciler must bring spirit and flesh together; must make life and love once more integral and innocent.

Finally, there had been a fissure between science and religion. On the one hand, religion had become a thing of ritual and dead observance—a lake without outlet or flow, stagnating into the salt of a Dead Sea. On the other hand, life without religion had reverted to the great apes: Darwin, contrary to his own purpose, had not so much shown men that they had come from the apes, as he had shown them the way back. "Survival of the fittest," "struggle for existence," "will to power," and the brute hugger-mugger of animals trampling each other into the abyss and losing the power and the glory that they should have found by giving themselves to God made life chaos. The churches, prattling of Jesus, knew nothing of his genius; they betrayed the lightning-brilliance of his vision, the sun-warmth of his love. Modernism, scorning Jesus and calling Harris a Jesus-monger, had plunged into exploitation, secularism, anarchy, insensate wars, like the Gadarene swine over the cliff. "Ever since our conquest of natural forces began, toward the end of the eighteenth century, and material wealth increased by leaps and bounds, our conduct has deteriorated. Up to that time we had done the gospel of Christ mouth-honor at least; and had to some slight extent shown consideration if not love to our fellowmen: we did not give tithes to charity; but we did give petty doles till suddenly science appeared to reinforce our selfishness with a new message: progress comes through the blotting out of the unfit, we were told, and self-assertion was preached as a duty: the idea of the Superman came into life and the Will to Power and thereby Christ's teaching of love and pity and gentleness was thrust into the background. At once we men gave ourselves over to wrong doing and our iniquity took monstrous forms. . . . Never, I believe, in the world's history was there such confusion in men's thoughts about conduct, never were there so many different ideals put forward for his guidance. It is imperatively necessary for us to bring clearness into this muddle and see why we have gone wrong and where." [5] Men must "give and forgive"; must return to the new commandment (which is the oldest) "that ye love one another." The Reconciler must see the world with the clarity of Science but must also feel in his soul the sweet-thoughted wisdom and moral grandeur of Jesus. And he must know, too, the mysticism that leads below red and beyond violet.

Thus Frank Harris desired the new man. This new man must not be a sensualist, a moralist, a pragmatist, or an intellectual—*only:* each one of these, separately, is but one aspect out of life's whole. The senses must be accepted and enriched; morality must be universal and motivated by love and light, it must not consist of static negations and prohibitions, but of dynamic impulses and affirmations; the intellect must be intensified and reverenced. Yet beyond all these is Life—Life that contains all, as Light contains the colors. The Reconciler seeks integrity: his word is *integral.*

Such was Frank Harris's Gospel. How, nevertheless, did he fail to realize perfectly what it was his glory to have seen? He, first of all men, would wish his limitations to be lovingly studied: for he knew that it is impossible to make a picture with white on white; and that all shadows point toward the sun.

The highest reach of Frank Harris's spirit touched mysticism. In story after story he points out the mystery and miracle which make us sub-men in a super-Nature. He said that plants have will and consciousness; that even the mineral has will and consciousness. He said that man modifies climate by changes in his spirit—blizzards and bleak cold have grown less as man has

[5] *Ibid,* Vol. I, Introduction, p. xi.

risen in stature; the very sky is higher where men are idealistic. He said that no man dies in the flesh until the work of the spirit is accomplished. He wrote: "Whatever we want in life, whatever we desire intensely and with persistence, we are sure to attain. 'All our youthful prayers are granted,' says Goethe, 'brimming measure in maturity.' That is the chief lesson of life. You can mould it to what you wish: *Knock and it shall be opened unto you. Ask and ye shall have.* You can make it hymn or epic, as you please, get joy from it, or sorrow or love, or fame—greatness of soul or fatness of purse—whatever you will; if you *will* it with all your might to the end." [6] And in an article for Locke Miller's magazine, *Views of Truth,* of which he was the European editor, Harris made his mysticism clear. He was writing about Joan of Arc. Were her voices impossible? He used the analogy of the radio, to which he had been listening only the other evening—a simple box with wires, and yet by it he heard the inaudible, he came into proximity with the distant. Paris, Madrid became suddenly audible to him over the many miles of air. Such sounds, then, had been always there—but men had not heard; they had not had instruments to augment their ears! How could he deny to Joan of Arc the natural power that others had not yet attained? Perhaps the "voices" are always there, for all to hear if they have delicate ears, if they have super-instruments, like Joan. The whole world is one miracle: how, then, could he deny miracles? In "The Holy Man" Harris says that when we love things they return our love: a saint finds it no miracle to walk on water.

Such was the highest insight of his spirit. Unfortunately his reach exceeded his grasp; his mind never attained the height of his soul. There was another Harris, the intellectual, who (like all intellectuals) stands this side integrity. He was a "modern" in the unfortunate nineteenth-century sense; he was St. Thomas among the disciples. He could not fully follow with his mind the implications of his soul's truth. If there are colors we cannot

[6] *My Life and Loves.*

see and sounds we cannot hear, why suppose that the "body" is the only body? If plants and minerals have will and consciousness, why suppose that our own will and consciousness end when we shuffle off this mortal coil, when we drop this muddy vesture of decay? If a Holy Man in Russia by perfect love can walk on water, why deny the "miracles" of Jesus? In his intellect Harris accepted the easy materialism and sceptical naïveté of the nineteenth century—that most superstitious and credulous of centuries.

This maims what would otherwise be the highest modern vision of Jesus. The sweet-thoughted wisdom, the magical beauty, the passionate love, these Harris saw; but he shrank from the metaphysics of Jesus. He tried to show Jesus saved from death not by immortality but by mortality; not resurrected by God, but rescued by man. But metaphysics are the roots of His Gospel, as well as the sun toward which it climbs. Harris's Jesus was resuscitated, not resurrected: therefore, having found His life, He lost it. Harris's Jesus is a broken sentimentalist, trying vainly to salvage a few gleaming scraps from the lovely but frail vase of illusion. If Jesus' Gospel had no metaphysical foundation, it was not a Gospel but a lie; if the metaphysical basis was false, his ethics (which grow out of it and are congruous with it) are a lie. His Gospel would have been a rainbowed pretense at which the world—wistfully, as at another fair but fragile dream—would rightly smile.

If Frank Harris had transcended the nineteenth century, if he had gone toward the worlds not realized, the truths that perish never, the intimations of immortality, he would have been the first man of the future. Yet for all his failure, he remains close to the door. If he was St. Thomas, yet he loved his Lord, and wrote some beautiful pages of his ethical Gospel. And in his highest insight he knew more than his mind would admit.

In his own life Frank Harris was a protagonist of the Tragedy of Modern Man.

His writing is the outer record of this inner struggle. His highest vision lifted him toward the future; knowledge, lust, ambition, scorn, conflict, despair, the weight of the world dragged him back. Living in the tension of genius, he was extreme: his, therefore, was the war between the best and the worst, never the equilibrium of the merely good. He had the nth power of expression, as well as the nth power to experience. Longing for mysticism, he subordinated it to "reason"; longing for the joyous integrity of love wherein spirit and flesh find the innocence of Eden, he often fell into lust and the mere pride of sensation; longing for the victory that is not won with hands, he could not escape the ambition of worldly place and power, or the luxuries of the flesh; longing for forgiveness, pity, loving-kindness, he was often hot with scorn and indignation and hate of those who had hurt him (and of some who had not); longing for faith, he often fell into the nihilism of those to whom earth is all. He saw and desired the highest; yet ambition, pride of intellect, the parade of science, the hunger and lust that defaced the nineteenth century were raised in him by genius to terrible tension. He might have quoted of himself the words he heard Verlaine recite:

Suis-je né trop tôt ou trop tard?
Qu'est-ce que je fais en ce monde?
Oh, vous tous, ma peine est profonde:
Priez pour le pauvre Gaspard.

He was Mr. Penry—yet also the world that denied Mr. Penry. He was Hagedorn or Piranello, the genius of Heaven who by some quirk of madness stumbled into Hell. Thus his life was a vicarious atonement: that terrific and sublime tragedy wherein our human fate, crucified between the nineteenth and the twentieth centuries, is made visible.

The life of Shakespeare as Harris saw it was similar. Shakespeare's life was kindled by love and aspiration; it was tortured and half wrecked by ambition and lust. In that conflict both

Shakespeare and Harris were defeated, and their defeat and torture furnish amusement to halfmen who forget or ignore or are incapable of knowing what they sought and what they saw. But Harris's greatness can be measured by his failure as surely as by his victory: only the great fall far. He was—like Shakespeare, like Goethe—a symbolic man: in him the nineteenth and twentieth centuries struggled in tragic tension. The death of the nineteenth century dragged him down—ambition, lust, unbelief, all that had to die; the birth of the twentieth century uplifted him— a new innocence and a reconciliation, where freedom is one with economic justice, where love uses the body for the meaning of the spirit, where art is a vital power, where intellect is transcended by the meaning of the whole man, were coming into being. In his life the dead past and the unborn future wrestled; his outer life was the theater of their tragic crisis, and in that struggle he failed and died—and lives.

Frank Harris's salvation, through all, was his invulnerable virtue. Even when his worldly self sought place, money, the mere flesh of love, the fallibility of finite knowledge, his soul destroyed and made impossible the very things he sought. If he sought political eminence, he could not pay the price: he had to tell the truth, to speak the brave defiance, to serve justice. If he won money, he could not keep it: folly made him poor again. If he became immersed in the mere pleasure of love's biology, the word of a Byron Smith or a Carlyle, or the call of an ideal that made him question his conquest drove him onward. When he was threatened by success God saved him by failure. In spite of his worldliness, he was unworldly; in spite of his need for money, he was generous; in spite of his ambition, he aspired. He spoke the terrible truth. He was on the side of the poor, the outcast, the world's victims, the Joans and not the Cauchons, Jesus and never Pilate. He never urged on the hounds of time: he stood between them and the hunted deer. Never, for friendship or advantage, did he lower the inexorability of beauty or truth; always he gave the best that was in him to the unrewarded service of art. And he never made that art a sterile thing: it was seership and prophecy. In spite of hatred or love, abuse or acclaim, poverty or riches, persecution or power, slander or overpraise, exile or arrival, loss or gain, age or youth, he was incorrigible and incorruptible— Cyrano who carried to God, unspotted from the world, in spite of all, his White Plume.

The affirmative wisdom of Frank Harris is best condensed in the too little-known *Beatitudes:*

"Blessed are they that mourn: for they shall give comfort.

"Blessed are they that love: for they shall be loved.

"Blessed are the meek: for they shall dwell with peace.

"Blessed are they that do hunger and thirst after beauty: for they shall find it on every side.

"Blessed are the merciful: for the dumb shall praise them.

"Blessed are the peacemakers: for their kingdom shall come upon earth.

"Blessed are they that are persecuted for truth's sake: for they shall inherit the future.

"Blessed are they that stumble and fall by the way: for they shall know compassion, and pity shall lead them by the hand."[7]

Even more beautiful are the *Beatitudes of a Modern:*

"Blessed are the strong: for they are as suns shining.

"Blessed are the brave: for they shall not know death.

"Blessed are the prudent: for their children shall exalt them.

"Blessed are the healthy: for they beget hope.

"Blessed are the rich: for they can help with both hands.

"Blessed are the wise: for they drink life from many wells.

"Blessed are they that laugh: for mirth and joy are sisters.

"Blessed are they that love justice: for the hours work with them.

"Blessed are the sensuous: for their roots are strong, and their continuance sure."

[7] *Beatitudes of a Saint.*

Chapter XV

COME, LOVELY AND SOOTHING
DEATH
(1929-1931)

In a white villa by a blue sea Frank Harris waited for death.
Dr. Hort told Allan Dowling that for two years he had not
understood why Harris was still alive: anyone else in the same
condition would have died. It was, on a higher plane, what—in
athletics and war—we call "heart."

The world was too little with him: few friends visited him
toward the end, or even wrote. Shaw came in genial greatness;
Emma Goldman and Alexander Berkman were true and constant; Allan Dowling was a comrade of sunny hours or in darker
days.

Harris believed himself poor; he was harassed and worried by
the fear that like Oscar Wilde he was "dying beyond his means."

His leg intermittently swelled and ached with the agony of
phlebitis, till he could not move without torture; he was a man
chained to pain. His lungs half failed him; he suffered from
asthma and bronchitis. He, the fighter, seemed sinking into death
as a cowboy sinks into a quicksand.

He was shaken with pain. Ulcers on his stomach tortured him;
yet he would not agree to an operation. Horrible hiccoughs shook
him, night and day. Mrs. Harris felt that she could not escape

310

them even in sleep, for they pursued her through her dreams. She
served him with unwearied devotion; but all that she could do
seemed only the sand forts that a child builds upon the shore,
swept away by the next inrush of the great waves.

Dr. Hort warned that Harris must not get up, even though he
might seem temporarily better; not walk or run, "for otherwise
he may drop dead."

Resolutely Frank Harris gathered his failing powers and strove
to complete his life of Shaw. But his heart was not in it, or he
would have lived to finish it. It kept him alive for two years, but
he wearied of it; before he completed it, life wrote *Finis* after
her own greater work.

In those last days and hours, memories flickered through his
fading brain: of the toss of flaming torches in the Claddagh; of
the fierce constriction of air and the hammering in the boiling
sand under Brooklyn Bridge; of air like wine over the plains of
Texas, and the rush of Blue Dick through the wind; of women
he had loved and possessed, of great men he had known; of a
sun-haze of exquisite landscapes; of appetites and ambitions, of
true aspiration; of the high calling of art wherein God's Spies
take upon themselves the mystery of things. Lines of poetry
flickered like lightning through the mist of his memory: "Like a
sick eagle staring at the sky. . . ." "Dateless oblivion and divine
repose. . . ." "But something ere the end, some work of noble
note may yet be done. . . ." "Men must endure their going hence
even as their coming hither: ripeness is all."

And through the days hazy like nights walked a gallant company. Montes was there with his fierce somber soul, a splash of
crimson on a background of ebony; Mr. Penry came with his
quiet terrible eyes; Louis Lingg whispered through the red stubs
of his jaws, "Courage, comrade—it is nothing: Death is only
another hill to climb." Joan of Arc came, pitying him as she had
pitied the soldier who stood too close to the flame that was killing
her. And Sonia came—greatest of his dreams of women—saying,

"You are stronger even than I: the slow hours did not break you."
Shakespeare moved majestically over the stage of his dying brain
—the world-worn, the passion-weary, the lord of infinite virtue.
Heine laughed in triumphant mockery: *"Dieu vous pardonnera:
c'est son métier."* James Thomson, somber-eyed, watched in compassion him who had felt compassion. Oscar Wilde, a lumpish
Puck in velveteens, drawled from sunny scrolls of wit. Burton—
dark terrible Dick Burton—muttered obscenities about blue ba-
boons. Byron Smith beckoned—and turned away. Carlyle struck
him with the fierce lightning of a glance. Shaw tossed generous
malice of laughter: "Here lies a man of letters who hated cruelty
and injustice and bad art, and never spared them in his own
interests. R.I.P." What memories, what creations, what friends!
Could he not truly say: "In a sun-haze of exquisite memories, I,
too, like a God, look upon the world and say that it was all good."

So Frank Harris fought death. But his body, now, was a mere
cage for Bagheera, the black panther: why live—merely to stay
alive?

August 25, 1931. . . . The twilight would soon sink redly into
the blue sea. Frank Harris had passed a fevered, fretful day. Toward the last, about five in the afternoon, his deeper self wakened
him into awareness. To die in bed?—What a fate for a fighter!
The cowboys of the plains knew better; they wished to die with
their boots on. The Sioux would not die so, either, but in the
saddle—giving wounds and taking death, making death itself a
road of life. Frank Harris rose out of sleep: he struggled up, half
sitting, half standing, propped against the bed. He caught up an
empty glass, and in final ferocity hurled it against the wall. It
struck. It shattered. Warned by the sudden sound, Nellie Harris
came. She saw Frank half lying, half standing; she saw the
empty shattered glass. . . .

That night the great heart weakened and failed while the great
mind slept. Frank Harris died in the early morning of August 26.

Emma Goldman came that day to tell Allan Dowling that

Mrs. Harris had arranged for a church funeral and burial, but that she had no money to pay for the grave. The church would accept her note only if some responsible person would add his signature. Allan Dowling went surety for the grave; later, Mrs. Harris sold some of the furniture and paid off the note. Bernard Shaw, hearing of Frank's death, sent fifty pounds. He wrote:

"Dear Mrs. Harris,

"They have just telephoned me that you have finished the strange adventure of being married to Frank.

"Death does not always select the convenient moment when there is plenty of ready money in the house to meet its expenses. Hence the enclosure. You can repay it out of the profits of the biography.

"Now you can begin another life with the wisdom garnered from your first experiment; so run up the half-masted flag to the top of the staff, and away with melancholy.

Ever

G. B. S."

Alexander Berkman ("Sasha") went with Allan Dowling to see the dead Harris for the last time. "Somehow he looked very, very small in his coffin—an impression of him which I had never had while he was alive; and it must have affected me, because I remember Sasha saying to me, 'We all have to come to it, you know.' " (Only a few years later, in Nice, Sasha had "come to it" too, by his own hand.)

There were between twenty and thirty people at the funeral, but "no one of note: it was out of season and there were not many people in Nice, apart from the regulars."[1] Emma Goldman and Sasha, not believing in the Church, did not attend. Monseigneur Barry Doyle, brother of Sir Arthur Conan Doyle, was there. "I remember a tall, dark, young Frenchman who came down from Paris, I believe, and who seemed to be one of Harris's

[1] Allan Dowling.

most fervent admirers, but I cannot remember his name." [2] Nellie Harris was escorted on one side by Mrs. Hort, and on the other side by a woman who was always known as "Auntie," who kept a tea-shop in Venice and befriended D. H. Lawrence and other artists and writers. So this mortal put on immortality.

Frank Harris, the Welshman born in Ireland, who ran away to America and won fame in England, but who dwelt in a country not made with hands, was buried, ironically, in the English cemetery at Nice. Something of England held him even at the end. Yet the virtue of that clay is not contained there: it quickens the earth into life wherever men read and love beauty, like the hidden motivation of spring.

But even at his death Frank Harris was not born. The world broke into cackle of gaucherie and gossip; the wits of journalism wisecracked unwisely: their motto seemed, *De mortuis nil nisi malum.* The soldiers threw dice for the robes of notoriety; the mob jested and forgot. The stone was rolled against the tomb, and no one foresaw the years when the Angel shall push it aside and say, "He is not here: he is risen."

"We are immortal only when we die:" (he had written) *"it is the dead who steer the living."*

[2] *Ibid.*

INDEX